GREAT
SPEECHES

GREAT SPEECHES

WORDS THAT SHAPED THE WORLD

Edited and with an Introduction by
Edward Humphreys

ARCTURUS

Arcturus Publishing Limited hereby excludes all liability to the extent permitted by law for any errors or omissions in this book and for any loss, damage or expense (whether direct or indirect) suffered by a third party relying on information contained in this book.

Winston Churchill, David Lloyd George and Margaret Thatcher, reproduced by kind permission of Crown Copyright; Martin Luther King speeches are reprinted by arrangement with the Heirs to the Estate of Martin Luther King Jr., c/o Writers House as agent for the proprietor New York, N.Y.; Pope John Paul II, Speech at Yad Vashem (2000) © Libreria Editrice Vaticana, 2009.

Every effort has been made to contact copyright holders. The publishers will be glad to correct any omissions in future editions.

PICTURE CREDITS

Clipart 60; Corbis 15, 17, 20, 24, 26, 31, 33, 43, 45, 51, 57, 64, 69, 71, 75, 83, 96, 102, 112, 116, 118, 122, 123, 134, 139, 144, 153, 159, 161, 162, 164, 171, 179, 188; Mary Evans 93; Topfoto 40, 42.

ARCTURUS

This edition published in 2012 by Arcturus Publishing Limited
26/27 Bickels Yard, 151–153 Bermondsey Street,
London SE1 3HA

Project Editor: Ella Fern

ISBN: 978-1-84858-925-4
AD000233EN

Printed in Singapore

CONTENTS

INTRODUCTION

Early in his political career, Winston Churchill, then Conservative Member of Parliament for Oldham, rose in the House of Commons and delivered a speech in which he argued that, to the United Kingdom, the Navy was of greater importance than the Army. He had worked on the speech for several weeks, rewriting and revising. When the time came for delivery, Churchill knew the address – of almost one hour's length – by heart. His performance was nearly flawless, the only error occurring when he chose to quote his father, Lord Randolph Churchill. Opening a book, he spoke his father's words, but these too he had memorized and, as a consequence, he closed the volume before finishing the quotation. Churchill had mastered the art of delivery, but not yet the use of props.

This piece of oratory, delivered on 13 May 1901, established Churchill as a speaker of note. The *Daily Telegraph* would later describe the future Prime Minister as 'the best orator in the House'.

This volume contains over forty of the finest and most important English-language speeches of the last four centuries. Three of them – more than by any other person – were delivered by Winston Churchill. Another, Edward VIII's abdication speech, had the benefit of the great man's input. It is also worth noting that Churchill is referred to in several other speeches here, including those of Ronald Reagan and Al Gore, who incorporate Churchill's words.

Each of the thirty-four men and women who feature in this book were important in their respective times; all played significant roles in history. It says something of the danger of public life that nine of the names included here died as a result of their expressed beliefs.

Assassination, execution and war lend weight to many of the memorable words and phrases presented in these pages.

Martin Luther King's 'I've Been to the Mountaintop' speech, delivered the evening before he was assassinated, seems horribly prophetic. The Reverend's oration was impromptu, delivered to a crowd that refused to disperse without hearing him speak. King's death prompted another great improvised speech, that delivered by Robert Kennedy in Indianapolis. Told of the assassination while en route to speak before a gathering of poor African-Americans, Kennedy's advisors provided suggestions as to what he might say on arrival. All were ignored. The Senator from New York used no notes, but looked at and spoke directly to the crowd.

Kennedy was keenly aware of whom he was addressing that cold April evening in 1968. Speeches are, of course, delivered toward very specific audiences. Charles I's statement at Westminster Hall in January 1649, was obviously not made with the 21st-century reader in mind, nor was he addressing the British citizenry over which he ruled; rather, the doomed monarch was speaking to the unsympathetic judiciary that would ultimately condemn him to death.

For the speaker, failure to recognize the audience will inevitably lead to an unsuccessful speech. And the reader who is unaware of the intended audience will not grasp either the context or the significance.

Though witnessed by others, it was to General William Henry Harrison that Tecumseh addressed his 1810 speech, dealing with Indian land rights. Harrison's failure to heed the words contributed, little more than a year later, to Tecumseh's War. The bloodshed escalated when Tecumseh's confederacy joined the Canadians and British in fighting the United States Army during the War of 1812. The Shawnee Chief and American General met for the last time in 1813 at the Battle of the Thames, fought in present-day Ontario. There, Tecumseh lost his life, a tragedy that Harrison would use to his advantage when he entered politics. As the man who won the ultimate victory over the Chief, Harrison amassed sufficient votes to gain the presidency of the United States.

We know the words of Tecumseh and Charles I because they were transcribed at the time; while those of King and Kennedy were recorded on film and audio tape. However, the accuracy of several other famous speeches must be questioned. A number of different versions exist of Elizabeth I's Golden Speech; the same applies to so relatively recent an oration as Abraham Lincoln's Gettysburg Address. Perhaps the most quoted speech in American history, it has been published with significant variations.

Others should be questioned further.

The words of Sojourner Truth's 'Ain't I a Woman?', spoken in 1851, were not set down on paper until abolitionist Frances Dana Gage picked up her pen twelve years later. Patrick Henry's 'Give Me Liberty, or Give Me Death!' is even more problematic. There is no question that the radical revolutionary leader delivered an inspiring speech at the Virginia House of Burgesses on 23 March 1775, but we cannot say with any certainty what words were used. The most famous of American Revolutionary speeches, it was not set down until 1817, forty-two years after it was delivered, and eighteen years after Henry's death. It first appeared in *Sketches of the Life and Character of Patrick Henry*, a biography written by author and statesman William Wirt, who attempted to recreate the speech through the receding memories of those who had been present at the time.

If legend reflects reality, Henry's words elicited cries of 'To arms! To arms!' among those who had been undecided about whether to support the Revolution. The great power and influence of some other orations have proved to be less immediate. The key elements of Harold Macmillan's 'The Wind of Change' speech in 1960 were present in an address he made the previous month in Accra, Ghana, but didn't receive attention until repeated before the Parliament of South Africa in February. Similarly, Ronald Reagan's 1987 'Tear Down this Wall', arguably his most famous speech, received little notice from the press of the day. Indeed, it wasn't until Berliners were permitted to destroy the Berlin Wall, over two years later, that Reagan's words began to receive attention.

While some speeches gain prominence over time, others come to be viewed differently. One example might be Churchill's 'Iron Curtain' speech. Now considered an important warning to the nations of the West, at the time it was criticized as sabre-rattling.

It is very easy to look down on those who did not recognize the validity of Churchill's words; and so we must remember that it may be difficult, living in the instant, to gauge the importance of a speech. Ultimately, it is history that will determine.

ELIZABETH I

THE GOLDEN SPEECH

The Presence Chamber, London, 30 November 1601

Four hundred years after her death, Elizabeth I remains
the greatest of all English monarchs in terms of
eloquence and oratorical skill; it is therefore somewhat
amusing that one of her personal mottoes was *video et
taceo* ('I see, and say nothing'). The Golden Speech was
the 68-year-old queen's final address to her Parliament,
delivered before the 141 members of the House of
Commons. The name of the speech can be traced back to
a commonwealth pamphlet that included the header:
'This speech ought to be set in letters of gold'. Several
versions of the Golden Speech exist, including an early
pamphlet, the publication of which Elizabeth herself may
have overseen. The words presented here follow those
recorded by parliamentary diarist Hayward Townshend.

MR SPEAKER, We have heard your declaration
and perceive your care of our estate. I do assure
you there is no prince that loves his subjects
better, or whose love can countervail our love. There is no
jewel, be it of never so rich a price, which I set before this
jewel: I mean your love. For I do esteem it more than any
treasure or riches; for that we know how to prize, but love
and thanks I count invaluable. And, though God hath
raised me high, yet this I count the glory of my Crown,
that I have reigned with your loves. This makes me that I
do not so much rejoice that God hath made me to be a
Queen, as to be a Queen over so thankful a people.
Therefore I have cause to wish nothing more than to
content the subject and that is a duty which I owe. Neither
do I desire to live longer days than I may see your

prosperity and that is my only desire. And as I am that person still yet, under God, hath delivered you and so I trust by the almighty power of God that I shall be his instrument to preserve you from every peril, dishonour, shame, tyranny and oppression, partly by means of your intended helps which we take very acceptably because it manifesteth the largeness of your good loves and loyalties unto your sovereign.

Of myself I must say this: I never was any greedy, scraping grasper, nor a strait fast-holding prince, nor yet a waster. My heart was never set on any worldly goods. What you bestow on me, I will not hoard it up, but receive it to bestow on you again. Therefore render unto them I beseech you Mr Speaker, such thanks as you imagine my heart yieldeth, but my tongue cannot express. Mr Speaker, I would wish you and the rest to stand up for I shall yet trouble you with longer speech. Mr Speaker, you give me thanks but I doubt me I have greater cause to give you thanks, than you me, and I charge you to thank them of the Lower House from me. For had I not received a knowledge from you, I might have fallen into the lapse of an error, only for lack of true information.

Since I was Queen, yet did I never put my pen to any grant, but that upon pretext and semblance made unto me, it was both good and beneficial to the subject in general though a private profit to some of my ancient servants, who had deserved well at my hands. But the contrary being found by experience, I am exceedingly beholden to such subjects as would move the same at first. And I am not so simple to suppose but that there be some of the Lower House whom these grievances never touched. I think they spake out of zeal to their countries and not out of spleen or malevolent affection as being parties grieved. That my grants should be grievous to my people and oppressions to be privileged under colour of our patents, our Kingly dignity shall not suffer it. Yea, when I heard it, I could give no rest unto my thoughts until I had reformed it. Shall they, think you, escape unpunished that have oppressed you, and have been respectless of their duty and regardless our honour? No, I assure you, Mr Speaker, were it not more for conscience' sake than for any glory or increase of love that I desire, these errors, troubles, vexations and oppressions done by these varlets and lewd persons not worthy of the name of subjects should not escape without condign punishment. But I perceive they dealt with me like physicians who, ministering a drug, make it more acceptable by giving it a good aromatical savour, or when they give pills do gild them all over.

I have ever used to set the Last Judgement Day before mine eyes and so to rule as I shall be judged to answer before a higher judge, and now if my Kingly bounties have been abused and my grants turned to the hurt of my people contrary to my will and meaning, and if any in authority under me have neglected or perverted what I have

Elizabeth I as depicted by an anonymous artist, c. 1557. Known as the Darnley Portrait – *after a former owner – it is thought to have been painted from life.*

committed to them, I hope God will not lay their culps and offences in my charge. I know the title of a King is a glorious title, but assure yourself that the shining glory of princely authority hath not so dazzled the eyes of our understanding, but that we well know and remember that we also are to yield an account of our actions before the great judge. To be a King and wear a crown is a thing more glorious to them that see it than it is pleasant to them that bear it. For myself I was never so much enticed with the glorious name of a King or royal authority of a Queen as delighted that God hath made me his instrument to maintain his truth and glory and to defend his Kingdom as I said from peril, dishonour, tyranny and oppression. There will never Queen sit in my seat with more zeal to my country, care to my subjects and that will sooner with willingness venture her life for your good and safety than myself. For it is my desire to live nor reign no longer than my life and reign shall be for your good. And though you have had, and may have, many princes more mighty and wise sitting in this seat, yet you never had nor shall have, any that will be more careful and loving.

For I, oh Lord, what am I, whom practices and perils past should not fear? Or what can I do? That I should speak for any glory, God forbid. And I pray to you Mr Comptroller, Mr Secretary and you of my Council, that before these gentlemen go into their countries, you bring them all to kiss my hand.

11

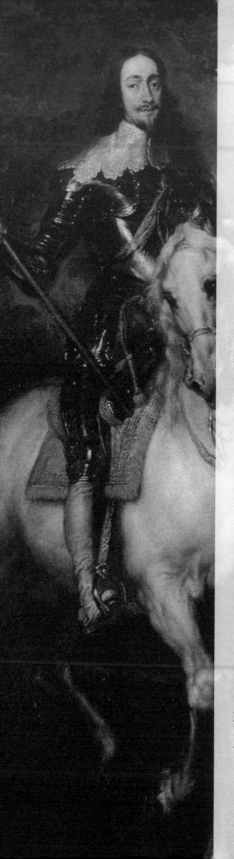

CHARLES I

STATEMENT AT THE TRIAL OF CHARLES STUART,
KING OF ENGLAND
Westminster Hall, London, 20 January 1649

Like his father, James I, Charles was an unwavering
believer in the Divine Right of Kings; he dissolved
Parliament three times, and for more than a decade
attempted to rule Great Britain alone. Forever
overestimating his support and shifting his alliances,
Charles led his country into a period marred by a series
of civil wars. He was defeated in the First English Civil
War (1642-6), and yet managed to survive and fight
again. However, Charles' good fortune was not with him
at the close of the Second English Civil War (1648-9).
Imprisoned, he was charged with 'High Treason and
other High Crimes' before a court established by
Parliament. The trial began with a reading of the
charges, a delivery Charles attempted to prevent. He was
overruled by John Bradshaw, Sergeant at Law and Lord
President. Obliged to listen, he fidgeted, but made no
sound until the Clerk read words describing the King as
a 'Tyrant and Traitor'; at this Charles laughed. This
statement, addressed to a court he would not recognize,
followed the reading of the charges. Found guilty, ten
days later Charles was publicly executed by beheading.

I WOULD KNOW BY what power I am called hither. I
would know by what authority, I mean lawful; there
are many unlawful authorities in the world; thieves
and robbers by the high-ways. Remember, I am your King,
your lawful King, and what sins you bring upon your
heads, and the judgement of God upon this land. Think
well upon it, I say, think well upon it, before you go further

from one sin to a greater. I have a trust committed to me by God, by old and lawful descent, I will not betray it, to answer a new unlawful authority; therefore resolve me that, and you shall hear more of me.

I do stand more for the liberty of my people, than any here that come to be my pretended judges. I do not come here as submitting to the Court. I will stand as much for the privilege of the House of Commons, rightly understood, as any man here whatsoever: I see no House of Lords here, that may constitute a parliament. Let me see a legal authority warranted by the Word of God, the Scriptures, or warranted by the constitutions of the Kingdom, and I will answer.

It is not a slight thing you are about. I am sworn to keep the peace, by that duty I owe to God and my country; and I will do it to the last breath of my body. And therefore ye shall do well to satisfy, first, God, and then the country, by what authority you do it. If you do it by an usurped authority, you cannot answer it; there is a God in heaven, that will call you, and all that give you power, to account.

If it were only my own particular case, I would have satisfied myself with the protestation I made the last time I was here, against the legality of the Court, and that a King cannot be tried by any superior jurisdiction on earth: but it is not my case alone, it is the freedom and the liberty of the people of England; and do you pretend what you will, I stand more for their liberties. For if power without law, may make laws, may alter the fundamental laws of the Kingdom, I do not know what subject he is in England that can be sure of his life, or any thing that he calls his own.

I do not know the forms of law; I do know law and reason, though I am no lawyer professed: but I know as much law as any gentleman in England, and therefore, under favour, I do plead for the liberties of the people of England more than you do; and therefore if I should impose a belief upon any man without reasons given for it, it were unreasonable. The Commons of England was never a Court of Judicature; I would know how they came to be so.

It was the liberty, freedom, and laws of the subject that ever I took – defended myself with arms. I never took up arms against the people, but for the laws. For the charge, I value it not a rush. It is the liberty of the people of England that I stand for. For me to acknowledge a new Court that I never heard of before, I that am your King, that should be an example to all the people of England, for to uphold justice, to maintain the old laws, indeed I do not know how to do it.

This many-a-day all things have been taken away from me, but that that I call more dear to me than my life, which is my conscience, and my honour: and if I had a respect to my life more than the peace of the Kingdom, and the liberty of the subject, certainly I should have made a particular defence for myself; for by that at leastwise I might have delayed an ugly sentence, which I

Anthony van Dyck's triple portrait of Charles I, commonly known as Charles I in Three Positions *(c. 1635). The Flemish master served as court painter in England and painted several portraits of the monarch.*

believe will pass upon me. Now, sir, I conceive that an hasty sentence once passed, may sooner be repented of than recalled: and truly, the self-same desire that I have for the peace of the Kingdom, and the liberty of the subject, more than my own particular ends, makes me now at least desire, before sentence be given, that I may be heard before the Lords and Commons. If I cannot get this liberty, I do protest, that these fair shows of liberty and peace are pure shows and that you will not hear your King.

JAMES WOLFE

Speech Before the Battle of the
Plains of Abraham
*The Plains of Abraham, outside Quebec City,
13 September 1759*

Major General James Wolfe's speech, delivered
immediately before battle commenced, took place
during the Seven Years' War, in the fourth month of a
British campaign designed to capture the capital of
New France. As June of 1759 drew to an end, Wolfe's
forces arrived at the Île d'Orléans, 20 kilometres
(12 miles) east of the city. Over the following months,
the General's energies were spent in failed attempts to
force the enemy to leave Quebec's fortifications. Wolfe
was finally successful when, one dark evening in late
summer, he commanded 3,300 men to scale a 53-metre
(174-foot) cliff – the 'steep and dangerous rocks' –
leading to the Plains of Abraham. There they were met
by a force superior in number, under Major General
Louis-Joseph de Montcalm-Gozon. Both Wolfe and
Montcalm were killed in the ensuing battle; four days
later, the city was surrendered.

I CONGRATULATE YOU, my brave countrymen and
fellow soldiers, on the spirit and success with which
you have executed this important part of our
enterprise. The formidable Heights of Abraham are now
surmounted; and the city of Quebec, the object of all our
toils, now stands in full view before us. A perfidious
enemy, who have dared to exasperate you by their
cruelties, but not to oppose you on equal ground, are now
constrained to face you on the open plain, without
ramparts or intrenchments to shelter them.

You know too well the forces which compose their army to dread their superior numbers. A few regular troops from old France, weakened by hunger and sickness, who, when fresh, were unable to withstand the British soldiers, are their general's chief dependence. Those numerous companies of Canadians, insolent, mutinous, unsteady, and ill-disciplined, have exercised his utmost skill to keep them together to this time; and, as soon as their irregular ardour is damped by one firm fire, they will instantly turn their backs, and give you no further trouble but in the pursuit. As for those savage tribes of

James Wolfe, the man whose victory at the Plains of Abraham brought about the end of New France.

Indians, whose horrid yells in the forest have struck many a bold heart with affright, terrible as they are with a tomahawk and scalping-knife to a flying and prostrate foe, you have experienced how little their ferocity is to be dreaded by resolute men upon fair and open ground: you can now only consider them as the just objects of a severe revenge for the unhappy fate of many slaughtered countrymen.

This day puts it into your power to terminate the fatigues of a siege which has so long employed your courage and patience. Possessed with a full confidence of the certain success which British valour must gain over such enemies, I have led you up these steep and dangerous rocks, only solicitous to show you the foe within your reach. The impossibility of a retreat makes no difference in the situation of men resolved to conquer or die; and, believe me, my friends, if your conquest could be bought with the blood of your general, he would most cheerfully resign a life which he has long devoted to his country.

PATRICK HENRY
'GIVE ME LIBERTY, OR GIVE ME DEATH!'
The Virginia House of Burgesses, St John's Church, Williamsburg, 23 March, 1775

During the spring of 1775, the Colony of Virginia was in crisis; the revolution was going poorly and the likelihood of military engagement was growing. Before the House of Burgesses – the colony's legislative body – lay the question of whether to take up arms or stand down. It is said that the House was in favour of the latter option until Representative Patrick Henry rose to deliver the speech presented here. However, Henry's words were not recorded, and for more than forty years no known attempts were made at recreating the speech. Although the verity of the address continues to be debated, its effect is certain. Less than four weeks later, with the support of Virginia, the American Revolutionary War began.

NO MAN THINKS more highly than I do of the patriotism, as well as abilities, of the very worthy gentlemen who have just addressed the House. But different men often see the same subject in different lights; and, therefore, I hope it will not be thought disrespectful to those gentlemen if, entertaining as I do opinions of a character very opposite to theirs, I shall speak forth my sentiments freely and without reserve. This is no time for ceremony. The question before the House is one of awful moment to this country. For my own part, I consider it as nothing less than a question of freedom or slavery; and in proportion to the magnitude of the subject ought to be the freedom of the debate. It is only in this way that we can hope to arrive at truth, and fulfill the great responsibility which we hold to God and our country. Should I keep back my opinions at such a time, through fear of giving offense, I should consider myself as guilty of treason towards my country, and of an act of disloyalty toward the Majesty of Heaven, which I revere above all earthly kings.

Mr President, it is natural to man to indulge in the illusions of hope. We are apt to shut our eyes against a painful truth, and listen to the song of that siren till she transforms us into beasts. Is this the part of wise men, engaged in a great and arduous struggle for liberty? Are we disposed to be of the number of those who, having eyes, see not, and, having ears, hear not, the things which so nearly concern their temporal salvation? For my part, whatever anguish of spirit it may cost, I am willing to know the whole truth; to know the worst, and to provide for it.

I have but one lamp by which my feet are guided, and that is the lamp of experience. I know of no way of judging of the future but by the past. And judging by the past, I wish to know what there has been in the conduct of the British ministry for the last ten years to justify those hopes with which gentlemen have been pleased to solace themselves and the House. Is it that insidious smile with which our petition has been lately received? Trust it not, sir; it will prove a snare to your feet. Suffer not yourselves to be betrayed with a kiss. Ask yourselves how this gracious reception of our petition comports with those warlike preparations which cover

our waters and darken our land. Are fleets and armies necessary to a work of love and reconciliation? Have we shown ourselves so unwilling to be reconciled that force must be called in to win back our love? Let us not deceive ourselves, sir. These are the implements of war and subjugation; the last arguments to which kings resort. I ask gentlemen, sir, what means this martial array, if its purpose be not to force us to submission? Can gentlemen assign any other possible motive for it? Has Great Britain any enemy, in this quarter of the world, to call for all this accumulation of navies and armies? No, sir, she has none. They are meant for us: they can be meant for no other. They are sent over to bind and rivet upon us those chains which the British ministry have been so long forging. And what have we to oppose to them? Shall we try argument? Sir, we have been trying that for the last ten years. Have we anything new to offer upon the subject? Nothing. We have held the subject up in every light of which it is capable; but it has been all in vain. Shall we resort to entreaty and humble supplication? What terms shall we find which have not been already exhausted? Let us not, I beseech you, sir, deceive ourselves. Sir, we have done everything that could be done to avert the storm which is now coming on. We have petitioned; we have remonstrated; we have supplicated; we have prostrated ourselves before the throne, and have implored its interposition to arrest the tyrannical hands of the ministry and Parliament. Our petitions have been slighted; our remonstrances have produced additional violence and insult; our supplications have been disregarded; and we have been spurned, with contempt, from the foot of the throne! In vain, after these things, may we indulge the fond hope of peace and reconciliation. There is no longer any room for hope. If we wish to be free – if we mean to preserve inviolate those inestimable privileges for which we have been so long contending – if we mean not basely to abandon the noble struggle in which we have been so long engaged, and which we have pledged ourselves never to abandon until the glorious object of our contest shall be obtained – we must fight! I repeat it, sir, we must fight! An appeal to arms and to the God of hosts is all that is left us!

They tell us, sir, that we are weak; unable to cope with so formidable an adversary. But when shall we be stronger? Will it be the next week, or the next year? Will it be when we are totally disarmed, and when a British guard shall be stationed in every house? Shall we gather strength by irresolution and inaction? Shall we acquire the means of effectual resistance by lying supinely on our backs and hugging the delusive phantom of hope, until our enemies shall have bound us hand and foot? Sir, we are not weak if we make a proper use of those means which the God of nature hath placed in our power. The millions of people, armed in the holy cause of liberty, and in such a country as that which we possess, are invincible by any force which our enemy can send against us. Besides, sir, we shall not fight our battles alone. There is a just God who presides over the destinies of nations, and who will raise up friends to fight our battles for us. The battle, sir, is not to the strong alone; it is to the vigilant, the active, the brave. Besides, sir, we have no election. If we were base enough to desire it, it is now too late to retire from the contest. There is no retreat but in submission and slavery! Our chains are forged! Their clanking may be heard on the plains of Boston! The war is inevitable – and let it come! I repeat it, sir, let it come.

It is in vain, sir, to extenuate the matter. Gentlemen may cry: 'Peace! Peace!' – but there is no peace. The war is actually begun! The next gale that sweeps from the north will bring to our ears the clash of resounding arms! Our brethren are already in the field! Why stand we here idle? What is it that gentlemen wish? What would they have? Is life so dear, or peace so sweet, as to be purchased at the price of chains and slavery? Forbid it, Almighty God! I know not what course others may take; but as for me, give me liberty, or give me death!

TECUMSEH

'SELL A COUNTRY! WHY NOT SELL THE AIR,
THE CLOUDS, THE GREAT SEA…?'
Vincennes, Indiana Territory, 12 August 1810

On 30 September 1809, a number of disparate Native American groups signed the Treaty of Fort Wayne, thus ceding three million acres to the United States in exchange for $5,200, together with annuities of $1,750 and a small quantity of salt. The next year, the Shawnee chief Tecumseh, who had not been present during the negotiations, challenged the Treaty in this speech, delivered before an audience of unknown number, to the American negotiator, William Henry Harrison, Governor of Indiana Territory and Superintendent of Indian Affairs. In doing so, the great Native leader refers to several past grievances, including the 1782 massacre of 'the Jesus Indians of the Delawares' by Pennsylvanian militiamen; the 1786 Treaty of Fort Finney, in which the Shawnee, under threat of war, had been forced to relinquish land in the Ohio Country; the 1786 murder of Shawnee leader, Moluntha; and the broken 1796 Treaty of Greenville. Also mentioned is Winnemac, a chief of the Potawatomi, and the leading Native advocate of the Treaty of Fort Wayne. Although Winnemac's tribe received a significant portion of the slim compensation offered, the Potawatomi and the other tribes represented by the Treaty did not live on the land involved.

BROTHER, I WISH YOU to give me close attention, because I think you do not clearly understand. I want to speak to you about promises that the Americans have made.

You recall the time when the Jesus Indians of the Delawares lived near the Americans, and had confidence in their promises of friendship, and thought they were secure, yet the Americans murdered all the men, women, and children, even as they prayed to Jesus?

The same promises were given to the Shawnee one time. It was at Fort Finney, where some of my people were forced to make a treaty. Flags were given to my people, and they were told they were now the children of the Americans. We were told, if any white people mean to harm you, hold up these flags and you will then be safe from all danger. We did this in good faith. But what happened? Our beloved chief Moluntha stood with the American flag in front of him and that very peace treaty in his hand, but his head was chopped by an American officer, and that American officer was never punished.

Brother, after such bitter events, can you blame me for placing little confidence in the promises of Americans? That happened before the Treaty of Greenville. When they buried the tomahawk at Greenville, the Americans said they were our new fathers, not the British anymore, and would treat us well. Since that treaty, here is how the Americans have treated us well: They have killed many Shawnee, many Winnebagoes, many Miamis, many Delawares, and have taken land from them. When they killed them, no American ever was punished, not one.

It is you, the Americans, by such bad deeds, who push the red men to do mischief. You do not want unity among tribes, and you destroy it. You try to make differences between them. We, their leaders, wish them to unite and consider their land the common property of all, but you try to keep them from this. You separate the tribes and deal with them that way, one by one, and advise them not to come into this union. Your states have set an example of forming a union among all the Fires, why should you censure the Indians for following that example?

But, Brother, I mean to bring all the tribes together, in spite of you, and until I have finished, I will not go to visit your president. Maybe I will when I have finished. Maybe. The reason I tell you this, you want, by making your distinctions of Indian tribes and allotting to each particular tract of land, to set them against each other, and thus to weaken us.

You never see an Indian come, do you, and endeavour to make the white people divide up?

You are always driving the red people this way! At last you will drive them into the Great Lake, where they can neither stand nor walk.

Tecumseh as depicted in a portrait that is thought to be based on a lost 1807 pencil sketch made from life by Pierre Le Dru, a Canadian fur trader.

Brother, you ought to know what you are doing to the Indians. Is it by direction of the president you make these distinctions? It is a very bad thing, and we do not like it. Since my residence at Tippecanoe, we have tried to level all distinctions, to destroy village chiefs, by whom all such mischief is done. It is they who sell our lands to the Americans. Brother, these lands that were sold and the goods that were given for them were done by only a few. The Treaty of Fort Wayne was made through the threats of Winnemac, but in the future we are going to punish those chiefs who propose to sell the land.

The only way to stop this evil is for all the red men to unite in claiming an equal right in the land. That is how it was at first, and should be still, for the land never was divided, but was for the use of everyone. Any tribe could go to an empty land and make a home there. No groups among us have a right to sell, even to one another, and surely not to outsiders who want all, and will not do with less.

Sell a country! Why not sell the air, the clouds, and the Great Sea, as well as the earth? Did not the Great Good Spirit make them all for the use of his children?

Brother, I was glad to hear what you told us. You said that if we could prove that the land was sold by people who had no right to sell it, you would restore it. I will prove that those who did sell did not own it.

Did they have a deed? A title? No! You say those prove someone owns land.

Those chiefs only spoke a claim, and so you pretended to believe their claim, only because you wanted the land. But the many tribes with me will not agree with those claims. They have never had a title to sell, and we agree this proves you could not buy it from them. If the land is not given back to us, you will see, when we return to our home from here, how it will be settled.

It will be like this:

We shall have a great council, at which all tribes will be present. We shall show to those who sold that they had no rights to the claims they set up, and we shall see what will be done to those chiefs who did sell the land to you. I am not alone in this determination, it is the determination of all the warriors and red people who listen to me.

Brother, I now wish you to listen to me. If you do not wipe out that treaty, it will seem that you wish to kill all the chiefs who sold the land! I tell you so because I am authorized by all tribes to do so! I am the head of them all! All my warriors will meet together with me in two or three moons from now. Then I will call for those chiefs who sold you this land, and we shall know what to do with them. If you do not restore the land, you will have had a hand in killing them!

I am Shawnee! I am a warrior! My forefathers were warriors. From them I took my birth into this world. From my tribe I take nothing. I am the master of my own destiny! And of that I might make the destiny of my red people, of our nation, as great as I conceive to in my mind, when I think of Weshemoneto, who rules this universe! The being within me hears the voice of the ages, which tells me that once, always, and until lately, there were no white men on all this island, that it then belonged to the red man, children of the same parents, placed on it by the Great Good Spirit who made them, to keep it, to traverse it, to enjoy its yield, and to people it with the same race. Once they were a happy race! Now they are made miserable by the white people, who are never contented but are always coming in! You do this always, after promising not to anyone, yet you ask us to have confidence in your promises. How can we have confidence in the white people? When Jesus Christ came upon the earth, you killed him, the son of your own God, you nailed him up! You thought he was dead, but you were mistaken. And only after you thought you killed him did you worship him, and start killing those who would not worship him. What kind of people is this for us to trust?

Now, Brother, everything I have said to you is the truth, as Weshemoneto has inspired me to speak only truth to you. I have declared myself freely to you about my intentions. And I want to know your intentions. I want to know what you are going to do about taking our land. I want to hear you say that you understand now, and you will wipe out that pretended treaty, so that the tribes can be at peace with each other, as you pretend you want them to be. Tell me, Brother. I want to know now.

SOJOURNER TRUTH

'Ain't I a Woman?'

The Akron Convention, Akron, Ohio, 29 May 1851

The only black person in attendance, Sojourner Truth's appearance at the two-day Akron Convention, devoted to the rights of women, evoked whispered protest. One of the organizers, Frances Dana Gage, later recalled private pleas from delegates that she should not permit the former slave to speak. Truth was silent the first day. She spent the second in much the same way, seemingly deep in contemplation as a clergyman – the 'little man in black' – spoke of the superior intellect of men and the sin of Eve. He supplemented his argument against women's rights, stating: 'if God had desired the equality of woman, He would have given some token of His will through the birth, life, and death of the Savior.' At this Sojourner Truth rose to speak, and was recognized over objections from the delegates.

WELL, CHILDREN, WHERE THERE IS so much racket there must be something out of kilter. I think that 'twixt the negroes of the South and the women at the North, all talking about rights, the white men will be in a fix pretty soon. But what's all this here talking about?

That man over there says that women need to be helped into carriages, and lifted over ditches, and to have the best place everywhere. Nobody ever helps me into carriages, or over mud-puddles, or gives me any best place! And ain't I a woman? Look at me! Look at my arm! I have ploughed and planted, and gathered into barns, and no man could head me! And ain't I a woman? I could work as much and eat as much as a man – when I could get it –

and bear the lash as well! And ain't I a woman? I have borne thirteen children, and seen most all sold off to slavery, and when I cried out with my mother's grief, none but Jesus heard me! And ain't I a woman?

Then they talk about this thing in the head; what's this they call it?

[*From the audience:* 'Intellect.']

That's it, honey. What's that got to do with women's rights or negroes' rights? If my cup won't hold but a pint, and yours holds a quart, wouldn't you be mean not to let me have my little half measure full?

Then that little man in black there, he says women can't have as much rights as men, 'cause Christ wasn't a woman! Where did your Christ come from? Where did your Christ come from? From God and a woman! Man had nothing to do with Him.

An engraving of Sojourner Truth. Likely made several decades after her death, it was first published in 1897.

If the first woman God ever made was strong enough to turn the world upside down all alone, these women together ought to be able to turn it back, and get it right side up again! And now they is asking to do it, the men better let them.

Obliged to you for hearing me, and now old Sojourner ain't got nothing more to say.

FREDERICK DOUGLASS

'WHAT, TO THE SLAVE, IS YOUR FOURTH OF JULY?'
Corinthian Hall, Rochester, New York, 5 July 1852

In 1852, the Rochester Ladies' Anti-Slavery Society invited Frederick Douglass to speak at their Independence Day meeting. However, the great orator requested that he should not speak on the Fourth of July, choosing to deliver his speech the following day. What began with praise for the Founding Fathers and the principles held in the Declaration of Independence, evolved into an attack on American hypocrisy embodied in the very holiday being celebrated. This scathing attack, the most powerful and effective of all anti-slavery speeches, was well received by his audience and soon published as a pamphlet. At 10,499 words, it is one of Douglass' longest speeches. The excerpt that follows, roughly one-fifth of the whole, is that included in his second autobiography, *My Bondage and My Freedom* (1855).

A Christian and a scholar, Douglass incorporated quotations from the Bible, William Shakespeare, the Quaker poet John Greenleaf Whittier and several other sources in his speech. In this excerpt are found words from Isaiah ('lame man leap as an hart') and Psalm 137 ('By the rivers of Babylon…'), together with a quotation from abolitionist editor William Lloyd Garrison ('I will not equivocate; I will not excuse…').

FELLOW CITIZENS, PARDON ME, allow me to ask, why am I called upon to speak here today? What have I, or those I represent, to do with your national independence? Are the great principles of political freedom and of natural justice, embodied in that Declaration of Independence, extended to us? And am I, therefore, called upon to bring our humble offering to the national altar, and to confess the benefits and express devout gratitude for the blessings resulting from your independence to us?

Would to God, both for your sakes and ours, that an affirmative answer could be truthfully returned to these questions! Then would my task be light, and my burden easy and delightful. For who is there so cold, that a nation's sympathy could not warm him? Who so obdurate and dead to the claims of gratitude, that would not thankfully acknowledge such priceless benefits? Who so stolid and selfish, that would not give his voice to swell the hallelujahs of a nation's jubilee, when the chains of servitude had been torn from his limbs? I am not that man. In a case like that, the dumb might eloquently speak, and the 'lame man leap as an hart'.

But, such is not the state of the case. I say it with a sad sense of the disparity between us. I am not included within the pale of this glorious anniversary! Your high independence only reveals the immeasurable distance between us. The blessings in which you, this day, rejoice, are not enjoyed in common. The rich inheritance of justice, liberty, prosperity and independence, bequeathed by your fathers, is shared by you, not by me. The sunlight that brought life and healing to you, has brought stripes and death to me. This Fourth of July is yours, not mine. You may rejoice, I must mourn. To drag a man in fetters into the grand illuminated temple of liberty, and call upon him to join you in joyous anthems, were inhuman mockery and sacrilegious irony. Do you mean, citizens, to mock me, by asking me to speak today? If so, there is a parallel to your conduct. And let me warn you that it is dangerous to copy the example of a nation whose crimes, lowering up to heaven, were thrown down by the breath of the Almighty, burying that nation in irrecoverable ruin! I can today take up the plaintive lament of a peeled and woe-smitten people!

'By the rivers of Babylon, there we sat down. Yea! we wept when we remembered Zion. We hanged our harps upon the willows in the midst thereof. For there, they that carried us away captive, required of us a song; and they who wasted us required of us mirth, saying, Sing us one of the songs of Zion. How can we sing the Lord's song in a strange land? If I forget thee, O Jerusalem, let my right hand forget her cunning. If I do not remember thee, let my tongue cleave to the roof of my mouth.'

Fellow citizens, above your national, tumultuous joy, I hear the mournful wail of

27

millions whose chains, heavy and grievous yesterday, are, today, rendered more intolerable by the jubilee shouts that reach them. If I do forget, if I do not faithfully remember those bleeding children of sorrow this day, 'may my right hand forget her cunning, and may my tongue cleave to the roof of my mouth!' To forget them, to pass lightly over their wrongs, and to chime in with the popular theme, would be treason most scandalous and shocking, and would make me a reproach before God and the world. My subject, then, fellow citizens, is *American slavery.* I shall see, this day, and its popular characteristics, from the slave's point of view. Standing, there, identified with the American bondman, making his wrongs mine, I do not hesitate to declare, with all my soul, that the character and conduct of this nation never looked blacker to me than on this Fourth of July! Whether we turn to the declarations of the past, or to the professions of the present, the conduct of the nation seems equally hideous and revolting. America is false to the past, false to the present, and solemnly binds herself to be false to the future. Standing with God and the crushed and bleeding slave on this occasion, I will, in the name of humanity which is outraged, in the name of liberty which is fettered, in the name of the constitution and the Bible, which are disregarded and trampled upon, dare to call in question and to denounce, with all the emphasis I can command, everything that serves to perpetuate slavery – the great

sin and shame of America! 'I will not equivocate; I will not excuse;' I will use the severest language I can command; and yet not one word shall escape me that any man whose judgment is not blinded by prejudice, or who is not at heart a slaveholder, shall not confess to be right and just.

But I fancy I hear some one of my audience say: it is just in this circumstance that you and your brother abolitionists fail to make a favorable impression on the public mind. Would you argue more, and denounce less, would you persuade more, and rebuke less, your cause would be much more likely to succeed. But, I submit, where all is plain there is nothing to be argued. What point in the anti-slavery creed would you have me argue? On what branch of the subject do the people of this country need light? Must I undertake to prove that the slave is a man? That point is conceded already. Nobody doubts it. The slaveholders themselves acknowledge it in the enactment of laws for their government. They acknowledge it when they punish disobedience on the part of the slave. There are seventy-two crimes in the State of Virginia, which, if committed by a black man – no matter how ignorant he be – subject him to the punishment of death; while only two of the same crimes will subject a white man to the like punishment. What is this but the acknowledgement that the slave is a moral, intellectual and responsible being? The manhood of the slave is conceded. It is admitted in the fact that Southern statute books are covered with enactments forbidding, under severe fines and penalties, the teaching of the slave to read or to write. When you can point to any such laws, in reference to the beasts of the field, then I may consent to argue the manhood of the slave. When the dogs in your streets, when the fowls of the air, when the cattle on your hills, when the fish of the sea, and the reptiles that crawl, shall be unable to distinguish the slave from a brute, there will I argue with you that the slave is a man!

For the present, it is enough to affirm the equal manhood of the negro race. Is it not astonishing that, while we are ploughing, planting and reaping, using all kinds of mechanical tools, erecting houses, constructing bridges, building ships, working in metals of brass, iron, copper, silver and gold; that, while we are reading, writing and cyphering, acting as clerks, merchants and secretaries, having among us lawyers, doctors, ministers, poets, authors, editors, orators and teachers; that, while we are engaged in all manner of enterprises common to other men, digging gold in California, capturing the whale in the Pacific, feeding sheep and cattle on the hillside, living, moving, acting, thinking, planning, living in families as husbands, wives and children, and, above all, confessing and worshipping the Christian's God, and looking hopefully for life and immortality beyond the grave, we are called upon to prove that we are men!

Would you have me argue that man is

A photograph of Frederick Douglass that is thought to have been taken when the abolitionist and orator was 61 years old.

entitled to liberty? That he is the rightful owner of his own body? You have already declared it. Must I argue the wrongfulness of slavery? Is that a question for Republicans? Is it to be settled by the rules of logic and argumentation, as a matter beset with great difficulty, involving a doubtful application of the principle of justice, hard to be understood? How should I look today, in the presence of Americans, dividing, and subdividing a discourse, to show that men have a natural right to freedom? speaking of it relatively, and positively, negatively, and affirmatively. To do so, would be to make myself ridiculous, and lo offer an insult to

29

your understanding. There is not a man beneath the canopy of heaven, that does not know that slavery is wrong for him.

What, am I to argue that it is wrong to make men brutes, to rob them of their liberty, to work them without wages, to keep them ignorant of their relations to their fellow men, to beat them with sticks, to flay their flesh with the lash, to load their limbs with irons, to hunt them with dogs, to sell them at auction, to sunder their families, to knock out their teeth, to burn their flesh, to starve them into obedience and submission to their masters? Must I argue that a system thus marked with blood, and stained with pollution, is wrong? No! I will not. I have better employments for my time and strength, than such arguments would imply.

What, then, remains to be argued? Is it that slavery is not divine; that God did not establish it; that our doctors of divinity are mistaken? There is blasphemy in the thought. That which is inhuman cannot be divine! Who can reason on such a proposition? They that can, may; I cannot. The time for such argument is past.

At a time like this, scorching irony, not convincing argument, is needed. Oh, had I the ability, and could I reach the nation's ear, I would, today, pour out a fiery stream of biting ridicule, blasting reproach, withering sarcasm, and stern rebuke. For it is not light that is needed, but fire; it is not the gentle shower, but thunder. We need the storm, the whirlwind, and the earthquake. The feeling of the nation must be quickened; the conscience of the nation must be roused; the propriety of the nation must be startled; the hypocrisy of the nation must be exposed; and its crimes against God and man must be proclaimed and denounced.

What, to the American slave, is your Fourth of July? I answer: a day that reveals to him, more than all other days in the year, the gross injustice and cruelty to which he is the constant victim. To him, your celebration is a sham; your boasted liberty, an unholy license; your national greatness, swelling vanity; your sounds of rejoicing are empty and heartless; your denunciations of tyrants, brass-fronted impudence; your shouts of liberty and equality, hollow mockery; your prayers and hymns, your sermons and thanksgivings, with all your religious parade, and solemnity, are, to him, mere bombast, fraud, deception, impiety, and hypocrisy – a thin veil to cover up crimes which would disgrace a nation of savages. There is not a nation on the earth guilty of practices more shocking and bloody, than are the people of these United States, at this very hour.

Go where you may, search where you will, roam through all the monarchies and despotisms of the old world, travel through South America, search out every abuse, and when you have found the last, lay your facts by the side of the everyday practices of this nation, and you will say with me, that, for revolting barbarity and shameless hypocrisy, America reigns without a rival.

ABRAHAM LINCOLN

THE GETTYSBURG ADDRESS

The Soldiers' National Cemetery, Gettysburg, Pennsylvania,
19 November 1863

When Abraham Lincoln delivered this, perhaps the most
quoted of all American speeches, he was the president of
a divided country. The American Civil War had been
aflame for over two and a half years, at a cost of over a
quarter of a million souls. One of the bloodiest battles of
the conflict had been fought less than four months earlier
at Gettysburg, Pennsylvania. The three-day struggle left
close to 8,000 dead, well over three times the population
of the small town. Faced with the necessary task of
re-interring the dead from their battlefield graves, a
national cemetery was created. At the dedication
ceremony, before an estimated crowd of 15,000, Lincoln
made his famous address.

FOUR SCORE AND SEVEN YEARS AGO our fathers
brought forth on this continent a new nation,
conceived in Liberty, and dedicated to the
proposition that all men are created equal.

Now we are engaged in a great civil war, testing
whether that nation, or any nation, so conceived and so
dedicated, can long endure. We are met on a great
battlefield of that war. We have come to dedicate a portion
of that field, as a final resting place for those who here
gave their lives that that nation might live. It is altogether
fitting and proper that we should do this.

But, in a larger sense, we can not dedicate—we can
not consecrate—we can not hallow—this ground. The
brave men, living and dead, who struggled here, have
consecrated it, far above our poor power to add or detract.

The world will little note, nor long remember what we say here, but it can never forget what they did here. It is for us the living, rather, to be dedicated here to the unfinished work which they who fought here have thus far so nobly advanced. It is rather for us to be here dedicated to the great task remaining before us—that from these honored dead we take increased devotion to that cause for which they gave the last full measure of devotion—that we here highly resolve that these dead shall not have died in vain—that this nation, under God, shall have a new birth of freedom —and that government of the people, by the people, for the people, shall not perish from the earth.

Abraham Lincoln at his last portrait sitting, four days before his assassination.

SUSAN B. ANTHONY

ON A WOMAN'S RIGHT TO VOTE
The Districts of Monroe and Ontario,
New York State, May–June 1873

In the weeks leading up to *United States v. Susan B. Anthony*, the defendant toured the State of New York delivering this stump speech of over 10,000 words on fifty separate occasions. Drawing on a wealth of legal documents, opinions and decisions, she presents a number of arguments that would be later used in her trial for 'knowingly voting without having a lawful right to vote'. The charge stemmed from an incident that took place during elections of November, 1872. Anthony and fourteen other women had voted in Rochester, New York after successfully arguing their case with three inspectors of election. Before the month was out, the women voters had been arrested; all of them, save Anthony, chose to pay a fine of $500 rather than face imprisonment.

Although Anthony's arguments won over many in sympathetic crowds, they were not so effective against Ward Hunt, the presiding judge. Supported by her two lawyers, Anthony was found guilty and ordered to pay a fine of $100 and the costs of prosecution. When told that the convicted would never pay the 'unjust penalty', Hunt responded: 'Madam, the Court will not order you to stand committed until the fine is paid.' Anthony was released and, true to her word, the fine was never paid.

What follows is the beginning of Anthony's speech.

FRIENDS AND FELLOW CITIZENS: I stand before you tonight under indictment for the alleged crime of having voted at the last presidential election, without having a lawful right to vote. It shall be my work this evening to prove to you that in thus voting, I not only committed no crime, but, instead, simply exercised my citizen's rights, guaranteed to me and all United States citizens by the National Constitution, beyond the power of any state to deny.

Our democratic-republican government is based on the idea of the natural right of every individual member thereof to a voice and a vote in making and executing the laws. We assert the province of government to be to secure the people in the enjoyment of their unalienable rights. We throw to the winds the old dogma that governments can give rights. Before governments were organized, no one denies that each individual possessed the right to protect his own life, liberty and property. And when 100 or 1,000,000 people enter into a free government, they do not barter away their natural rights; they simply pledge themselves to protect each other in the enjoyment of them, through prescribed judicial and legislative tribunals. They agree to abandon the methods of brute force in the adjustment of their differences, and adopt those of civilization.

Nor can you find a word in any of the grand documents left us by the fathers that assumes for government the power to create or to confer rights. The Declaration of Independence, the United States Constitution, the constitutions of the several states and the organic laws of the territories, all alike propose to protect the people in the exercise of their God-given rights. Not one of them pretends to bestow rights:

All men are created equal, and endowed by their Creator with certain unalienable rights. Among these are life, liberty and the pursuit of happiness. To secure these, governments are instituted among men, deriving their just powers from the consent of the governed.

Here is no shadow of government authority over rights, nor exclusion of any class from their full and equal enjoyment. Here is pronounced the right of all men, and 'consequently,' as the Quaker preacher said, 'of all women,' to a voice in the government. And here, in this very first paragraph of the Declaration, is the assertion of the natural right of all to the ballot; for, how can 'the consent of the governed' be given, if the right to vote be denied? Again:

That whenever any form of government becomes destructive of these ends, it is the right of the people to alter or abolish it, and to institute a new government, laying its foundations on such principles, and organizing its powers in such forms as to them shall seem most likely to effect their safety and happiness.

Surely, the right of the whole people to vote is here clearly implied. For however destructive to their happiness this government might become, a disfranchised class could neither alter nor abolish it, nor institute a new one, except by the old brute force method of insurrection and rebellion. One-half of the people of this nation to-day are utterly powerless to blot from the statute books an unjust law, or to write there a new and a just one. The women, dissatisfied as they are with this form of government, that enforces taxation without representation, – that compels them to obey laws to which they have never given their consent, – that imprisons and hangs them without a trial by a jury of their peers, that robs them, in marriage, of the custody of their own persons, wages and children, – are this half of the people left wholly at the mercy of the other half, in direct violation of the spirit and letter of the declarations of the framers of this government, every one of which was based on the immutable principle of equal rights to all. By those declarations, kings, priests, popes, aristocrats, were all alike dethroned, and placed on a common level, politically, with the lowliest born subject or serf. By them, too, men, as such, were deprived of their divine right to rule, and placed on a political level with women. By the practice of those declarations all class and caste distinction will be abolished; and slave, serf, plebeian, wife, woman, all alike, bound from their subject position to the proud platform of equality.

The preamble of the Federal Constitution says:

We, the people of the United States, in order to form a more perfect union, establish justice, insure domestic tranquility, provide for the common defense, promote the general welfare, and secure the blessings of liberty to ourselves and our posterity, do ordain and establish this Constitution for the United States of America.

It was we, the people; not we, the white male citizens; nor yet we, the male citizens; but we, the whole people, who formed the Union. And we formed it, not to give the blessings of liberty, but to secure them; not to the half of ourselves and the half of our posterity, but to the whole people – women as well as men. And it is a downright bad to talk to women of their enjoyment of the blessings of liberty while they are denied the use of the only means of securing them provided by this democratic-republican government – the ballot.

EMMELINE PANKHURST

IN SUPPORT OF THE WOMEN'S ENFRANCHISEMENT BILL

Royal Albert Hall, London, 19 March 1908

Emmeline Pankhurst – Mrs Pankhurst, as she was known – was imprisoned thirteen times during her struggle for the rights of women. This speech was made the same day on which she had been released, quite unexpectedly, from her very first sentence. While the experience disturbed her greatly, this is not reflected in the tenor of this speech. Rather, Pankhurst celebrates a winter torchlight procession, two months past, at which she had spoken to 100,000 men and women, and expresses enthusiasm and support for the Women's Enfranchisement Bill, proposed legislation brought forward by H.Y. Stanger.

Two names from history appear in the speech: Annie Kenney sat with Pankhurst as one of the leaders of the Women's Social and Political Union, and Herbert Gladstone, who was Home Secretary and the youngest son of former Prime Minister William Gladstone. A self-described suffragist, the younger Gladstone had advised the Union in means to achieve their goal. Despite his support, the Women's Enfranchisement Bill failed; another decade would pass before women in the United Kingdom would be granted the right to vote.

FRIENDS, THIS MORNING I WAS IN PRISON! And I was thinking of this meeting here tonight, how in the solitude of my prison cell, while you women here were demanding your political freedom, my thoughts would be with you.

At two o'clock, the chief wardress came into my cell. She said: 'You are to go out.'

And I said: 'My time is not up until tomorrow morning. By whose authority am I to leave the prison?'

She said: 'There is an order for your release, and I suppose your friends procured it for you.'

'Not my friends,' I said.

Well, we had to come out. Was it because the government knew that we and you would be disappointed if we could not be here tonight, was it out of kindness that they did it? Well, one can hardly think so, because if they had felt that it wasn't fair to put political prisoners, who have broken no law, in the second division in solitary confinement to deprive them of paper and pen and pencil, to deprive them even from speaking to one another, I think the order for our release would have come earlier than the day before the law entitled us to have it. No, I suppose they chose the lesser of two evils, they thought they preferred one demonstration to two. So I think we may conclude that is the reason why my friends and I, who should have been sleeping in Holloway tonight, are at this meeting with you.

Well, while we have been in prison, you outside have been doing magnificent work. The bill – because these things filter even into prison – the bill has passed, after many years, its second reading. Well, that is something, but you women have not studied parliamentary procedure any more than some of the young Liberal MPs. You must not think too much of the second reading of the women's suffrage bill. We know, who understand parliamentary procedure, that that means little or nothing; that if we ever get beyond that state we women must do ten times more than we have done in the past to secure that the bill shall successfully come to a third reading.

While we have been in prison, I learn you have had two by-elections. One is over, and a great defeat to the Liberal government, the second is not concluded, so we women who proverbially are pushing will be pushing still until we know the result, but I understand that tomorrow we are to go along there, we women who have been in solitude so long, and do what we can to inflict upon the government another defeat.

I understand that members of the government have been saying that we must demonstrate as men did before they got the vote. Well, the night before I came to London, we had a demonstration in Yorkshire, on the historic site of the great franchise demonstration in the sixties. On Hunslet Moor in Leeds thousands of men demonstrated when they were agitating for the franchise. The night before I came up to London for the Women's Parliament, we women had a procession in Leeds. Well, I think the whole of Leeds joined in the procession. After the procession, with torches, we met on Hunslet Moor where Mr Herbert Gladstone had advised us to meet, and old men in Leeds who remembered that agitation said that never in the history of any agitation for reform had so many people congregated together on Hunslet Moor as met there that night.

But we women, because we are women, must do far more than the men ever did, to show that we are determined to gain their citizen rights. So I am glad to think that this programme for the summer months has been made, which if carried out successfully will prove to the satisfaction even of members of the government that women indeed want the vote, and mean to have it. And we may well be ready to spare no effort in our determination to get the vote.

For more than fifty years, women have been demanding that common elementary right. We have always needed the vote, we have always wanted it, but never so much as we need it today. Today we have the new kind of politics, very different from the old-fashioned politics – because today politics means, as it never has meant before, interference with us all in our daily lives. You have proposals out of Parliament, and in Parliament, for the regulation of our lives as we have never had before. No doubt with the best intentions – every body intends well – but we women need new representation in order to see that this new kind of legislation is not to be worse tyranny and a greater oppression than any kind of legislation that has gone before.

They say women have no sense of humour, but if it were not so serious, what is being done by men would create a sense of humour in women. I am sorry if some of the gentlemen in the audience may feel their susceptibilities wounded by what I am going to say now, but to a woman it is humorous to see how men seem to think they are fitted to deal with questions which ever since the human race existed have been left to women to manage, and which women understand. How children, even, are to be brought into the world men in Parliament think they can decide now! The rearing and bearing of children, the care of the sick, the care of the old, the making of our homes, and the keeping of our homes, men are going to make laws to decide, without even giving us the elementary right of deciding who the men are to be who are to make these momentous decisions!

I need only give you one instance. This bill which the government is introducing to decide the question of the controls of that splendid body of women who nurse the sick in our hospitals, rules and regulations are to be made for them, without even thinking it necessary to ask experienced women what these rules and regulations are to be.

Well, I for one friends, looking round at the muddles men have made, looking round now at the starving children, looking round now at the sweated and decrepit members of my sex, I say men have had the control of these things long enough and no woman with any spark of womanliness in her will consent to let this state of things go on any longer.

So this year we are going to settle the business. We are tired and we want to be of use, we want to have this power in order that we may try to make this world a much better place for men and women than it is today. So I appeal to you women in this magnificent auditorium, every one of you to do your part. You need not go to prison. Yet I believe if you all did, as we have done – and it doesn't need much courage, as some of you think – if you all made up your minds to do it, we would only have to do it once.

Well, we have got this programme planned out. You are going to hear more about it from other speakers because I have been shut away so I don't understand the details as fully, I cannot tell you as much about it as they can, but I know this, that we cannot carry out this programme, which means the bringing together of 150,000 determined women in June, unless we have the wherewithal to do it.

Now, politicians know better than women, because we are new to practical politics many of us, how much it costs in time and energy and money to carry out an agitation like this, but let me tell you this, that we want you all, we want your services, we want your energy, we want your time, we want your help, we want your money and after all that is the least part of it.

So in conclusion, I want to say I am very glad to be here tonight. It makes me very happy to see what a few years ago I thought I should never live to see. They said: 'You will never rouse women'. Well, we have done what they thought, and what they hoped

impossible: we women are roused. Perhaps it is difficult to rouse women, and they are longsuffering and patient; now that we are roused, we will never be quiet again.

There is a resolution to be put to the meeting later on, and it is my duty to move it from the chair. It is as follows:

> *This meeting of women assembled in the Royal Albert Hall demand that constitutional rights be granted to women, and calls upon the government to adopt and carry into law the Women's Enfranchisement Bill now before Parliament.*

I move that resolution and call upon Miss Annie Kenney, who at the opening of the London campaign, at a great Liberal demonstration, from that box yonder, had the courage to put out a banner and say: 'Will the Liberal government give votes to women?'

I call upon Miss Annie Kenney to second the resolution.

Emmeline Pankhurst during the time of her struggle for women's suffrage.

PATRICK PEARSE

'IRELAND UNFREE SHALL NEVER BE AT PEACE'

Glasnevin Cemetery, Dublin, 1 August 1915

Though one of the foremost Irish leaders of his day, Jeremiah O'Donovan Rossa is best remembered through Patrick Pearse's panegyric to the fallen Fenian. Delivered at the graveside, the oration marked the culmination of a series of events begun five weeks earlier with Rossa's death in New York City. As the body was en route to Dublin, preparations were made to transform the funeral into a gathering in support of Irish independence. Pearse was selected to speak, not because he was the most prominent leader, but because he had the greatest gift for oration. He composed the speech himself, the sole input coming from senior revolutionary leader Tom Clarke, who instructed: 'Make it as hot as hell, throw all discretion to the winds.'

It is not so much a eulogy, but an affirmation that Rossa's struggle would continue under a new generation. In doing so, Pearse makes mention of two other past leaders in the struggle for independence: Wolfe Tone, the 18th-century figure credited as the father of Irish Republicanism, and the 19th-century journalist and activist John Mitchel.

Delivered before thousands, Pearse's words are frequently credited with rallying Republican forces, ultimately contributing to the Easter Rising the following year.

IT HAS SEEMED RIGHT, before we turn away from this place in which we have laid the mortal remains of O'Donovan Rossa, that one among us should, in the name of all, speak the praise of that valiant man, and endeavour to formulate the thought and the hope that are in us as we stand around his grave. And if there is anything that makes it fitting that I, rather than some other, rather than one of the grey-haired men who were young with him and shared in his labour and in his suffering, should speak here, it is perhaps that I may be taken as speaking on behalf of a new generation that has been re-baptised in the Fenian faith, and that has accepted the responsibility of carrying out the Fenian programme. I propose to you then that, here by the grave of this unrepentant Fenian, we renew our baptismal vows; that, here by the grave of this unconquered and unconquerable man, we ask of God, each one for himself, such unshakable purpose, such high and gallant courage, such unbreakable strength of soul as belonged to O'Donovan Rossa.

Deliberately here we avow ourselves, as he avowed himself in the dock, Irishmen of one allegiance only. We of the Irish Volunteers, and you others who are associated with us in today's task and duty, are bound together and must stand together henceforth in brotherly union for the achievement of the freedom of Ireland. And we know only one definition of freedom: it is Tone's definition, it is Mitchel's definition, it is Rossa's definition. Let no man blaspheme the cause that the dead generations of Ireland served by giving it any other name and definition than their name and their definition.

We stand at Rossa's grave not in sadness but rather in exaltation of spirit that it has been given to us to come thus into so close a communion with that brave and splendid Gael. Splendid and holy causes are served by men who are themselves splendid and holy. O'Donovan Rossa was splendid in the proud manhood of him, splendid in the heroic grace of him, splendid in the Gaelic strength and clarity and truth of him. And all that splendour and pride and strength was compatible with a humility and a simplicity of devotion to Ireland, to all that was olden and beautiful and Gaelic in Ireland, the holiness and simplicity of patriotism of a Michael O'Clery or of an Eoghan O'Growney. The clear true eyes of this man almost alone in his day visioned Ireland as we of today would surely have her: not free merely, but Gaelic as well; not Gaelic merely, but free as well.

In a closer spiritual communion with him now than ever before or perhaps ever again, in a spiritual communion with those of his day, living and dead, who suffered with him in English prisons, in communion of spirit too with our own dear comrades who suffer in English prisons today, and speaking on their behalf as well as our own, we pledge to Ireland our love, and we pledge to English rule in Ireland our hate. This is a place of

41

Patrick Pearse, in the uniform of an Irish Volunteer Officer, addresses a recruiting meeting in Dublin in 1915.

peace, sacred to the dead, where men should speak with all charity and with all restraint; but I hold it a Christian thing, as O'Donovan Rossa held it, to hate evil, to hate untruth, to hate oppression, and, hating them, to strive to overthrow them. Our foes are strong and wise and wary; but, strong and wise and wary as they are, they cannot undo the miracles of God who ripens in the hearts of young men the seeds sown by the young men of a former generation. And the seeds sown by the young men of '65 and '67 are coming to their miraculous ripening to-day. Rulers and defenders of realms had need to be wary if they would guard against such processes. Life springs from death; and from the graves of patriot men and women spring living nations. The defenders of this realm have worked well in secret and in the open. They think that they have pacified Ireland. They think that they have purchased half of us and intimidated the other half. They think that they have foreseen everything, think that they have provided against everything; but the fools, the fools, the fools! – they have left us our Fenian dead, and while Ireland holds these graves, Ireland unfree shall never be at peace.

DAVID LLOYD GEORGE

ON THE CAUSE OF THE GREAT WAR

St Andrew's Hall, Glasgow, 29 June 1917

Liberal Prime Minister David Lloyd George delivered this speech as the First World War was poised to enter its fourth year. Before the conflict, he had been considered a pacifist; indeed as Chancellor of the Exchequer he had argued for a massive reduction in naval expenditures. There was, however, a major change in stance once war was declared. In 1915, Lloyd George was appointed Minister of Munitions and the year after that, upon the death of Field Marshal Herbert Kitchener, became Secretary of State for War. Believing himself a greater wartime leader than his own Prime Minister, H. H. Asquith, in 1916 he drew support from Conservatives and disaffected Liberals to take the office himself.

Lloyd George's great eloquence, displayed here, masks the fact that Welsh, not English, was his mother tongue.

I T IS A SATISFACTION FOR Britain in these terrible times that no share of the responsibility for these events rests on her.

She is not the Jonah in this storm. The part taken by our country in this conflict, in its origin, and in its conduct, has been as honourable and chivalrous as any part ever taken in any country in any operation.

We might imagine from declarations which were made by the Germans, aye! and even by a few people in this country, who are constantly referring to our German comrades, that this terrible war was wantonly and wickedly provoked by England – never Scotland, never Wales and never Ireland.

Wantonly provoked by England to increase her

possessions, and to destroy the influence, the power, and the prosperity of a dangerous rival.

There never was a more foolish travesty of the actual facts. It happened three years ago, or less, but there have been so many bewildering events crowded into those intervening years that some people might have forgotten, perhaps, some of the essential facts, and it is essential that we should now and again restate them, not merely to refute the calumniators of our native land, but in order to sustain the hearts of her people by the unswerving conviction that no part of the guilt of this terrible bloodshed rests on the conscience of their native land.

What are the main facts? There were six countries which entered the war at the beginning. Britain was last, and not the first.

Before she entered the war Britain made every effort to avoid it; begged, supplicated, and entreated that there should be no conflict.

I was a member of the Cabinet at the time, and I remember the earnest endeavours we made to persuade Germany and Austria not to precipitate Europe into this welter of blood. We begged them to summon a European conference to consider.

Had that conference met, arguments against provoking such a catastrophe were so overwhelming that there would never have been a war. Germany knew that, so she rejected the conference, although Austria was prepared to accept it. She suddenly declared war, and yet we are the people who wantonly provoked this war, in order to attack Germany.

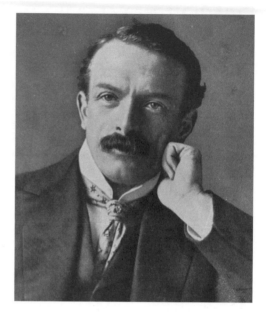

David Lloyd George in 1908, eight years before becoming Prime Minister of the United Kingdom.

We begged Germany not to attack Belgium, and produced a treaty, signed by the King of Prussia, as well as the King of England, pledging himself to protect Belgium against an invader, and we said: 'If you invade Belgium we shall have no alternative but to defend it.'

The enemy invaded Belgium, and now they say: 'Why, forsooth, you, England, provoked this war.'

It is not quite the story of the wolf and the lamb. I will tell you why: because Germany expected to find a lamb and found a lion.

WOODROW WILSON

The Fourteen Points

The United States Capitol, Washington, DC, 8 January 1918

When President Woodrow Wilson made this speech before a joint session of Congress, it was clear that the First World War, which the Americans had joined nine months earlier, was drawing to an end. More than a basis through which peace might be negotiated, Wilson's address contained his vision of a world in which further conflict might be avoided. Ultimately, the President's Fourteen Points, laid out here, would serve as a foundation for the Treaty of Versailles.

Wilson formulated his Fourteen Points with the aid of the 'Inquiry', a group of 150 academics. No American politicians were involved, nor were any Allied leaders consulted. While French Prime Minister Georges Clemenceau and David Lloyd George, Prime Minister of the United Kingdom, took issue with select points, Wilson's greatest obstacle was domestic in origin. This was manifested in the United States Senate's refusal to ratify the Treaty of Versailles; the main objection being obligations imposed by the associated membership in the League of Nations.

First proposed as the fourteenth point – a 'general association of nations' – Wilson received the 1919 Nobel Peace Prize for his promotion of the League of Nations, a body his own country never joined.

GENTLEMEN OF THE CONGRESS: Once more, as repeatedly before, the spokesmen of the Central Empires have indicated their desire to discuss the objects of the war and the possible basis of a general peace. Parleys have been in progress at Brest-Litovsk between Russian representatives and representatives of the Central Powers to which the attention of all the belligerents has been invited for the purpose of ascertaining whether it may be possible to extend these parleys into a general conference with regard to terms of peace and settlement.

The Russian representatives presented not only a perfectly definite statement of the principles upon which they would be willing to conclude peace, but also an equally definite program of the concrete application of those principles. The representatives of the Central Powers, on their part, presented an outline of settlement which, if much less definite, seemed susceptible of liberal interpretation until their specific program of practical terms was added. That program proposed no concessions at all, either to the sovereignty of Russia or to the preferences of the populations with whose fortunes it dealt, but meant, in a word, that the Central Empires were to keep every foot of territory their armed forces had occupied – every province, every city, every point of vantage as a permanent addition to their territories and their power.

It is a reasonable conjecture that the general principles of settlement which they at first suggested originated with the more liberal statesmen of Germany and Austria, the men who have begun to feel the force of their own peoples' thought and purpose, while the concrete terms of actual settlement came from the military leaders who have no thought but to keep what they have got. The negotiations have been broken off. The Russian representatives were sincere and in earnest. They cannot entertain such proposals of conquest and domination.

The whole incident is full of significance. It is also full of perplexity. With whom are the Russian representatives dealing? For whom are the representatives of the Central Empires speaking? Are they speaking for the majorities of their respective parliaments or for the minority parties, that military and imperialistic minority which has so far dominated their whole policy and controlled the affairs of Turkey and of the Balkan States which have felt obliged to become their associates in this war?

The Russian representatives have insisted, very justly, very wisely, and in the true spirit of modern democracy, that the conferences they have been holding with the Teutonic and Turkish statesmen should be held within open, not closed, doors, and all the world has been audience, as was desired. To whom have we been listening, then? To those who speak the spirit and intention of the resolutions of the German Reichstag of the 9th of July last, the spirit and intention of the liberal leaders and parties of Germany, or to those who resist and defy that spirit and intention and insist upon conquest and subjugation? Or are we listening, in fact, to both, unreconciled and in open and hopeless contradiction? These are very serious and pregnant questions. Upon the answer to them depends the peace of the world.

But whatever the results of the parleys at Brest-Litovsk, whatever the confusions of counsel and of purpose in the utterances of the spokesmen of the Central Empires, they have again attempted to acquaint the world with their objects in the war and have again challenged their adversaries to say what their objects are and what sort of settlement they would deem just and satisfactory. There is no good reason why that challenge should not be responded to, and responded to with the utmost candor. We did not wait for it. Not once, but again and again we have laid our whole thought and purpose before the world, not in general terms only, but each time with sufficient definition to make it clear what sort of definite terms of settlement must necessarily spring out of them. Within the last week Mr Lloyd George has spoken with admirable candor and in admirable spirit for the people and Government of Great Britain.

There is no confusion of counsel among the adversaries of the Central Powers, no uncertainty of principle, no vagueness of detail. The only secrecy of counsel, the only lack of fearless frankness, the only failure to make definite statement of the objects of the war, lies with Germany and her allies. The issues of life and death hang upon these definitions. No statesman who has the least conception of his responsibility ought for a moment to permit himself to continue this tragical and appalling outpouring of blood and treasure unless he is sure beyond a peradventure that the objects of the vital sacrifice are part and parcel of the very life of society and that the people for whom he speaks think them right and imperative as he does.

There is, moreover, a voice calling for these definitions of principle and of purpose which is, it seems to me, more thrilling and more compelling than any of the many moving voices with which the troubled air of the world is filled. It is the voice of the Russian people. They are prostrate and all but helpless, it would seem, before the grim power of Germany, which has hitherto known no relenting and no pity. Their power, apparently, is shattered. And yet their soul is not subservient. They will not yield either in principle or in action. Their conception of what is right, of what is humane and honorable for them to accept, has been stated with a frankness, a largeness of view, a generosity of spirit, and a universal human sympathy which must challenge the admiration of every friend of mankind; and they have refused to compound their ideals or desert others that they themselves may be safe.

They call to us to say what it is that we desire, in what, if in anything, our purpose and our spirit differ from theirs; and I believe that the people of the United States would wish me to respond, with utter simplicity and frankness. Whether their present leaders believe it or not, it is our heartfelt desire and hope that some way may be opened whereby we may be privileged to assist the people of

47

Russia to attain their utmost hope of liberty and ordered peace.

It will be our wish and purpose that the processes of peace, when they are begun, shall be absolutely open and that they shall involve and permit henceforth no secret understandings of any kind. The day of conquest and aggrandizement is gone by; so is also the day of secret covenants entered into in the interest of particular governments and likely at some unlooked-for moment to upset the peace of the world. It is this happy fact, now clear to the view of every public man whose thoughts do not still linger in an age that is dead and gone, which makes it possible for every nation whose purposes are consistent with justice and the peace of the world to avow now or at any other time the objects it has in view.

We entered this war because violations of right had occurred which touched us to the quick and made the life of our own people impossible unless they were corrected and the world secured once for all against their recurrence.

What we demand in this war, therefore, is nothing peculiar to ourselves. It is that the world be made fit and safe to live in; and particularly that it be made safe for every peace-loving nation which, like our own, wishes to live its own life, determine its own institutions, be assured of justice and fair dealing by the other peoples of the world, as against force and selfish aggression.

All the peoples of the world are in effect partners in this interest, and for our own part we see very clearly that unless justice be done to others it will not be done to us.

The program of the world's peace, therefore, is our program; and that program, the only possible program, as we see it, is this:

1. Open covenants of peace, openly arrived at, after which there shall be no private international understandings of any kind, but diplomacy shall proceed always frankly and in the public view.

2. Absolute freedom of navigation upon the seas, outside territorial waters, alike in peace and in war, except as the seas may be closed in whole or in part by international action for the enforcement of international covenants.

3. The removal, so far as possible, of all economic barriers and the establishment of an equality of trade conditions among all the nations consenting to the peace and associating themselves for its maintenance.

4. Adequate guarantees given and taken that national armaments will be reduced to the lowest points consistent with domestic safety.

5. A free, open-minded, and absolutely impartial adjustment of all colonial claims, based upon a strict observance of the principle that in determining all such questions of sovereignty the interests of the population concerned must have equal weight with the equitable claims of the government whose title is to be determined.

6. The evacuation of all Russian territory

and such a settlement of all questions affecting Russia as will secure the best and freest co-operation of the other nations of the world in obtaining for her an unhampered and unembarrassed opportunity for the independent determination of her own political development and national policy, and assure her of a sincere welcome into the society of free nations under institutions of her own choosing; and, more than a welcome, assistance also of every kind that she may need and may herself desire. The treatment accorded Russia by her sister nations in the months to come will be the acid test of their goodwill, of their comprehension of her needs as distinguished from their own interests, and of their intelligent and unselfish sympathy.

7. Belgium, the whole world will agree, must be evacuated and restored, without any attempt to limit the sovereignty which she enjoys in common with all other free nations. No other single act will serve as this will serve to restore confidence among the nations in the laws which they have themselves set and determined for the government of their relations with one another. Without this healing act the whole structure and validity of international law is forever impaired.

8. All French territory should be freed and the invaded portions restored, and the wrong done to France by Prussia in 1871 in the matter of Alsace-Lorraine, which has unsettled the peace of the world for nearly fifty years, should be righted, in order that peace may once more be made secure in the interest of all.

9. A re-adjustment of the frontiers of Italy should be effected along clearly recognizable lines of nationality.

10. The peoples of Austria-Hungary, whose place among the nations we wish to see safeguarded and assured, should be accorded the freest opportunity of autonomous development.

11. Rumania, Serbia, and Montenegro should be evacuated; occupied territories restored; Serbia accorded free and secure access to the sea; and the relations of the several Balkan states to one another determined by friendly counsel along historically established lines of allegiance and nationality; and international guarantees of the political and economic independence and territorial integrity of the several Balkan states should be entered into.

12. The Turkish portions of the present Ottoman Empire should be assured a secure sovereignty, but the other nationalities which are now under Turkish rule should be assured an undoubted security of life and an absolutely unmolested opportunity of autonomous development, and the Dardanelles should be permanently opened as a free passage to the ships and commerce of all nations under international guarantees.

13. An independent Polish state should be erected which should include the territories inhabited by indisputably Polish populations, which should be assured a free

and secure access to the sea, and whose political and economic independence and territorial integrity should be guaranteed by international covenant.

14. A general association of nations must be formed under specific covenants for the purpose of affording mutual guarantees of political independence and territorial integrity to great and small states alike.

In regard to these essential rectifications of wrong and assertions of right, we feel ourselves to be intimate partners of all the governments and peoples associated together against the Imperialists. We cannot be separated in interest or divided in purpose. We stand together until the end.

For such arrangements and covenants we are willing to fight and to continue to fight until they are achieved; but only because we wish the right to prevail and desire a just and stable peace such as can be secured only by removing the chief provocations to war, which this program does remove.

We have no jealousy of German greatness, and there is nothing in this program that impairs it. We grudge her no achievement or distinction of learning or of pacific enterprise such as have made her record very bright and very enviable. We do not wish to injure her or to block in any way her legitimate influence or power. We do not wish to fight her either with arms or with hostile arrangements of trade, if she is willing to associate herself with us and the other peace-loving nations of the world in covenants of justice and law and fair dealing.

We wish her only to accept a place of equality among the peoples of the world – the new world in which we now live – instead of a place of mastery.

Neither do we presume to suggest to her any alteration or modification of her institutions. But it is necessary, we must frankly say, and necessary as a preliminary to any intelligent dealings with her on our part, that we should know whom her spokesmen speak for when they speak to us, whether for the Reichstag majority or for the military party and the men whose creed is imperial domination.

We have spoken now, surely, in terms too concrete to admit of any further doubt or question. An evident principle runs through the whole program I have outlined. It is the principle of justice to all peoples and nationalities, and their right to live on equal terms of liberty and safety with one another, whether they be strong or weak.

Unless this principle be made its foundation, no part of the structure of international justice can stand. The people of the United States could act upon no other principle, and to the vindication of this principle they are ready to devote their lives, their honor, and everything that they possess. The moral climax of this, the culminating and final war for human liberty has come, and they are ready to put their own strength, their own highest purpose, their own integrity and devotion to the test.

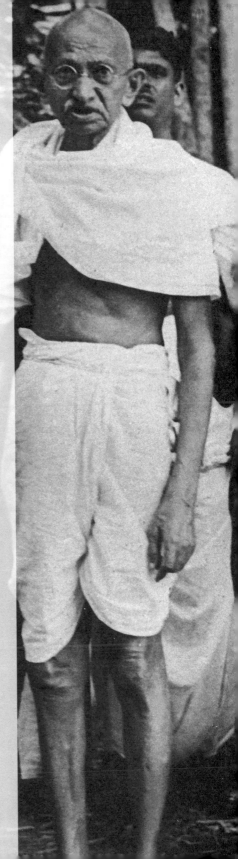

MOHANDAS GANDHI

STATEMENT AT THE GREAT TRIAL

Courtroom of the District and Sessions Judge,
Ahmedabad, India, 18 March 1922

Mohandas Gandhi's Satyagraha movement of non-
violence and non-co-operation was in its second year when,
in 1922, policemen in the northern Indian town of Chauri
Chaura fired on a group of protesters. A chase ensued,
leading the police to lock themselves in their local station.
The crowd set the building afire, killing twenty-two
policemen. Gandhi quickly called off all further protest,
but not before a warrant had been issued for his arrest on
the charge of 'bringing or attempting to excite disaffection
towards His Majesty's Government established by law in
British India', the offences being three articles published
between September 1921 and February 1922 in *Young
India*. In the ensuing trial of Gandhi and Shri Banker
(printer and publisher of *Young India*), Sir J.T. Strangman,
the prosecuting counsel, acknowledged that Gandhi had
insisted the campaign be non-violent, but went on to
question 'of what value is it to insist on non-violence, if
incessantly you preach disaffection towards the
Government and hold it up as a treacherous Government,
and if you openly and deliberately seek to instigate others
to overthrow it?' Having considered the prosecution's
argument and Gandhi's admission of guilt, Justice C.N.
Bloomfield found the prisoner guilty and sentenced him to
six years in prison. The judge concluded: 'if, in due course,
events in India should make it possible for the
Government to reduce the period and release you, no one
will be better pleased than I'. Gandhi served two years.

Included here are the remarks made by Gandhi before
reading his written statement. The statement itself begins
with the words: 'I owe it perhaps to the Indian public…'

BEFORE I READ THIS STATEMENT I would like to state that I entirely endorse the learned Advocate-General's remarks in connection with my humble self, I think that he has made. Because it is very true and I have no desire whatsoever to conceal from this court the fact that to preach disaffection towards the existing system of government has become almost a passion with me, and the Advocate-General is entirely in the right when he says that my preaching of disaffection did not commence with my connection with *Young India,* but that it commenced much earlier. And in the statement that I am about to read, it will be my painful duty to admit before this court that it commenced much earlier than the period stated by the Advocate-General.

It is a painful duty with me but I have to discharge that duty knowing the responsibility that rests upon my shoulders, and I wish to endorse all the blame that the learned Advocate-General has thrown on my shoulders in connection with the Bombay occurrences, Madras occurrences and the Chauri Chaura occurrences. Thinking over these things deeply and sleeping over them night after night, it is impossible for me to dissociate myself from the diabolical crimes of Chauri Chaura or the mad outrages of Bombay.

He is quite right when he says, that as a man of responsibility, a man having received a fair share of education, having had a fair share of experience of this world, I should have known the consequences of every one of my acts.

I know them. I knew that I was playing with fire. I ran the risk and if I was set free I would still do the same. I have felt it this morning that I would have failed in my duty, if I did not say what I said here just now.

I wanted to avoid violence. Non-violence is the first article of my faith. It is also the last article of my creed. But I had to make my choice. I had either to submit to a system which I considered had done an irreparable harm to my country, or incur the risk of the mad fury of my people bursting forth when they understood the truth from my lips. I know that my people have sometimes gone mad. I am deeply sorry for it and I am, therefore, here to submit not to a light penalty, but to the highest penalty. I do not ask for mercy. I do not plead any extenuating act.

I am here, therefore, to invite and cheerfully submit to the highest penalty that can be inflicted upon me for what in law is a deliberate crime, and what appears to me to be the highest duty of a citizen. The only course open to you, the Judge, is, as I am going to say in my statement, either to resign your post, or inflict on me the severest penalty if you believe that the system and law you are assisting to administer are good for the people. I do not except that kind of conversion. But by the time I have finished with my statement you will have a glimpse of what is raging within my breast to run this

The young Gandhi (left) with Rabindranath Tagore, an Indian writer, poet and musician who was awarded the Nobel Prize for Literature in 1913.

maddest risk which a sane man can run.

I owe it perhaps to the Indian public and to the public in England, to placate which this prosecution is mainly taken up, that I should explain why from a staunch loyalist and co-operator, I have become an uncompromising disaffectionist and non-co-operator. To the court too I should say why I plead guilty to the charge of promoting disaffection towards the Government established by law in India.

My public life began in 1893 in South Africa in troubled weather. My first contact with British authority in that country was not of a happy character. I discovered that as a man and an Indian, I had no rights. More correctly I discovered that I had no rights as a man because I was an Indian.

But I was not baffled. I thought that this treatment of Indians was an excrescence upon a system that was intrinsically and mainly good. I gave the Government my voluntary and hearty co-operation, criticising it freely where I felt it was faulty but never wishing its destruction.

Consequently when the existence of the Empire was threatened in 1899 by the Boer challenge, I offered my services to it, raised a volunteer ambulance corps and served at several actions that took place for the relief of Ladysmith. Similarly in 1906, at the time of the Zulu 'revolt', I raised a stretcher bearer party and served till the end of the 'rebellion'. On both the occasions I received medals and was even mentioned in dispatches. For my work in South Africa I was given by Lord Hardinge a Kaisar-i-Hind gold medal. When the war broke out in 1914 between England and Germany, I raised a volunteer ambulance corps in London, consisting of the then resident Indians in London, chiefly students. Its work was acknowledged by the authorities to be valuable. Lastly, in India when a special appeal was made at the war Conference in Delhi in 1918 by Lord Chelmsford for recruits, I struggled at the cost of my health to raise a corps in Kheda, and the response was being made when the hostilities ceased and orders were received that no more

recruits were wanted. In all these efforts at service, I was actuated by the belief that it was possible by such services to gain a status of full equality in the Empire for my countrymen.

The first shock came in the shape of the Rowlatt Act – a law designed to rob the people of all real freedom. I felt called upon to lead an intensive agitation against it. Then followed the Punjab horrors, beginning with the massacre at Jallianwala Bagh and culminating in crawling orders, public flogging and other indescribable humiliations. I discovered too that the plighted word of the Prime Minister to the Musalmans of India regarding the integrity of Turkey and the holy places of Islam was not likely to be fulfilled. But in spite of the forebodings and the grave warnings of friends, at the Amritsar Congress in 1919, I fought for co-operation and working of the Montagu-Chelmsford reforms, hoping that the Prime Minister would redeem his promise to the Indian Musalmans, that the Punjab wound would be healed, and that the reforms, inadequate and unsatisfactory though they were, marked a new era of hope in the life of India.

But all that hope was shattered. The Khilafat promise was not to be redeemed. The Punjab crime was whitewashed and most culprits went not only unpunished but remained in service, and some continued to draw pensions from the Indian revenue and in some cases were even rewarded. I saw too

STATEMENT AT THE GREAT TRIAL

that not only did the reforms not mark a change of heart, but they were only a method of further robbing India of her wealth and of prolonging her servitude.

I came reluctantly to the conclusion that the British connection had made India more helpless than she ever was before, politically and economically. A disarmed India has no power of resistance against any aggressor if she wanted to engage, in an armed conflict with him. So much is this the case that some of our best men consider that India must take generations, before she can achieve Dominion status. She has become so poor that she has little power of resisting famines. Before the British advent India spun and wove in her millions of cottages, just the supplement she needed for adding to her meagre agricultural resources. This cottage industry, so vital for India's existence, has been ruined by incredibly heartless and inhuman processes as described by English witnesses. Little do town dwellers know how the semi-starved masses of India are slowly sinking to lifelessness. Little do they know that their miserable comfort represents the brokerage they get for their work they do for the foreign exploiter, that the profits and the brokerage are sucked from the masses. Little do they realise that the Government established by law in British India is carried on for this exploitation of the masses. No sophistry, no jugglery in figures, can explain away the evidence that the skeletons in many villages present to the naked eye. I have no doubt whatsoever that both England and the town dweller of India will have to answer, if there is a God above, for this crime against humanity, which is perhaps unequalled in history. The law itself in this country has been used to serve the foreign exploiter. My unbiased examination of the Punjab Marital Law cases has led me to believe that at least 95 per cent of convictions were wholly bad. My experience of political cases in India leads me to the conclusion, in nine out of every ten, the condemned men were totally innocent. Their crime consisted in the love of their country. In ninety-nine cases out of a hundred, justice has been denied to Indians as against Europeans in the courts of India. This is not an exaggerated picture. It is the experience of almost every Indian who has had anything to do with such cases. In my opinion, the administration of the law is thus prostituted, consciously or unconsciously, for the benefit of the exploiter.

The greater misfortune is that the Englishmen and their Indian associates in the administration of the country do not know that they are engaged in the crime I have attempted to describe. I am satisfied that many Englishmen and Indian officials honestly believe that they are administering one of the best systems devised in the world, and that India is making steady, though slow, progress. They do not know, a subtle but effective system of terrorism and an organised display of force on the one hand, and the deprivation of all powers of retaliation or self-defence on the other, has emasculated the people and induced in them the habit of simulation. This awful habit has added to the ignorance and the self-deception of the administrators. Section 124 A, under which I am happily charged, is perhaps the prince among the political sections of the Indian Penal Code designed to suppress the liberty of the citizen. Affection cannot be manufactured or regulated by law. If one has no affection for a person or system, one should be free to give the fullest expression to his disaffection, so long as he does not contemplate, promote, or incite to violence. But the section under which Mr Banker and I are charged is one under which mere promotion of disaffection is a crime. I have studied some of the cases tried under it; I know that some of the most loved of India's patriots have been convicted under it. I consider it a privilege, therefore, to be charged under that section. I have endeavoured to give in their briefest outline the reasons for my disaffection. I have no personal ill will against any single administrator, much less can I have any disaffection towards the King's person. But I hold it to be a virtue to be disaffected towards a Government which in its totality has done more harm to India than any previous system. India is less manly under the British rule than she ever was before. Holding such a belief, I consider it to be a sin to have affection for the system. And it has been a precious privilege for me to be able to write what I have in the various articles tendered in evidence against me.

In fact, I believe that I have rendered a service to India and England by showing in non-co-operation the way out of the unnatural state in which both are living. In my opinion, non-co-operation with evil is as much a duty as is co-operation with good. But in the past, non-co-operation has been deliberately expressed in violence to the evil-doer. I am endeavouring to show to my countrymen that violent non-co-operation only multiplies evil, and that as evil can only be sustained by violence, withdrawal of support of evil requires complete abstention from violence. Non-violence implies voluntary submission to the penalty for non-co-operation with evil. I am here, therefore, to invite and submit cheerfully to the highest penalty that can be inflicted upon me for what in law is deliberate crime, and what appears to me to be the highest duty of a citizen. The only course open to you, the Judge and the assessors, is either to resign your posts and thus dissociate yourselves from evil, if you feel that the law you are called upon to administer is an evil and that in reality I am innocent, or to inflict on me the severest penalty, if you believe that the system and the law you are assisting to administer are good for the people of this country, and that my activity is, therefore, injurious to the common weal.

FRANKLIN DELANO ROOSEVELT

FIRST INAUGURAL ADDRESS

The United States Capitol, Washington, DC,
4 March 1933

Of the four inaugural addresses delivered by Franklin D. Roosevelt, the first is considered one of the finest delivered by any president of the United States. It followed a taxing campaign during which the candidate travelled the country, delivering over 200 speeches in promotion of economic reform. By election day, the United States had entered the fourth year of the Great Depression; millions of people were unemployed and nearly half of the country's 24,000 banks had collapsed. Roosevelt's victory was decisive. He captured 472 electoral college votes to President Herbert Hoover's 59, winning all but six of the 48 states. Approaching 18 per cent, Roosevelt's margin of victory in the popular vote remains the largest over an incumbent president.

Roosevelt continued to tour the country during the five months between victory and inauguration. On 15 February 1933, a bricklayer named Giuseppe Zangara attempted to assassinate the president-elect. Five people were wounded in the attack, including Roosevelt's friend Anton Cermak, the Mayor of Chicago. Cermak died the day after the inauguration.

PRESIDENT HOOVER, Mr Chief Justice, my friends: This is a day of national consecration, and I am certain that my fellow Americans expect that on my induction into the presidency I will address them with a candor and a decision which the present situation of our Nation impels.

This is pre-eminently the time to speak the truth, the whole truth, frankly and boldly. Nor need we shrink from honestly facing conditions in our country today. This great nation will endure as it has endured, will revive and will prosper.

So, first of all, let me assert my firm belief that the only thing we have to fear is fear itself – nameless, unreasoning, unjustified terror which paralyzes needed efforts to convert retreat into advance. In every dark hour of our national life a leadership of frankness and vigor has met with that understanding and support of the people themselves which is essential to victory. I am convinced that you will again give that support to leadership in these critical days.

In such a spirit on my part and on yours we face our common difficulties. They concern, thank God, only material things. Values have shrunken to fantastic levels; taxes have risen; our ability to pay has fallen; government of all kinds is faced by serious curtailment of income; the means of exchange are frozen in the currents of trade; the withered leaves of industrial enterprise lie on every side; farmers find no markets for their produce; the savings of many years in thousands of families are gone.

More important, a host of unemployed citizens face the grim problem of existence, and an equally great number toil with little return. Only a foolish optimist can deny the dark realities of the moment.

Yet our distress comes from no failure of substance. We are stricken by no plague of locusts. Compared with the perils which our forefathers conquered because they believed and were not afraid, we have still much to be thankful for. Nature still offers her bounty and human efforts have multiplied it. Plenty is at our doorstep, but a generous use of it languishes in the very sight of the supply. Primarily this is because the rulers of the exchange of mankind's goods have failed, through their own stubbornness and their own incompetence, have admitted their failure, and abdicated. Practices of the unscrupulous money changers stand indicted in the court of public opinion, rejected by the hearts and minds of men.

True they have tried, but their efforts have been cast in the pattern of an outworn tradition. Faced by failure of credit they have proposed only the lending of more money. Stripped of the lure of profit by which to induce our people to follow their false leadership, they have resorted to exhortations, pleading tearfully for restored confidence. They know only the rules of a generation of self-seekers. They have no vision, and when there is no vision the people perish.

The money changers have fled from their high seats in the temple of our civilization. We may now restore that temple to the ancient truths. The measure of the restoration lies in the extent to which we apply social values more noble than mere monetary profit.

Happiness lies not in the mere possession of money; it lies in the joy of achievement, in the thrill of creative effort. The joy and moral stimulation of work no longer must be forgotten in the mad chase of evanescent profits. These dark days will be worth all they cost us if they teach us that our true destiny is not to be ministered unto but to minister to ourselves and to our fellow men.

Recognition of the falsity of material wealth as the standard of success goes hand in hand with the abandonment of the false belief that public office and high political position are to be valued only by the standards of pride of place and personal profit; and there must be an end to a conduct in banking and in business which too often has given to a sacred trust the likeness of callous and selfish wrongdoing. Small wonder that confidence languishes, for it thrives only on honesty, on honor, on the sacredness of obligations, on faithful protection, on unselfish performance; without them it cannot live.

Restoration calls, however, not for changes in ethics alone. This nation asks for action, and action now.

Our greatest primary task is to put people to work. This is no unsolvable problem if we face it wisely and courageously. It can be accomplished in part by direct recruiting by the Government itself, treating the task as we would treat the emergency of a war, but at the same time, through this employment, accomplishing greatly needed projects to stimulate and reorganize the use of our natural resources.

Hand in hand with this we must frankly recognize the overbalance of population in our industrial centers and, by engaging on a national scale in a redistribution, endeavor to provide a better use of the land for those best fitted for the land. The task can be helped by definite efforts to raise the values of agricultural products and with this the power to purchase the output of our cities. It can be helped by preventing realistically the tragedy of the growing loss through foreclosure of our small homes and our farms. It can be helped by insistence that the federal, state, and local governments act forthwith on the demand that their cost be drastically reduced. It can be helped by the unifying of relief activities which today are often scattered, un-economical, and unequal. It can be helped by national planning for and supervision of all forms of transportation and of communications and other utilities which have a definitely public character. There are many ways in which it can be helped, but it can never be helped merely by talking about it. We must act and act quickly.

Finally, in our progress toward a resumption of work we require two safeguards against a return of the evils of the old order; there must be a strict supervision of all banking and credits and investments; there must be an end to speculation with other people's money, and there must be provision for an adequate but sound currency.

Franklin Delano Roosevelt during the twelve years he served as President of the United States.

There are the lines of attack. I shall presently urge upon a new Congress in special session detailed measures for their fulfillment, and I shall seek the immediate assistance of the several States.

Through this program of action we address ourselves to putting our own national house in order and making income balance outgo. Our international trade relations, though vastly important, are in point of time and necessity secondary to the establishment of a sound national economy. I favor as a practical policy the putting of first things first. I shall spare no effort to restore world trade by international economic readjustment, but the emergency at home cannot wait on that accomplishment.

The basic thought that guides these specific means of national recovery is not narrowly nationalistic. It is the insistence, as a first consideration, upon the interdependence of the various elements in all parts of the United States – a recognition of the old and permanently important manifestation of the American spirit of the pioneer. It is the way to recovery. It is the immediate way. It is the strongest assurance that the recovery will endure.

In the field of world policy I would dedicate this Nation to the policy of the good neighbor – the neighbor who resolutely respects himself and, because he does so, respects the rights of others – the neighbor who respects his obligations and respects the sanctity of his agreements in and with a world of neighbors.

If I read the temper of our people correctly, we now realize as we have never realized before our interdependence on each other; that we can not merely take but we must give as well; that if we are to go forward, we must move as a trained and loyal army willing to sacrifice for the good of a common discipline, because without such discipline no progress is made, no leadership becomes effective. We are, I know, ready and willing to submit our lives and property to such discipline, because it makes possible a leadership which aims at a larger good. This I propose to offer, pledging that the larger purposes will bind upon us all as a sacred obligation with a unity of duty hitherto evoked only in time of armed strife.

With this pledge taken, I assume unhesitatingly the leadership of this great army of our people dedicated to a disciplined attack upon our common problems.

Action in this image and to this end is feasible under the form of government which we have inherited from our ancestors. Our Constitution is so simple and practical that it is possible always to meet extraordinary needs by changes in emphasis and arrangement without loss of essential form. That is why our constitutional system has proved itself the most superbly enduring political mechanism the modern world has produced. It has met every stress of vast expansion of territory, of foreign wars, of bitter internal strife, of world relations.

It is to be hoped that the normal balance of executive and legislative authority may be wholly adequate to meet the unprecedented task before us. But it may be that an unprecedented demand and need for undelayed action may call for temporary departure from that normal balance of public procedure.

I am prepared under my constitutional duty to recommend the measures that a stricken nation in the midst of a stricken world may require. These measures, or such other measures as the Congress may build out of its experience and wisdom, I shall seek, within my constitutional authority, to bring to speedy adoption.

But in the event that the Congress shall fail to take one of these two courses, and in the event that the national emergency is still critical, I shall not evade the clear course of duty that will then confront me. I shall ask the Congress for the one remaining instrument to meet the crisis – broad executive power to wage a war against the emergency, as great as the power that would be given to me if we were in fact invaded by a foreign foe.

For the trust reposed in me I will return the courage and the devotion that befit the time. I can do no less.

We face the arduous days that lie before us in the warm courage of the national unity; with the clear consciousness of seeking old and precious moral values; with the clean satisfaction that comes from the stern performance of duty by old and young alike. We aim at the assurance of a rounded and permanent national life.

We do not distrust the future of essential democracy. The people of the United States have not failed. In their need they have registered a mandate that they want direct, vigorous action. They have asked for discipline and direction under leadership. They have made me the present instrument of their wishes. In the spirit of the gift I take it.

In this dedication of a nation we humbly ask the blessing of God. May He protect each and every one of us. May He guide me in the days to come.

EDWARD VIII

ABDICATION SPEECH

Radio broadcast from Windsor Castle, Windsor, Berkshire,
11 December 1936

Before his accession to the throne, Edward was a
popular, energetic prince; very much at home in the
post-war world that F. Scott Fitzgerald dubbed 'The
Jazz Age'. Seemingly in keeping with the times, he had
a number of romances, including Freda Dudley Ward,
Lady Furness and actress Mildred Harris, former wife
of Charlie Chaplin. Several of these affairs were with
married women, the last of whom was Wallis Simpson.
The future King met the American socialite in January
of 1931, less than three years into her second marriage.
In November of 1936, ten months after the death of
George V, Edward famously announced to his Prime
Minister, Stanley Baldwin, that he intended to marry
Mrs Simpson, who was at the time estranged from her
second husband. The crisis that ensued was resolved
only when, twenty-four days later, Edward issued an
Instrument for Abdication. The document, witnessed
by his three brothers – including his successor, Albert,
the future George VI – was given legislative form by
Parliament the very next day.

Edward's abdication speech was brief and took less
than seven minutes to read. The next day, the former
King left England for Austria.

A T LONG LAST I AM ABLE TO SAY a few words of
my own. I have never wanted to withhold
anything, but until now it has not been
constitutionally possible for me to speak.

A few hours ago I discharged my last duty as King and Emperor, and now that I have been succeeded by my brother, the Duke of York, my first words must be to declare my allegiance to him. This I do with all my heart.

You all know the reasons which have impelled me to renounce the Throne. But I want you to understand that in making up my mind I did not forget the country or the Empire, which, as Prince of Wales and lately as King, I have for twenty-five years tried to serve.

But you must believe me when I tell you that I have found it impossible to carry the heavy burden of responsibility and to discharge my duties as King as I would wish to do without the help and support of the woman I love.

And I want you to know that the decision I have made has been mine and mine alone. This was a thing I had to judge entirely for myself. The other person most nearly concerned has tried up to the last to persuade me to take a different course.

I have made this, the most serious decision of my life, only upon the single thought of what would, in the end, be best for all.

This decision has been made less difficult to me by the sure knowledge that my brother, with his long training in the public affairs of this country and with his fine qualities, will be able to take my place forthwith, without interruption or injury to the life and progress of the empire. And he has one matchless blessing, enjoyed by so many of you, and not bestowed on me – a happy home with his wife and children.

During these hard days I have been comforted by Her Majesty my mother and by my family. The Ministers of the Crown, and in particular, Mr Baldwin, the Prime Minister, have always treated me with full consideration. There has never been any constitutional difference between me and them, and between me and Parliament. Bred in the constitutional tradition by my father, I should never have allowed any such issue to arise.

Ever since I was Prince of Wales, and later on when I occupied the Throne, I have been treated with the greatest kindness by all classes of the people wherever I have lived or journeyed throughout the empire. For that I am very grateful.

I now quit altogether public affairs and I lay down my burden. It may be some time before I return to my native land, but I shall always follow the fortunes of the British race and Empire with profound interest, and if at any time in the future I can be found of service to His Majesty in a private station, I shall not fail.

And now, we all have a new King. I wish him and you, his people, happiness and prosperity with all my heart. God bless you all! God save the King!

DAVID LLOYD GEORGE
'The Prime Minister Should Give
an Example of Sacrifice'
The House of Commons, Westminster, 7 May 1940

Seventy-seven-year-old David Lloyd George was a
marginalized figure when he rose to make this, his last
great speech in the House of Commons. The last Liberal
Prime Minister of the United Kingdom, he had achieved
the office through the support of opposition parties, and
was eventually felled by scandal in which he was accused
of selling peerages and knighthoods. He was,
nevertheless, recognized as the man who had led the
country to victory in the Great War.

The new World War still in its first year, Lloyd
George delivers a lengthy list of governmental
ineptitude, beginning with a harsh criticism of the
Norwegian Campaign. Praise is limited to one man,
Winston Churchill, the First Lord of the Admiralty, who
it is implied, was alone in recognizing the growing
German threat. Lloyd George ends, famously, with the
suggestion that Prime Minister Neville Chamberlain
resign. Three days later, the embattled Chamberlain did
just that, and Churchill became Prime Minister.

I INTERVENE WITH RELUCTANCE IN THIS DEBATE. All
my Honourable Friends know very well that I
hesitated whether I should take part in it at all,
because I thought it was more desirable that we should
have a discussion in which Members not of front-bench
rank should take a good deal of the time. But I think that
it is my duty, having regard to the fact that I have some
experience of these matters.

I feel that I ought to say something, from such

experience as I have had in the past of the conduct of war in victory and in disaster, about what I think of the present situation and what really ought to be done. I have heard most of the speech of the Right Honourable Gentleman, the Secretary of State for Air, and I should think that the facts which he gave us justify the criticism against the Government and are no defence of the Government.

He said that we had practically no chance of making good in our Norwegian expedition unless we were able to have our air bases there which would enable us to put our fighters into the air in order to counteract the very destructive effect of the German aeroplanes. But we knew there were no air bases available. We know they were in the hands of the enemy.

The Right Honourable Gentleman admits that. He says that the Government knew beforehand that there were no air bases unless they were captured from the enemy, he even intimates that the object of the Trondheim expedition was to capture an air base. In that case we ought to have had picked men, and not a kind of a scratch team. We ought to have sent the very best man available, especially as we could not send the whole of our force in the first instalment.

The first instalment ought to have been picked men, because the Germans had picked men, as is generally accepted. We sent there, I think, a Territorial Brigade which had not had very much training. They were very young men, but they were the advance party of an expeditionary force which had to accomplish a task upon which the success of the whole force depended.

We ought also to have had combined action between the Army and the Navy. We had neither. We gambled on the chance of getting air bases. We did not take any measures that would guarantee success. This vital expedition, which would have made a vast difference to this country's strategical position, and an infinite difference to her prestige in the world, was made dependent upon this half-prepared, half-baked expeditionary force without any combination at all between the Army and the Navy.

There could not have been a more serious condemnation of the whole action of the Government in respect of Norway. They knew perfectly well that the Germans were preparing for a raid on some adjoining country, probably in the Balkans, and it is a severe condemnation of them that they should have gambled in this way. The Right Honourable Gentleman spoke about the gallantry of our men, and we are equally proud of them. It thrills us to read the stories. All the more shame that we should have made fools of them.

Now, the situation is a grave one – I agree with what was said about that by the Prime Minister – and it would be a fatal error on our part not to acknowledge it. In such experience as I have had of war direction I have never tried to minimise the extent of such a disaster. I try to get the facts, because unless you really face the facts you cannot overcome the difficulties and restore the position.

There is no case, in my judgement, for panic. I say that deliberately, after a good deal of reflection, but there is a grave case for pulling ourselves together. We cannot do that unless we tell the country the facts. They must realise the magnitude of our jeopardy. We have two immense empires federated in the struggle for liberty, the two greatest empires in the world, the British Empire and the French Empire, with almost inexhaustible resources, but not easily mobilised, not easily roused – especially ours.

You are not going to rouse the British Empire – because you will have to do it not merely in Britain, but throughout the world – to put forth the whole of its strength unless and until you tell it what the facts and realities are of the peril that confronts it. At the cost of unpleasantness, I am going to do that, not with a view to terrifying them or spreading dismay and consternation, but with a view to rousing real action and not sham action as we have had. It is no use saying that the balance of advantage is in our favour, or adding up the number of ships sunk on either side. That kind of petty-cash balance-sheer is not the thing to look at. There are more serious realities than that.

First of all, we are strategically in a very much worse position than we were before. Now see these words, as they pass along,

'strategically better', 'strategically worse', because victory or defeat may depend upon the application of those two words. The greatest triumph of this extraordinary man Hitler has been that he has succeeded in putting his country into an infinitely better strategical position to wage war than his predecessors did in 1914, and by what he has done now he has increased his own advantages and he has put us into greater jeopardy.

Let us face it like men of British blood. Graver perils than this have been fought through in the past. Let us face it; just look at it, Czechoslovakia, that spearhead, aimed at the heart of Germany, broken: a million of the finest troops in Europe of a very well-educated race of free man, all gone. Such advantage as there is in Czechoslovakia, with its great lines of fortifications and its Skoda works, which turned out the finest artillery in the 1914 war, are in the hands of Hitler. That is one strategic advantage which we have handed over to the enemy.

You have a Franco-Russian Alliance, negotiated by an old friend of mine, M. Barthou, by which Russia was to come to the aid of Czechoslovakia if France did. There would have been a two-front war for Germany. She knows what that means, because she had it before. That door is closed. We sent a third-class clerk to negotiate with the Prime Minister of the greatest country in the world, while Germany sent her Foreign Secretary with a resplendent retinue. That door is closed. Oil in Russian ships is now coming across the Black Sea for the aeroplanes of Germany.

Strategically, that was an immense victory for the Nazi Government.

The third – Rumania. We have tried to form one big syndicate, but Germany has been there starting, not one syndicate, but little syndicates here and there to develop the land, to increase production of work and to give her all sorts of machinery. She has practically got Rumania in her hands; and if she did not have it in her hands a month ago, by this failure in Norway you have handed over Rumania.

What else? Spain. I am hoping that my fears about that will not prove true.

Now you have Scandinavia and Norway, which were one of the great strategic possibilities of the war, and they are in German hands.

It is no use criticising Sweden. Sweden is now between Germany on the left and Germany on the right. What right have we to criticize the little powers? We promised to rescue them. We promised to protect them. We never sent an aeroplane to Poland. We were too late in Norway, although we had the warning of ships in the Baltic and barges crammed with troops. They have to think about themselves. They do not want German troops on their soil, and they are definitely frightened, and for good reasons.

It deprives us of a possible opening in that direction. That has gone. It brings the German aeroplanes and submarines 200 miles nearer our coast. It does more than that. There is the opening-up of the Baltic. I venture to say that that will be considered, in regard to the protection of our trade and commerce, a grave menace. Strategically, we are infinitely worse off.

With regard to our prestige, can you doubt that that has been impaired? You have only to read the friendly American papers to find out, highly friendly papers that were backing us up through thick and thin, in a country which was pro-Ally. I do not know whether Honourable Members ever listen to the British Broadcasting Corporation's relay of the American commentator, Raymond Gram Swing. He is very remarkable. He gave an account of the change in American opinion. He said that what has happened was a hammer-blow to Americans. They were perfectly dazed. Before that they were convinced that victory was going to be won by the Allies, and they had never any doubt about it. This is the first doubt that has entered their minds, and they said, 'It will be up to us to defend democracy.'

There is also the fact of the state of our preparations five years ago, in 1935. In 1935 a promise of rearmament was made; in 1936 active proposals were submitted to this House and were passed without a Division. The Government said they would commit us to £1,500,000,000. If they had asked for more and had said that it was necessary, then there was no party in this House that would have challenged it. And if any party had challenged it, you had your majority.

Is there anyone in this House who will say that he is satisfied with the speed and efficiency of the preparations in any respect for Air, for Army or for Navy? Everybody is disappointed. Everybody knows that whatever was done was done half-heartedly, ineffectively, without drive and unintelligently. For three to four years I thought to myself that the facts with regard to Germany were exaggerated by the First Lord, because the then Prime Minister – not this Prime Minister – said that they were not true. The First Lord, Mr Churchill, was right about it. Then came the war.

The Prime Minister must remember that he has met this formidable foe of ours in peace and in war. He has always been worsted. He is not in a position to put it on the ground of friendship. He has appealed for sacrifice. The nation is prepared for every sacrifice so long as it has leadership, as long as the Government show clearly what they are aiming at and so long as the nation is confident that those who are leading it are doing their best. I say solemnly that the Prime Minister should give an example of sacrifice, because there is nothing which can contribute more to victory in this war than that he should sacrifice the seals of office.

WINSTON CHURCHILL

'BLOOD, TOIL, TEARS AND SWEAT'

The House of Commons, Westminster, 13 May 1940

Three days after the resignation of Neville Chamberlain, Winston Churchill entered the House of Commons for the first time as Prime Minister and made this, the first of many inspiring and defiant wartime speeches.

'Blood, toil, tears and sweat', was not Churchill's expression, but was coined by Theodore Roosevelt, who first used it in an 1897 address before the Naval War College. A student of history and naval man himself, it is likely that Churchill would have read Roosevelt's speech.

I BEG TO MOVE, that this House welcomes the formation of a Government representing the united and inflexible resolve of the nation to prosecute the war with Germany to a victorious conclusion.

Mr Speaker: On Friday evening last I received His Majesty's commission to form a new Administration. It was the evident wish and will of Parliament and the nation that this should be conceived on the broadest possible basis and that it should include all parties, both those who supported the late Government and also the parties of the Opposition.

I have completed the most important part of this task. A War Cabinet has been formed of five Members, representing, with the Liberal Opposition, the unity of the nation. The three party Leaders have agreed to serve, either in the War Cabinet or in high executive office. The three Fighting Services have been filled. It was necessary that this should be done in one single day, on account of the extreme urgency and rigour of events. A number of other key positions were filled yesterday, and I am submitting a further list to His Majesty tonight. I hope to complete the appointment of the principal Ministers during tomorrow. The appointment of the other ministers usually takes a little longer, but I trust that, when Parliament meets again, this part of my task will be completed, and that the Administration will be complete in all respects.

Sir, I considered it in the public interest to suggest that the House should be summoned to meet today. Mr Speaker agreed and took the necessary steps, in accordance with the powers conferred upon him by the Resolution of the House. At the end of the proceedings today, the Adjournment of the House will be proposed until Tuesday, the 21st May with, of course, provision for earlier meeting if need be. The business to be considered during that week will be notified to Members at the earliest opportunity.

I now invite the House by the Resolution which stands in my name, to record its approval of the steps taken and to declare its confidence in the new Government.

Sir, to form an Administration of this scale and complexity is a serious undertaking in itself. But it must be remembered that we are in the preliminary stage of one of the greatest battles in history; that we are in action at many points in Norway and in Holland; that we have to be prepared in the Mediterranean; that the air battle is continuous; and that many preparations have to be made here at home.

In this crisis I hope I may be pardoned if I do not address the House at any length today. I hope that any of my friends and colleagues, or former colleagues, who are affected by the political reconstruction, will make all allowances for any lack of ceremony with which it has been necessary to act.

I would say to the House, as I said to those who've joined this Government, I have nothing to offer but blood, toil, tears, and sweat.

We have before us an ordeal of the most grievous kind. We have before us many, many long months of struggle and of suffering. You ask, what is our policy? I will say it is to wage war by sea, land and air, with all our might and with all the strength that God can give us; to wage war against a monstrous tyranny, never surpassed in the dark and lamentable catalogue of human crime. That is our policy.

You ask, what is our aim? I can answer in one word: victory. Victory at all costs, victory in spite of all terror, victory, however long and hard the road may be; for without victory there is no survival. Let that be realised. No survival for the British Empire; no survival for all that the British Empire has stood for; no survival for the urge and impulse of the ages, that mankind will move forward towards its goal.

But I take up my task with buoyancy and hope. I feel sure that our cause will not be suffered to fail among men. At this time I feel entitled to claim the aid of all, and I say, 'Come then, let us go forward together with our united strength.'

WINSTON CHURCHILL

'THIS WAS THEIR FINEST HOUR'
The House of Commons, Westminster, 18 June 1940

As dawn approached on the morning of 10 May 1940, German forces began their assault on western Europe. Luxembourg, the Netherlands and Belgium fell over the next few days. By 13 May, the German military had crossed the River Meuse and had swept into France. Prime Minister Winston Churchill crossed the English Channel, delivering this assessment to Parliament shortly after his return.

Churchill's purpose is not, as he says, recrimination; however, the mere reporting of the facts leaves little doubt that the failure to confront the German blitzkrieg rests with the French High Command and its leader General Maurice Gamelin.

'What General Weygand called the Battle of France is over', the Prime Minister reports. History sees things differently, but only because what is now referred to as the 'Battle of France' extends beyond the engagements described here to the French capitulation on 25 June.

History also has something to say about General Maxime Weygand who, the day before Churchill's speech, was made Supreme Commander of the French military. The General continued his fight against the Germans for several more weeks, before seeking an armistice. He served for three months as Minister of National Defence in Vichy France, and was later sent as Delegate General to the North African colonies. Weygand co-operated with the Germans and deported his opponents to concentration camps in Algeria and Morocco.

I SPOKE THE OTHER DAY of the colossal military disaster which occurred when the French High Command failed to withdraw the northern Armies from Belgium at the moment when they knew that the French front was decisively broken at Sedan and on the Meuse. This delay entailed the loss of fifteen or sixteen French divisions and threw out of action for the critical period the whole of the British Expeditionary Force. Our Army and 120,000 French troops were indeed rescued by the British Navy from Dunkirk but only with the loss of their cannon, vehicles and modern equipment. This loss inevitably took some weeks to repair, and in the first two of those weeks the Battle in France has been lost. When we consider the heroic resistance made by the French Army against heavy odds in this battle, the enormous losses inflicted upon the enemy and the evident exhaustion of the enemy, it may well be the thought that these 25 divisions of the best-trained and best-equipped troops might have turned the scale. However, General Weygand had to fight without them. Only three British divisions or their equivalent were able to stand in the line with their French comrades. They have suffered severely, but they have fought well. We sent every man we could to France as fast as we could re-equip and transport their formations.

I am not reciting these facts for the purpose of recrimination. That I judge to be utterly futile and even harmful. We cannot afford it. I recite them in order to explain why it was we did not have, as we could have had, between twelve and fourteen British divisions fighting in the line in this great battle instead of only three. Now I put all this aside. I put it on the shelf, from which the historians, when they have time, will select their documents to tell their stories. We have to think of the future and not of the past. This also applies in a small way to our own affairs at home. There are many who would hold an inquest in the House of Commons on the conduct of the Governments – and of Parliaments, for they are in it, too – during the years which led up to this catastrophe. They seek to indict those who were responsible for the guidance of our affairs. This also would be a foolish and pernicious process. There are too many in it. Let each man search his conscience and search his speeches. I frequently search mine.

Of this I am quite sure, that if we open a quarrel between the past and the present, we shall find that we have lost the future. Therefore, I cannot accept the drawing of any distinctions between members of the present Government. It was formed at a moment of crisis in order to unite all the Parties and all sections of opinion. It has received the almost unanimous support of both Houses of Parliament. Its Members are going to stand together, and, subject to the authority of the House of Commons, we are going to govern the country and fight the war. It is absolutely necessary at a time like this that every Minister who tries each day to do his duty shall be respected; and their subordinates must know that their chiefs are not threatened men, men who are here today and gone tomorrow, but that their directions must be punctually and faithfully obeyed. Without this concentrated power we cannot face what lies before us. I should not think it would be very advantageous for the House to prolong this Debate this afternoon under conditions of public stress. Many facts are not clear that will be clear in a short time. We are to have a secret Session on Thursday, and I should think that would be a better opportunity for the many earnest expressions of opinion which Members will desire to make and for the House to discuss vital matters without having everything read the next morning by our dangerous foes.

The disastrous military events which have happened during the past fortnight have not come to me with any sense of surprise. Indeed, I indicated a fortnight ago as clearly as I could to the House that the worst possibilities were open; and I made it perfectly clear then that whatever happened in France would make no difference to the resolve of Britain and the British Empire to fight on, 'if necessary for years, if necessary alone'.

During the last few days we have successfully brought off the great majority of the troops we had on the line of communication in France; and seven-eighths of the troops we have sent to France since the beginning of the war – that is to say, about 350,000 out of 400,000 men – are safely back in this country. Others are still fighting with the French, and fighting with considerable success in their local encounters against the enemy. We have also brought back a great mass of stores, rifles and munitions of all kinds which had been accumulated in France during the last nine months.

We have, therefore, in this Island today a very large and powerful military force. This force comprises all our best-trained and our finest troops, including scores of thousands of those who have already measured their quality against the Germans and found themselves at no disadvantage. We have under arms at the present time in this Island over a million and a quarter men. Behind these we have the Local Defence Volunteers, numbering half a million, only a portion of whom, however, are yet armed with rifles or other firearms. We have incorporated into our Defence Forces every man for whom we have a weapon. We expect very large additions to our weapons in the near future, and in preparation for this we intend forthwith to call up, drill and train further large numbers. Those who are not called up, or else are employed during the vast business of munitions production in all its branches – and their ramifications are innumerable – will serve their country best by remaining at their ordinary work until they receive their summons. We have also over here Dominions armies. The Canadians had actually landed in France, but have now been safely withdrawn, much disappointed, but in perfect order, with

73

all their artillery and equipment. And these very high-class forces from the Dominions will now take part in the defence of the Mother Country.

Lest the account which I have given of these large forces should raise the question: Why did they not take part in the great battle in France? I must make it clear that, apart from the divisions training and organizing at home, only twelve divisions were equipped to fight upon a scale which justified their being sent abroad. And this was fully up to the number which the French had been led to expect would be available in France at the ninth month of the war. The rest of our forces at home have a fighting value for home defence which will, of course, steadily increase every week that passes. Thus, the invasion of Great Britain would at this time require the transportation across the sea of hostile armies on a very large scale, and after they had been so transported they would have to be continually maintained with all the masses of munitions and supplies which are required for continuous battle – as continuous battle it will surely be.

Here is where we come to the Navy – and after all, we have a Navy. Some people seem to forget that we have a Navy. We must remind them. For the last thirty years I have been concerned in discussions about the possibilities of oversea invasion, and I took the responsibility on behalf of the Admiralty, at the beginning of the last war, of allowing all regular troops to be sent out of the

country. That was a very serious step to take, because our Territorials had only just been called up and were quite untrained. Therefore, this Island was for several months particularly denuded of fighting troops. The Admiralty had confidence at that time in their ability to prevent a mass invasion even though at that time the Germans had a magnificent battle fleet in the proportion of ten to sixteen, even though they were capable of fighting a general engagement every day and any day, whereas now they have only a couple of heavy ships worth speaking of – the *Scharnhorst* and the *Gneisenau*. We are also told that the Italian Navy is to come out and gain sea superiority in these waters. If they seriously intend it, I shall only say that we shall be delighted to offer Signor Mussolini a free and safeguarded passage through the Strait of Gibraltar in order that he may play the part to which he aspires. There is a general curiosity in the British Fleet to find out whether the Italians are up to the level they were at in the last war or whether they have fallen off at all.

Therefore, it seems to me that as far as seaborne invasion on a great scale is concerned, we are far more capable of meeting it today than we were at many periods in the last war and during the early months of this war, before our other troops were trained, and while the B.E.F. had proceeded abroad. Now, the Navy have never pretended to be able to prevent raids by bodies of 5,000 or 10,000 men flung

Churchill visiting the ruins of Coventry Cathedral in 1940, after much of the city was destroyed by German bombs.

suddenly across and thrown ashore at several points on the coast some dark night or foggy morning. The efficacy of sea power, especially under modern conditions, depends upon the invading force being of large size. It has to be of large size, in view of our military strength, to be of any use. If it is of large size, then the Navy have something they can find and meet and, as it were, bite on. Now, we must remember that even five divisions, however lightly equipped, would require 200 to 250 ships, and with modern air reconnaissance and photography it would not be easy to collect such an armada, marshal it, and conduct it across the sea without any powerful naval forces to escort it; and there would be very great possibilities, to put it mildly, that this armada would be intercepted long before it reached the coast, and all the men drowned in the sea or, at the worst blown to pieces with their equipment while they were trying to land. We also have a great system of minefields, recently strongly reinforced, through which we alone know the channels. If the enemy tries to sweep passages through these minefields, it will be the task of the Navy to destroy the minesweepers and any other forces employed to protect them. There should be no difficulty in this, owing to our great superiority at sea.

Those are the regular, well-tested, well-proved arguments on which we have relied during many years in peace and war. But the question is whether there are any new methods by which those solid assurances can be circumvented. Odd as it may seem, some attention has been given to this by the Admiralty, whose prime duty and responsibility is to destroy any large seaborne expedition before it reaches, or at the moment when it reaches, these shores. It would not be a good thing for me to go into details of this. It might suggest ideas to other people which they have not thought of, and they would not be likely to give us any of their ideas in exchange. All I will say is that untiring vigilance and mind-searching must be devoted to the subject, because the enemy is crafty and cunning and full of novel treacheries and stratagems. The House may be assured that the utmost ingenuity is being displayed and imagination is being evoked from large numbers of competent officers, well-trained in tactics and thoroughly up to date, to measure and counterwork novel possibilities. Untiring vigilance and untiring searching of the mind is being, and must be, devoted to the subject, because, remember, the enemy is crafty and there is no dirty trick he will not do.

Some people will ask why, then, was it that the British Navy was not able to prevent the movement of a large army from Germany into Norway across the Skagerrak? But the conditions in the Channel and in the North Sea are in no way like those which prevail in the Skagerrak. In the Skagerrak, because of the distance, we could give no air support to our surface ships, and consequently, lying as we did close to the enemy's main air power, we were compelled to use only our submarines. We could not enforce the decisive blockade or interruption which is possible from surface vessels. Our submarines took a heavy toll but could not, by themselves, prevent the invasion of Norway. In the Channel and in the North Sea, on the other hand, our superior naval surface forces, aided by our submarines, will operate with close and effective air assistance.

This brings me, naturally, to the great question of invasion from the air, and of the impending struggle between the British and German Air Forces. It seems quite clear that no invasion on a scale beyond the capacity of our land forces to crush speedily is likely to take place from the air until our Air Force has been definitely overpowered. In the meantime, there may be raids by parachute troops and attempted descents of airborne soldiers. We should be able to give those gentry a warm reception both in the air and on the ground, if they reach it in any condition to continue the dispute. But the great question is: Can we break Hitler's air weapon? Now, of course, it is a very great pity that we have not got an Air Force at least equal to that of the most powerful enemy within striking distance of these shores. But we have a very powerful Air Force which has proved itself far superior in quality, both in men and in many types of machine, to what we have met so far in the numerous and fierce air battles which have been fought with the Germans. In France, where we were at a considerable disadvantage and lost many machines on the ground when they were standing round the aerodromes, we were accustomed to inflict in the air losses of as much as two and two-and-a-half to one. In the fighting over Dunkirk, which was a sort of no-man's-land, we undoubtedly beat the German Air Force, and gained the mastery of the local air, inflicting here a loss of three or four to one, day after day. Anyone who looks at the photographs which were published a week or so ago of the re-embarkation, showing the masses of troops assembled on the beach and forming an ideal target for hours at a time, must realise that this re-embarkation would not have been possible unless the enemy had resigned all hope of recovering air superiority at that time and at that place.

In the defence of this Island the advantages to the defenders will be much greater than they were in the fighting around Dunkirk. We hope to improve on the rate of three or four to one which was realised at Dunkirk; and in addition all our injured machines and their crews which get down safely – and, surprisingly, a very great many injured machines and men do get down safely in modern air fighting – all of these will fall, in an attack upon these Islands, on friendly soil and live to fight another day; whereas all the injured enemy machines and their complements will be total losses as far as the war is concerned.

During the great battle in France, we gave very powerful and continuous aid to the French Army, both by fighters and bombers; but in spite of every kind of pressure we never would allow the entire metropolitan fighter strength of the Air Force to be consumed. This decision was painful, but it was also right, because the fortunes of the battle in France could not have been decisively affected even if we had thrown in our entire fighter force. That battle was lost by the unfortunate strategical opening, by the extraordinary and unforeseen power of the armoured columns, and by the great preponderance of the German Army in numbers. Our fighter Air Force might easily have been exhausted as a mere accident in that great struggle, and then we should have found ourselves at the present time in a very serious plight. But as it is, I am happy to

77

inform the House that our fighter strength is stronger at the present time relatively to the Germans, who have suffered terrible losses, than it has ever been; and consequently we believe ourselves possessed of the capacity to continue the war in the air under better conditions than we have ever experienced before. I look forward confidently to the exploits of our fighter pilots – these splendid men, this brilliant youth – who will have the glory of saving their native land, their island home, and all they love, from the most deadly of all attacks.

There remains, of course, the danger of bombing attacks, which will certainly be made very soon upon us by the bomber forces of the enemy. It is true that the German bomber force is superior in numbers to ours; but we have a very large bomber force also, which we shall use to strike at military targets in Germany without intermission. I do not at all underrate the severity of the ordeal which lies before us; but I believe our countrymen will show themselves capable of standing up to it, like the brave men of Barcelona, and will be able to stand up to it, and carry on in spite of it, at least as well as any other people in the world. Much will depend upon this; every man and every woman will have the chance to show the finest qualities of their race, and render the highest service to their cause. For all of us, at this time, whatever our sphere, our station, our occupation or our duties, it will be a help to remember the famous lines:

'He nothing common did or mean, Upon that memorable scene.'

I have thought it right upon this occasion to give the House and the country some indication of the solid, practical grounds upon which we base our inflexible resolve to continue the war. There are a good many people who say: 'Never mind. Win or lose, sink or swim, better die than submit to tyranny – and such a tyranny.' And I do not dissociate myself from them. But I can assure them that our professional advisers of the three Services unitedly advise that we should carry on the war, and that there are good and reasonable hopes of final victory. We have fully informed and consulted all the self-governing Dominions, these great communities far beyond the oceans who have been built up on our laws and on our civilisation, and who are absolutely free to choose their course, but are absolutely devoted to the ancient Motherland, and who feel themselves inspired by the same emotions which lead me to stake our all upon duty and honour. We have fully consulted them, and I have received from their Prime Ministers, Mr Mackenzie King of Canada, Mr Menzies of Australia, Mr Fraser of New Zealand, and General Smuts of South Africa – that wonderful man, with his immense profound mind, and his eye watching from a distance the whole panorama of European affairs – I have received from all these eminent men, who all have governments behind them elected on wide franchises, who are all there because they represent the will of their people, messages couched in the most moving terms in which they endorse our decision to fight on, and declare themselves ready to share our fortunes and to persevere to the end. That is what we are going to do.

We may now ask ourselves: In what way has our position worsened since the beginning of the war? It has worsened by the fact that the Germans have conquered a large part of the coast line of Western Europe, and many small countries have been overrun by them. This aggravates the possibilities of air attack and adds to our naval preoccupations. It in no way diminishes, but on the contrary definitely increases, the power of our long-distance blockade. Similarly, the entrance of Italy into the war increases the power of our long-distance blockade. We have stopped the worst leak by that. We do not know whether military resistance will come to an end in France or not, but should it do so, then of course the Germans will be able to concentrate their forces, both military and industrial, upon us. But for the reasons I have given to the House these will not be found so easy to apply. If invasion has become more imminent, as no doubt it has, we, being relieved from the task of maintaining a large army in France, have far larger and more efficient forces to meet it.

If Hitler can bring under his despotic control the industries of the countries he has conquered, this will add greatly to his already vast armament output. On the other hand, this will not happen immediately, and we are now assured of immense, continuous and increasing support in supplies and munitions of all kinds from the United States; and especially of aeroplanes and pilots from the Dominions and across the oceans coming from regions which are beyond the reach of enemy bombers.

I do not see how any of these factors can operate to our detriment on balance before the winter comes; and the winter will impose a strain upon the Nazi regime, with almost all Europe writhing and starving under its cruel heel, which, for all their ruthlessness, will run them very hard. We must not forget that from the moment when we declared war on the 3rd September it was always possible for Germany to turn all her Air Force upon this country, together with any other devices of invasion she might conceive, and that France could have done little or nothing to prevent her doing so. We have, therefore, lived under this danger, in principle and in a slightly modified form, during all these months. In the meanwhile, however, we have enormously improved our methods of defence, and we have learned what we had no right to assume at the beginning, namely, that the individual aircraft and the individual British pilot have a sure and definite superiority. Therefore, in casting up this dread balance sheet and contemplating our dangers with a disillusioned eye, I see great reason for intense vigilance and exertion, but none whatever for panic or despair.

During the first four years of the last war the Allies experienced nothing but disaster and disappointment. That was our constant fear: one blow after another, terrible losses, frightful dangers. Everything miscarried. And yet at the end of those four years the morale of the Allies was higher than that of the Germans, who had moved from one aggressive triumph to another, and who stood everywhere triumphant invaders of the lands into which they had broken. During that war we repeatedly asked ourselves the question: 'How are we going to win?' And no one was able ever to answer it with much precision, until at the end, quite suddenly, quite unexpectedly, our terrible foe collapsed before us, and we were so glutted with victory that in our folly we threw it away.

We do not yet know what will happen in France or whether the French resistance will be prolonged, both in France and in the French Empire overseas. The French Government will be throwing away great opportunities and casting adrift their future if they do not continue the war in accordance with their Treaty obligations, from which we have not felt able to release them. The House will have read the historic declaration in which, at the desire of many Frenchmen – and of our own hearts – we have proclaimed our willingness at the darkest hour in French history to conclude a union of common citizenship in this struggle. However matters may go in France or with the French Government, or other French Governments, we in this Island and in the British Empire will never lose our sense of comradeship with the French people. If we are now called upon to endure what they have been suffering, we shall emulate their courage, and if final victory rewards our toils they shall share the gains, aye, and freedom shall be restored to all. We abate nothing of our just demands; not one jot or tittle do we recede. Czechs, Poles, Norwegians, Dutch, Belgians have joined their causes to our own. All these shall be restored.

What General Weygand called the Battle of France is over. I expect that the Battle of Britain is about to begin. Upon this battle depends the survival of Christian civilisation. Upon it depends our own British life, and the long continuity of our institutions and our Empire. The whole fury and might of the enemy must very soon be turned on us.

Hitler knows that he will have to break us in this Island or lose the war. If we can stand up to him, all Europe may be free and the life of the world may move forward into broad, sunlit uplands. But if we fail, then the whole world, including the United States, including all that we have known and cared for, will sink into the abyss of a new Dark Age made more sinister, and perhaps more protracted, by the lights of perverted science.

Let us therefore brace ourselves to our duties, and so bear ourselves that if the British Empire and its Commonwealth last for a thousand years, men will still say: 'This was their finest hour.'

FRANKLIN DELANO ROOSEVELT

ADDRESS TO CONGRESS AFTER THE
ATTACK ON PEARL HARBOR
The United States Capitol, Washington, D.C.,
8 December 1941

President Franklin Delano Roosevelt's speech,
incorporating a request to Congress for declaration of
war, was delivered less than twenty-four hours after he
had first learned of the Japanese attack on Pearl Harbor.
Entrusting his speechwriters Samuel I. Rosenman and
Robert E. Sherwood, the award-winning playwright and
screenwriter, to work on an address to be broadcast to the
American people, Roosevelt composed this speech
himself. The first draft was dictated on the afternoon of
the attack, then revised as events unfolded.

The President's speech contains an error in procedure
in that when the Vice President of the United States
takes his seat in the Senate he is considered its president
and should be addressed as Mr President.

MR VICE PRESIDENT, Mr Speaker, Members of
the Senate and the House of Representatives:
Yesterday, December 7, 1941 – a date which
will live in infamy – the United States of America was
suddenly and deliberately attacked by naval and air forces
of the Empire of Japan.

The United States was at peace with that nation, and,
at the solicitation of Japan, was still in conversation with
its government and its Emperor looking toward the
maintenance of peace in the Pacific.

Indeed, one hour after Japanese air squadrons had
commenced bombing in the American island of Oahu, the

Japanese Ambassador to the United States and his colleague delivered to our Secretary of State a formal reply to a recent American message. And, while this reply stated that it seemed useless to continue the existing diplomatic negotiations, it contained no threat or hint of war or of armed attack.

It will be recorded that the distance of Hawaii from Japan makes it obvious that the attack was deliberately planned many days or even weeks ago. During the intervening time the Japanese Government has deliberately sought to deceive the United States by false statements and expressions of hope for continued peace.

The attack yesterday on the Hawaiian Islands has caused severe damage to American naval and military forces. I regret to tell you that very many American lives have been lost. In addition, American ships have been reported torpedoed on the high seas between San Francisco and Honolulu.

Yesterday the Japanese Government also launched an attack against Malaya.

Last night, Japanese forces attacked Hong Kong.

Last night, Japanese forces attacked Guam.

Last night, Japanese forces attacked the Philippine Islands.

Last night, the Japanese attacked Wake Island.

And this morning, the Japanese attacked Midway Island.

Japan has therefore undertaken a surprise offensive extending throughout the Pacific area. The facts of yesterday and today speak for themselves. The people of the United States have already formed their opinions and well understand the implications to the very life and safety of our nation.

As Commander-in-Chief of the Army and Navy I have directed that all measures be taken for our defense. But always will our whole nation remember the character of the onslaught against us.

No matter how long it may take us to overcome this premeditated invasion, the American people, in their righteous might, will win through to absolute victory.

I believe that I interpret the will of the Congress and of the people when I assert that we will not only defend ourselves to the uttermost, but will make it very certain that this form of treachery shall never again endanger us.

Hostilities exist. There is no blinking at the fact that our people, our territory and our interests are in grave danger.

With confidence in our armed forces, with the unbounding determination of our people, we will gain the inevitable triumph. So help us God.

I ask that the Congress declare that since the unprovoked and dastardly attack by Japan on Sunday, December 7th, 1941, a state of war has existed between the United States and the Japanese Empire.

WINSTON CHURCHILL

'THE IRON CURTAIN'
Westminster College, Fulton, Missouri, 5 March 1946

Ten months after having been turned out of office by a
populace that considered him ill-suited for peace-time
governance, Churchill used his appearance at
Westminster College to alert the 'western democracies'
to Soviet expansionism. Although it drew applause in
Fulton, it was not so well received by the leading
politicians and opinion-makers of the day, many of
whom accused the former Prime Minister of
warmongering. Churchill titled this speech 'The Sinews
of Peace', but it has come to be known as 'The Iron
Curtain'. Churchill never claimed ownership of this
phrase. As a political term, 'Iron Curtain' has been traced
back to a 1914 article by Violet Paget in which she wrote
of the peoples of Britain and Germany as having been
separated by 'War's monstrous iron curtain'.

I AM GLAD TO COME TO Westminster College this
afternoon, and am complimented that you should give
me a degree. The name 'Westminster' somehow or
other seems familiar to me. I feel as if I've heard of it before.
Indeed, it was at Westminster that I received a very large
part of my education in politics, dialectic, rhetoric, and one
or two other things. So, in fact, we have both been educated
at the same, or similar, or, at any rate, kindred
establishments.

It is also an honour, perhaps almost unique, for a
private visitor to be introduced to an academic audience by
the President of the United States. Amid his heavy burdens,
duties, and responsibilities – unsought but not recoiled
from – the President has travelled a thousand miles to

dignify and magnify our meeting here today and to give me an opportunity of addressing this kindred nation, as well as my own countrymen across the ocean, and perhaps some other countries too. The President has told you that it is his wish, as I am sure it is yours, that I should have full liberty to give my true and faithful counsel in these anxious and baffling times. I shall certainly avail myself of this freedom, and feel the more right to do so because any private ambitions I may have cherished in my younger days have been satisfied beyond my wildest dreams. Let me, however, make it clear that I have no official mission or status of any kind, and that I speak only for myself. There is nothing here but what you see.

I can therefore allow my mind, with the experience of a lifetime, to play over the problems which beset us on the morrow of our absolute victory in arms, and to try to make sure with what strength I have that what has been gained with so much sacrifice and suffering shall be preserved for the future glory and safety of mankind.

The United States stands at this time at the pinnacle of world power. It is a solemn moment for the American democracy. For with primacy in power is also joined an awe-inspiring accountability to the future. If you look around you, you must feel not only the sense of duty done but also you must feel anxiety lest you fall below the level of achievement. Opportunity is here now, clear and shining for both our countries. To reject it

or ignore it or fritter it away will bring upon us all the long reproaches of the after-time. It is necessary that constancy of mind, persistency of purpose, and the grand simplicity of decision shall guide and rule the conduct of the English-speaking peoples in peace as they did in war. We must, and I believe we shall, prove ourselves equal to this severe requirement.

When American military men approach some serious situation they are wont to write at the head of their directive the words 'over-all strategic concept'. There is wisdom in this, as it leads to clarity of thought. What then is the overall strategic concept which we should inscribe today? It is nothing less than the safety and welfare, the freedom and progress, of all the homes and families of all the men and women in all the lands. And here I speak particularly of the myriad cottage or apartment homes where the wage-earner strives amid the accidents and difficulties of life to guard his wife and children from privation and bring the family up in the fear of the Lord, or upon ethical conceptions which often play their potent part.

To give security to these countless homes, they must be shielded from the two giant marauders, war and tyranny. We all know the frightful disturbance in which the ordinary family is plunged when the curse of war swoops down upon the bread-winner and those for whom he works and contrives. The awful ruin of Europe, with all its vanished glories, and of large parts of Asia glares us in the eyes. When the designs of wicked men or the aggressive urge of mighty states dissolve over large areas the frame of civilised society, humble folk are confronted with difficulties with which they cannot cope. For them is all distorted, all is broken, all is even ground to pulp.

When I stand here this quiet afternoon I shudder to visualise what is actually happening to millions now and what is going to happen in this period when famine stalks the earth. None can compute what has been called 'the unestimated sum of human pain'. Our supreme task and duty is to guard the homes of the common people from the horrors and miseries of another war. We are all agreed on that.

Our American military colleagues, after having proclaimed their 'overall strategic concept' and computed available resources, always proceed to the next step – namely, the method. Here again there is widespread agreement. A world organisation has already been erected for the prime purpose of preventing war. UNO, the successor of the League of Nations, with the decisive addition of the United States and all that that means, is already at work. We must make sure that its work is fruitful, that it is a reality and not a sham, that it is a force for action, and not merely a frothing of words, that it is a true temple of peace in which the shields of many nations can some day be hung up, and not merely a cockpit in a Tower of Babel. Before we cast away the solid assurances of national

armaments for self-preservation, we must be certain that our temple is built, not upon shifting sands or quagmires, but upon the rock. Anyone can see with his eyes open that our path will be difficult and also long, but if we persevere together as we did in the two world wars – though not, alas, in the interval between them – I cannot doubt that we shall achieve our common purpose in the end.

I have, however, a definite and practical proposal to make for action. Courts and magistrates may be set up but they cannot function without sheriffs and constables. The United Nations Organisation must immediately begin to be equipped with an international armed force. In such a matter we can only go step by step, but we must begin now. I propose that each of the Powers and States should be invited to delegate a certain number of air squadrons to the service of the world organisation. These squadrons would be trained and prepared in their own countries, but would move around in rotation from one country to another. They would wear the uniform of their own countries but with different badges. They would not be required to act against their own nation, but in other respects they would be directed by the world organisation. This might be started on a modest scale and would grow as confidence grew. I wished to see this done after the First World War, and I devoutly trust it may be done forthwith.

It would nevertheless be wrong and imprudent to entrust the secret knowledge or

85

experience of the atomic bomb, which the United States, Great Britain, and Canada now share, to the world organisation, while it is still in its infancy. It would be criminal madness to cast it adrift in this still agitated and un-united world. No one in any country has slept less well in their beds because this knowledge and the method and the raw materials to apply it, are at present largely retained in American hands. I do not believe we should all have slept so soundly had the positions been reversed and if some communist or neo-fascist state monopolised for the time being these dread agencies. The fear of them alone might easily have been used to enforce totalitarian systems upon the free democratic world, with consequences appalling to human imagination. God has willed that this shall not be and we have at least a breathing space to set our house in order before this peril has to be encountered: and even then, if no effort is spared, we should still possess so formidable a superiority as to impose effective deterrents upon its employment, or threat of employment, by others. Ultimately, when the essential brotherhood of man is truly embodied and expressed in a world organisation with all the necessary practical safeguards to make it effective, these powers would naturally be confided to that world organisation.

Now I come to the second danger of these two marauders which threatens the cottage, homes, and the ordinary people – namely, tyranny. We cannot be blind to the fact that the liberties enjoyed by individual citizens throughout the British Empire are not valid in a considerable number of countries, some of which are very powerful. With these States, control is enforced upon the common people by various kinds of all-embracing police governments. The power of the state is exercised without restraint, either by dictators or by compact oligarchies operating through a privileged party and a political police. It is not our duty at this time, when difficulties are so numerous, to interfere forcibly in the internal affairs of countries which we have not conquered in war. But we must never cease to proclaim in fearless tones the great principles of freedom and the rights of man which are the joint inheritance of the English-speaking world and which through Magna Carta, the Bill of Rights, the Habeas Corpus, trial by jury, the English common law find their most famous expression in the American Declaration of Independence.

All this means that the people of any country have the right, and should have the power by constitutional action, by free unfettered elections, with secret ballot, to choose or change the character or form of government under which they dwell; that freedom of speech and thought should reign; that courts of justice, independent of the executive, unbiased by any party, should administer laws which have received the broad assent of large majorities or are consecrated by time and custom. Here are the title deeds of freedom which should lie in every cottage home. Here is the message of the British and American peoples to mankind. Let us preach what we practise – let us practise what we preach.

Though I have now stated the two great dangers which menace the homes of the people: war and tyranny, I have not yet spoken of poverty and privation which are in many cases the prevailing anxiety. But if the dangers of war and tyranny are removed, there is no doubt that science and co-operation can bring in the next few years, certainly in the next few decades, to the world, newly taught in the sharpening school of war, an expansion of material well-being beyond anything that has yet occurred in human experience.

Now, at this sad and breathless moment, we are plunged in the hunger and distress which are the aftermath of our stupendous struggle; but this will pass and may pass quickly, and there is no reason except human folly or sub-human crime which should deny to all the nations the inauguration and enjoyment of an age of plenty. I have often used words which I learned fifty years ago from a great Irish-American orator, a friend of mine, Mr Bourke Cockran: 'There is enough for all. The earth is a generous mother; she will provide in plentiful abundance food for all her children if they will but cultivate her soil in justice and in peace.' So far I feel that we are in full agreement. Now, while still pursuing the method of realising our overall strategic concept, I come to the crux of what I have travelled here to say. Neither the sure

prevention of war, nor the continuous rise of world organisation will be gained without what I have called the fraternal association of the English-speaking peoples. This means a special relationship between the British Commonwealth and Empire and the United States. This is no time for generalities, and I will venture to be precise. Fraternal association requires not only the growing friendship and mutual understanding between our two vast but kindred systems of society, but the continuance of the intimate relationship between our military advisers, leading to common study of potential dangers, the similarity of weapons and manuals of instruction, and to the interchange of officers and cadets at technical colleges. It should carry with it the continuance of the present facilities for mutual security by the joint use of all Naval and Air Force bases in the possession of either country all over the world. This would perhaps double the mobility of the American Navy and Air Force. It would greatly expand that of the British Empire Forces and it might well lead, if and as the world calms down, to important financial savings. Already we use together a large number of islands; more may well be entrusted to our joint care in the near future.

The United States has already a Permanent Defense Agreement with the Dominion of Canada, which is so devotedly attached to the British Commonwealth and Empire. This Agreement is more effective than many of those which have often been made under formal alliances. This principle should be extended to all British Commonwealths with full reciprocity. Thus, whatever happens, and thus only, shall we be secure ourselves and able to work together for the high and simple causes that are dear to us and bode no ill to any. Eventually there may come – I feel eventually there will come – the principle of common citizenship, but that we may be content to leave to destiny, whose outstretched arm many of us can already clearly see.

There is however an important question we must ask ourselves. Would a special relationship between the United States and the British Commonwealth be inconsistent with our overriding loyalties to the world organisation? I reply that, on the contrary, it is probably the only means by which that organisation will achieve its full stature and strength. There are already the special United States relations with Canada which I have just mentioned, and there are the relations between the United States and the South American republics. We British have our twenty years Treaty of Collaboration and Mutual Assistance with Soviet Russia. I agree with Mr Bevin, the Foreign Secretary of Great Britain, that it might well be a fifty years treaty so far as we are concerned. We aim at nothing but mutual assistance and collaboration with Russia. The British have an alliance with Portugal unbroken since 1384, and which produced fruitful results at critical moments in the recent war. None of these clash with the general interest of a world agreement, or a world organisation; on the contrary they help

it. 'In my father's house are many mansions.' Special associations between members of the United Nations which have no aggressive point against any other country, which harbour no design incompatible with the Charter of the United Nations, far from being harmful, are beneficial and, as I believe, indispensable.

I spoke earlier of the Temple of Peace. Workmen from all countries must build that temple. If two of the workmen know each other particularly well and are old friends, if their families are intermingled, and if they have 'faith in each other's purpose, hope in each other's future and charity towards each other's shortcomings' – to quote some good words I read here the other day – why cannot they work together at the common task as friends and partners? Why cannot they share their tools and thus increase each other's working powers? Indeed they must do so or else the temple may not be built, or, being built, it may collapse, and we shall all be proved again unteachable and have to go and try to learn again for a third time in a school of war incomparably more rigorous than that from which we have just been released. The Dark Ages may return, the Stone Age may return on the gleaming wings of science, and what might now shower immeasurable material blessings upon mankind, may even bring about its total destruction. Beware, I say; time may be short. Do not let us take the course of allowing events to drift along until it is too late. If there is to be a fraternal association of the kind I have described, with all the extra strength and security which both our countries can derive from it, let us make sure that that great fact is known to the world, and that it plays its part in steadying and stabilising the foundations of peace. There is the path of wisdom. Prevention is better than cure.

A shadow has fallen upon the scenes so lately lighted by the Allied victory. Nobody knows what Soviet Russia and its communist international organisation intends to do in the immediate future, or what are the limits, if any, to their expansive and proselytising tendencies. I have a strong admiration and regard for the valiant Russian people and for my wartime comrade, Marshal Stalin. There is deep sympathy and goodwill in Britain – and I doubt not here also – towards the peoples of all the Russias and a resolve to persevere through many differences and rebuffs in establishing lasting friendships. We understand the Russian need to be secure on her western frontiers by the removal of all possibility of German aggression. We welcome Russia to her rightful place among the leading nations of the world. We welcome her flag upon the seas. Above all, we welcome, or should welcome, constant, frequent and growing contacts between the Russian people and our own peoples on both sides of the Atlantic. It is my duty however, for I am sure you would wish me to state the facts as I see them to you, to place before you certain facts about the present position in Europe.

From Stettin in the Baltic to Trieste in the Adriatic, an iron curtain has descended across the Continent. Behind that line lie all the capitals of the ancient states of Central and Eastern Europe. Warsaw, Berlin, Prague, Vienna, Budapest, Belgrade, Bucharest and Sofia, all these famous cities and the populations around them lie in what I must call the Soviet sphere, and all are subject in one form or another, not only to Soviet influence but to a very high and, in many cases, increasing measure of control from Moscow. Athens alone – Greece with its immortal glories – is free to decide its future at an election under British, American and French observation. The Russian-dominated Polish Government has been encouraged to make enormous and wrongful inroads upon Germany, and mass expulsions of millions of Germans on a scale grievous and undreamed-of are now taking place. The communist parties, which were very small in all these Eastern States of Europe, have been raised to pre-eminence and power far beyond their numbers and are seeking everywhere to obtain totalitarian control. Police governments are prevailing in nearly every case, and so far, except in Czechoslovakia, there is no true democracy.

Turkey and Persia are both profoundly alarmed and disturbed at the claims which are being made upon them and at the pressure being exerted by the Moscow Government. An attempt is being made by the Russians in Berlin to build up a quasi-communist party in

89

their zone of Occupied Germany by showing special favours to groups of left-wing German leaders. At the end of the fighting last June, the American and British Armies withdrew westwards, in accordance with an earlier agreement, to a depth at some points of 150 miles upon a front of nearly 400 miles, in order to allow our Russian allies to occupy this vast expanse of territory which the western democracies had conquered.

If now the Soviet Government tries, by separate action, to build up a pro-communist Germany in their areas, this will cause new serious difficulties in the British and American zones, and will give the defeated Germans the power of putting themselves up to auction between the Soviets and the western democracies. Whatever conclusions may be drawn from these facts – and facts they are – this is certainly not the liberated Europe we fought to build up. Nor is it one which contains the essentials of permanent peace.

The safety of the world requires a new unity in Europe, from which no nation should be permanently outcast. It is from the quarrels of the strong parent races in Europe that the world wars we have witnessed, or which occurred in former times, have sprung. Twice in our own lifetime we have seen the United States – against their wishes and their traditions, against arguments, the force of which it is impossible not to comprehend – twice we have seen them drawn by irresistible forces, into these wars in time to secure the victory of the good cause, but only after

frightful slaughter and devastation had occurred. Twice the United States has had to send several millions of its young men across the Atlantic to find the war; but now war can find any nation, wherever it may dwell between dusk and dawn. Surely we should work with conscious purpose for a grand pacification of Europe, within the structure of the United Nations and in accordance with our Charter. That, I feel, opens a course of policy of very great importance.

In front of the iron curtain which lies across Europe are other causes for anxiety. In Italy the Communist Party is seriously hampered by having to support the communist-trained Marshal Tito's claims to former Italian territory at the head of the Adriatic. Nevertheless, the future of Italy hangs in the balance. Again one cannot imagine a regenerated Europe without a strong France. All my public life I worked for a strong France and I never lost faith in her destiny, even in the darkest hours. I will not lose faith now. However, in a great number of countries, far from the Russian frontiers and throughout the world, communist fifth columns are established and work in complete unity and absolute obedience to the directions they receive from the communist centre. Except in the British Commonwealth and in the United States where communism is in its infancy, the communist parties or fifth columns constitute a growing challenge and peril to Christian civilisation. These are sombre facts for anyone to have to recite on the morrow of a victory gained by so much splendid comradeship in arms and in the cause of freedom and democracy; but we should be most unwise not to face them squarely while time remains.

The outlook is also anxious in the Far East and especially in Manchuria. The Agreement which was made at Yalta, to which I was a party, was extremely favourable to Soviet Russia, but it was made at a time when no one could say that the German war might not extend all through the summer and autumn of 1945 and when the Japanese war was expected to last for a further eighteen months from the end of the German war. In this country you are all so well informed about the Far East, and such devoted friends of China, that I do not need to expatiate on the situation there.

I have, however, felt bound to portray the shadow which, alike in the West and in the East, falls upon the world. I was a Minister at the time of the Versailles Treaty and a close friend of Mr Lloyd George, who was the head of the British delegation at Versailles. I did not, myself, agree with many things that were done, but I have a very strong impression in my mind of that situation, and I find it painful to contrast it with that which prevails now. In those days, there were high hopes and unbounded confidence that the wars were over, and that the League of Nations would become all-powerful. I do not see or feel that same confidence or even the same hopes in the haggard world at the present time.

On the other hand, I repulse the idea that a new war is inevitable – still more that it is imminent. It is because I am sure that our fortunes are still in our own hands and that we hold the power to save the future, that I feel the duty to speak out now that I have the occasion and the opportunity to do so. I do not believe that Soviet Russia desires war. What they desire is the fruits of war and the indefinite expansion of their power and doctrines. But what we have to consider here today while time remains, is the permanent prevention of war and the establishment of conditions of freedom and democracy as rapidly as possible in all countries. Our difficulties and dangers will not be removed by closing our eyes to them. They will not be removed by mere waiting to see what happens; nor will they be removed by a policy of appeasement. What is needed is a settlement, and the longer this is delayed, the more difficult it will be and the greater our dangers will become.

From what I have seen of our Russian friends and allies during the war, I am convinced that there is nothing they admire so much as strength, and there is nothing for which they have less respect than for weakness, especially military weakness. For that reason, the old doctrine of a balance of power is unsound. We cannot afford, if we can help it, to work on narrow margins, offering temptations to a trial of strength. If the western democracies stand together in strict adherence to the principles of the United

91

Nations Charter, their influence for furthering those principles will be immense and no one is likely to molest them. If, however, they become divided or falter in their duty, and if these all-important years are allowed to slip away, then indeed catastrophe may overwhelm us all.

Last time I saw it all coming and cried aloud to my own fellow-countrymen and to the world, but no one paid any attention. Up till the year 1933 or even 1935, Germany might have been saved from the awful fate which has overtaken her, and we might all have been spared the miseries Hitler let loose upon mankind. There never was a war in all history easier to prevent by timely action than the one which has just desolated such great areas of the globe. It could have been prevented, in my belief, without the firing of a single shot, and Germany might be powerful, prosperous and honoured today; but no one would listen and one by one we were all sucked into the awful whirlpool. We surely must not let that happen again. This can only be achieved by reaching now, in 1946, a good understanding on all points with Russia under the general authority of the United Nations Organisation and by the maintenance of that good understanding through many peaceful years, by the world instrument, supported by the whole strength of the English-speaking world and all its connections. There is the solution, which I respectfully offer to you in this address, to which I have given the title 'The Sinews of Peace'.

Let no man underrate the abiding power of the British Empire and Commonwealth. Because you see the forty-six millions in our island harassed about their food supply, of which they only grow one half, even in wartime, or because we have difficulty in restarting our industries and export trade after six years of passionate war effort, do not suppose that we shall not come through these dark years of privation as we have come through the glorious years of agony. Do not suppose that half a century from now, you will not see seventy or eighty millions of Britons spread about the world, united in defence of our traditions, our way of life, and of the world causes which you and we espouse. If the population of the English-speaking Commonwealths be added to that of the United States with all that such co-operation implies in the air, on the sea, all over the globe, and in science, and in industry, and in moral force, there will be no quivering, precarious balance of power to offer its temptation to ambition or adventure. On the contrary, there will be an overwhelming assurance of security. If we adhere faithfully to the Charter of the United Nations and walk forward in sedate and sober strength, seeking no one's land or treasure, seeking to lay no arbitrary control upon the thoughts of men – if all British moral and material forces and convictions are joined with your own in fraternal association – the highroads of the future will be clear, not only for us but for all; not only for our times, but for a century to come.

JAWAHARLAL NEHRU

'A TRYST WITH DESTINY'
Parliament House, New Delhi, 14 August 1947

Jawaharlal Nehru's speech to the Constituent Assembly
was made in the final minutes of India's colonial history;
at the stroke of midnight, shortly after he had finished
speaking, it became an independent nation. At 58,
Nehru had spent half his life in the struggle for
independence. A total of ten years had been spent in
prison; the most recent sentence had been his longest.
The man who became India's first Prime Minister had
last emerged from imprisonment little more than two
years earlier.

Absent at the historic occasion was Mohandas
Gandhi, whom Nehru quotes, beginning with the words:
'The ambition of the greatest man...'

Also absent were Earl Mountbatten of Burma, the
final Viceroy of India, and Lady Mountbatten. They
had remained at Viceroy's House, where they had spent
much of the evening watching a Hollywood movie,
My Favourite Brunette, starring Bob Hope and
Dorothy Lamour.

L ONG YEARS AGO we made a tryst with destiny, and
now the time comes when we shall redeem our
pledge, not wholly or in full measure, but very
substantially.

At the stroke of the midnight hour, when the world
sleeps, India will awake to life and freedom. A moment
comes, which comes but rarely in history, when we step
out from the old to the new, when an age ends, and when
the soul of a nation, long suppressed, finds utterance.

It is fitting that at this solemn moment we take the

pledge of dedication to the service of India and her people and to the still larger cause of humanity.

At the dawn of history India started on her unending quest, and trackless centuries are filled with her striving and the grandeur of her success and her failures. Through good and ill fortune alike she has never lost sight of that quest or forgotten the ideals which gave her strength. We end today a period of ill fortune and India discovers herself again. The achievement we celebrate today is but a step, an opening of opportunity, to the greater triumphs and achievements that await us. Are we brave enough and wise enough to grasp this opportunity and accept the challenge of the future?

Freedom and power bring responsibility. The responsibility rests upon this Assembly, a sovereign body representing the sovereign people of India. Before the birth of freedom we have endured all the pains of labour and our hearts are heavy with the memory of this sorrow. Some of those pains continue even now. Nevertheless, the past is over and it is the future that beckons to us now.

That future is not one of ease or resting but of incessant striving so that we may fulfil the pledges we have so often taken and the one we shall take today. The service of India means the service of the millions who suffer. It means the ending of poverty and ignorance and disease and inequality of opportunity.

The ambition of the greatest man of our generation has been to wipe every tear from every eye. That may be beyond us, but as long as there are tears and suffering, so long our work will not be over.

And so we have to labour and to work, and work hard, to give reality to our dreams. Those dreams are for India, but they are also for the world, for all the nations and peoples are too closely knit together today for any one of them to imagine that it can live apart.

Peace has been said to be indivisible; so is freedom, so is prosperity now, and so also is disaster in this one world that can no longer be split into isolated fragments.

To the people of India, whose representatives we are, we make an appeal to join us with faith and confidence in this great adventure. This is no time for petty and destructive criticism, no time for ill will or blaming others. We have to build the noble mansion of free India where all her children may dwell.

The appointed day has come – the day appointed by destiny – and India stands forth again, after long slumber and struggle, awake, vital, free and independent. The past clings on to us still in some measure and we have to do much before we redeem the pledges we have so often taken. Yet the turning-point is past, and history begins anew for us, the history which we shall live and act and others will write about.

It is a fateful moment for us in India, for all Asia and for the world. A new star rises, the star of freedom in the East, a new hope comes into being, a vision long cherished materialises. May the star never set and that hope never be betrayed!

We rejoice in that freedom, even though clouds surround us, and many of our people are sorrow-stricken and difficult problems encompass us. But freedom brings responsibilities and burdens and we have to face them in the spirit of a free and disciplined people.

On this day our first thoughts go to the architect of this freedom, the father of our nation, who, embodying the old spirit of India, held aloft the torch of freedom and lighted up the darkness that surrounded us.

We have often been unworthy followers of his and have strayed from his message, but not only we but succeeding generations will remember this message and bear the imprint in their hearts of this great son of India, magnificent in his faith and strength and courage and humility. We shall never allow that torch of freedom to be blown out, however high the wind or stormy the tempest.

Our next thoughts must be of the unknown volunteers and soldiers of freedom who, without praise or reward, have served India even unto death.

We think also of our brothers and sisters who have been cut off from us by political boundaries and who unhappily cannot share at present in the freedom that has come. They are of us and will remain of us whatever may happen, and we shall be sharers in their good and ill fortune alike.

The future beckons to us. Whither do we go and what shall be our endeavour? To bring freedom and opportunity to the common man, to the peasants and workers of India; to fight and end poverty and ignorance and disease; to build up a prosperous, democratic and progressive nation, and to create social, economic and political institutions which will ensure justice and fullness of life to every man and woman.

We have hard work ahead. There is no resting for any one of us till we redeem our pledge in full, till we make all the people of India what destiny intended them to be.

We are citizens of a great country on the verge of bold advance, and we have to live up to that high standard. All of us, to whatever religion we may belong, are equally the children of India with equal rights, privileges and obligations. We cannot encourage communalism or narrow-mindedness, for no nation can be great whose people are narrow in thought or in action.

To the nations and peoples of the world we send greetings and pledge ourselves to co-operate with them in furthering peace, freedom and democracy.

And to India, our much-loved motherland, the ancient, the eternal and the ever-new, we pay our reverent homage and we bind ourselves afresh to her service.

Jai Hind [Victory to India].

ELEANOR ROOSEVELT

ON THE ADOPTION OF THE UNIVERSAL DECLARATION
OF HUMAN RIGHTS

*The United Nations General Assembly, Palais de Chaillot,
Paris, 9 December 1948*

After the Second World War, Eleanor Roosevelt
distinguished herself as chair of the Commission on
Human Rights, which was entrusted with the task of
drafting a Universal Declaration of Human Rights.
Roosevelt's speech, delivered on the eve of the
Declaration's adoption, reflects something of the
complexities and politics involved in drafting the
document, particularly in relation to the Soviet Union.

MR PRESIDENT, fellow delegates: The long and
meticulous study and debate, of which this
Universal Declaration of Human Rights is the
product, means that it reflects the composite views of the
many men and governments who have contributed to its
formulation. Not every man nor every government can
have what he wants in a document of this kind. There are,
of course, particular provisions in the Declaration before
us with which we are not fully satisfied. I have no doubt
this is true of other delegations, and it would still be true
if we continued our labors over many years.

Taken as a whole the delegation of the United States
believes that this is a good document – even a great
document – and we propose to give it our full support.
The position of the United States on the various parts of
the Declaration is a matter of record in the Third
Committee. I shall not burden the Assembly, and
particularly my colleagues of the Third Committee, with a
restatement of that position here.

I should like to comment briefly on the amendments proposed by the Soviet delegation. The language of these amendments has been dressed up somewhat, but the substance is the same as the amendments which were offered by the Soviet delegation in committee and rejected after exhaustive discussion. Substantially the same amendments have been previously considered and rejected in the Human Rights Commission. We in the United States admire those who fight for their convictions, and the Soviet delegation has fought for their convictions. But in the older democracies we have learned that sometimes we bow to the will of the majority. In doing that, we do not give up our convictions. We continue sometimes to persuade, and eventually we may be successful. But we know that we have to work together and we have to progress. So, we believe that when we have made a good fight, and the majority is against us, it is perhaps better tactics to try to co-operate.

I feel bound to say that I think perhaps it is somewhat of an imposition on this Assembly to have these amendments offered again here, and I am confident that they will be rejected without debate.

The first two paragraphs of the amendment to Article 3 deal with the question of minorities, which Committee 3 decided required further study, and has recommended, in a separate resolution, their reference to the Economic and Social Council and the Human Rights Commission. As set out in the Soviet amendment, this provision clearly states group, and not individual, rights.

The Soviet amendment to Article 20 is obviously a very restrictive statement of the right to freedom of opinion and expression. It sets up standards which would enable any state practically to deny all freedom of opinion and expression without violating the article. It introduces the terms 'democratic views', 'democratic systems', 'democratic state', and 'fascism', which we know all too well from debates in this Assembly over the past two years, on warmongering and related subjects, are liable to the most flagrant abuse and diverse interpretations.

The statement of the Soviet delegate here tonight is a very good case in point on this. The Soviet amendment of Article 22 introduces new elements into the article without improving the committee text and again introduces specific reference to discrimination.

As was repeatedly pointed out in Committee 3, the question of discrimination is comprehensively covered in Article 2 of the Declaration, so that its restatement elsewhere is completely unnecessary and also has the effect of weakening the comprehensive principles stated in Article 2.

The new article proposed by the Soviet delegation is but a restatement of state obligation, which the Soviet delegation attempted to introduce into practically every article in the Declaration. It would convert the Declaration into a document stating obligations on states, thereby changing completely its character as a statement of principles to serve as a common standard of achievement for the members of the United Nations.

The Soviet proposal for deferring consideration of the Declaration to the fourth session of the Assembly requires no comment. An identical text was rejected in Committee 3 by a vote of six in favor and 26 against.

We are all agreed, I am sure, that the Declaration, which has been worked on with such great effort and devotion, and over such a long period of time, must be approved by this Assembly at this session.

Certain provisions of the Declaration are stated in such broad terms as to be acceptable only because of the provisions in Article 30 providing for limitation on the exercise of the rights for the purpose of meeting the requirements of morality, public order, and the general welfare. An example of this is the provision that everyone has the right to equal access to the public service in his country. The basic principle of equality and of non-discrimination as to public employment is sound, but it cannot be accepted without limitation. My government, for example, would consider that this is unquestionably subject to limitation in the interest of public order and the general welfare. It would not consider that the exclusion from public employment of persons holding subversive political beliefs, and not loyal to the basic principles and practices of the constitution and laws of the country, would in any way infringe upon this right.

Likewise, my government has made it clear in the course of the development of the Declaration that it does not consider that the economic and social and cultural rights stated in the Declaration imply an obligation on governments to assure the enjoyment of these rights by direct governmental action. This was made quite clear in the Human Rights Commission text of Article 23 which served as a so-called 'umbrella' article to the articles on economic and social rights. We consider that the principle has not been affected by the fact that this article no longer contains a reference to the articles which follow it. This in no way affects our whole-hearted support for the basic principles of economic, social, and cultural rights set forth in these articles.

In giving our approval to the Declaration today, it is of primary importance that we keep clearly in mind the basic character of the document. It is not a treaty; it is not an international agreement. It is not and does not purport to be a statement of law or of legal obligation. It is a declaration of basic principles of human rights and freedoms, to be stamped with the approval of the General Assembly by formal vote of its members, and to serve as a common standard of achievement for all peoples of all nations.

We stand today at the threshold of a great event both in the life of the United Nations and in the life of mankind. This Universal Declaration of Human Rights may well become the international Magna Carta of all men everywhere. We hope its proclamation by the General Assembly will be an event comparable to the proclamation of the Declaration of the Rights of Man by the French people in 1789, the adoption of the Bill of Rights by the people of the United States, and the adoption of comparable declarations at different times in other countries.

At a time when there are so many issues on which we find it difficult to reach a common basis of agreement, it is a significant fact that fifty-eight states have found such a large measure of agreement in the complex field of human rights. This must be taken as testimony of our common aspiration, first voiced in the Charter of the United Nations, to lift men everywhere to a higher standard of life and to a greater enjoyment of freedom.

Man's desire for peace lies behind this Declaration. The realization that the flagrant violation of human rights by Nazi and fascist countries sowed the seeds of the last world war has supplied the impetus for the work which brings us to the moment of achievement here today.

In a recent speech in Canada, Gladstone Murray said:

The central fact is that man is fundamentally a moral being, that the light we have is imperfect does not matter so long as we are always trying to improve it. We are equal in sharing the moral freedom that distinguishes us as men. Man's status makes each individual an end in himself. No man is by nature simply the servant of the state

or of another man. The ideal and fact of freedom – and not technology – are the true distinguishing marks of our civilization.

This Declaration is based upon the spiritual fact that man must have freedom in which to develop his full stature and through common effort to raise the level of human dignity. We have much to do to fully achieve and to assure the rights set forth in this declaration. But having them put before us with the moral backing of fifty-eight nations will be a great step forward.

As we here bring to fruition our labors on this Declaration of Human Rights, we must at the same time rededicate ourselves to the unfinished task which lies before us. We can now move on with new courage and inspiration to the completion of an international covenant on human rights and of measures for the implementation of human rights.

In conclusion, I feel that I cannot do better than to repeat the call to action by Secretary Marshall in his opening statement to this Assembly:

Let this third regular session of the General Assembly approve by an overwhelming majority the Declaration of Human Rights as a standard of conduct for all; and let us, as Members of the United Nations, conscious of our own shortcomings and imperfections, join our effort in good faith to live up to this high standard.

99

ALBERT EINSTEIN

PEACE IN THE ATOMIC AGE

Mrs Roosevelt Meets the Public, 12 February 1950

The greatest physicist of his age, Albert Einstein knew
well the horrible destructive power that could be
unleashed by the atom. After the United States' use of
the atom bomb on the cities of Hiroshima and Nagasaki
in August 1945, Einstein advocated a world government
or, at the very least, what he refers to here as a body
'empowered to decide questions of immediate concern
to the security of the nations'.

In his address, Einstein argues against the concept
of security through armament, recognizing that the
United States was the first to develop the atomic bomb.
Indeed, the physicist played a role in this accomplishment
by way of a letter sent in 1939 to President Franklin
Delano Roosevelt, in which Einstein explained the
possibilities of just such a weapon.

The brief speech was delivered on the premier
episode of *Mrs Roosevelt Meets the Public*, a live
Sunday afternoon television show hosted by
Eleanor Roosevelt.

I AM GRATEFUL TO YOU, Mrs Roosevelt, for the
opportunity to express my conviction in this most
important political question.

The idea of achieving security through national
armament is, at the present state of military technique, a
disastrous illusion. On the part of the United States, this
illusion has been particularly fostered by the fact that this
country succeeded first in producing an atomic bomb. The
belief seemed to prevail that in the end it were possible to
achieve decisive military superiority.

In this way, any potential opponent would be intimidated, and security, so ardently desired by all of us, brought to us, and to all of humanity. The maxim which we have been following during these last five years has been, in short: security through superior military power, whatever the cost.

The armament race between the USA and the USSR, originally supposed to be a preventive measure, assumes hysterical character. On both sides, the means to mass destruction are perfected with feverish haste – behind the respective walls of secrecy. The H-bomb appears on the public horizon as a probably attainable goal.

If successful, radioactive poisoning of the atmosphere and hence annihilation of any life on earth has been brought within the range of technical possibilities. The ghostlike character of this development lies in its apparently compulsory trend. Every step appears as the unavoidable consequence of the preceding one. In the end, there beckons more and more clearly, general annihilation.

Is there any way out of this impasse created by man himself? All of us, and particularly those who are responsible for an attitude of the US and the USSR, should realize that we may have vanquished an external enemy, but have been incapable of getting rid of the mentality created by the war.

It is impossible to achieve peace as long as every single action is taken with a possible future conflict in view. The leading point of view of all political actions should therefore be: What can we do to bring about a peaceful co-existence and even loyal co-operation of the nations?

The first problem is to do away with mutual fear and distrust. Solemn renunciation of violence (not only with respect to means of mass destruction) is undoubtedly necessary.

Such renunciation, however, can only be effective if at the same time a supra-national judicial and executive body is set up, empowered to decide questions of immediate concern to the security of the nations. Even a declaration of the nations to collaborate loyally in the realization of such a 'restricted world government' would considerably reduce the imminent danger of war.

In the last analysis, every kind of peaceful co-operation among men is primarily based on mutual trust and only secondly on institutions such as courts of justice and police. This holds for nations as well as for individuals. And the basis of trust is loyal give and take.

And what about international control? Well, it may be useful as a police measure but cannot be considered a prime factor. In any event, it may be wise not to overestimate its importance. The example of Prohibition comes to mind and gives one pause.

HAROLD MACMILLAN

'THE WIND OF CHANGE'
The Parliament of South Africa, Cape Town,
3 February 1960

Prime Minister Harold Macmillan spent the first month of 1960 visiting British colonies in Africa and was nearing the end of his journey when he arrived at Cape Town, in the Union of South Africa. Up to this point, the United Kingdom had stood with Australia as the only British Commonwealth members that had not condemned apartheid at the United Nations. While the South African government had been hoping for a signal from Macmillan that this toleration would continue, it became clear in early discussions that this was not to be. The situation was made more tense by the British Prime Minister's speech, in which he outlined with great clarity his government's policy toward decolonization. This encouraged an immediate response from Henrik Verwoerd, the Prime Minister of South Africa, in which he put forth that the black nationalists of Africa owed a debt to 'the white men of Africa', who had brought education, industrial development and culture to the continent.

In 1961, South Africa became a republic and left the Commonwealth. By the end of that same year, the colonies of Nigeria, Somalia, Sierra Leone and Tanzania had achieved independence.

IT IS A GREAT PRIVILEGE to be invited to address the members of both Houses of Parliament in the Union of South Africa. It is a unique privilege to do so in 1960, just a half century after the Parliament of the Union came to birth. I am most grateful to you all for giving me this opportunity, and I am especially grateful to your Prime Minister who invited me to visit this country and arranged for me to address you here today. My tour of Africa – parts of Africa – the first ever made by a British Prime Minister in office, is now, alas, nearing its end, but it is fitting that it should culminate in the Union Parliament here in Cape Town, in this historic city so long Europe's gateway to the Indian Ocean, and to the East.

As in all the other countries that I have visited, my stay has been all too short. I wish it had been possible for me to spend a longer time here, to see more of your beautiful country and to get to know more of your people, but in the past week I have travelled many hundreds of miles and met many people in all walks of life. I have been able to get at least some idea of the great beauty of your countryside, with its farms and its forests, mountains and rivers, and the clear skies and wide horizons of the veldt. I have also seen some of your great and thriving cities, and am most grateful to your Government for all the trouble they have taken in making the arrangements which have enabled me to see so much in so short a time.

Some of the younger members of my staff have told me that it has been a heavy programme, but I can assure you that my wife and I have enjoyed every moment of it. Moreover, we have been deeply moved by the warmth of our welcome. Wherever we have been, in town or in country, we have been received in a spirit of friendship and affection which has warmed our hearts, and we value this the more because we know it is an expression of your goodwill, not just to ourselves but to all the people of Britain.

It is, as I have said, a special privilege for me to be here in 1960, when you are celebrating what I might call the golden wedding of the Union. At such a time it is natural and right that you should pause to take stock of your position, to look back at what you have achieved, to look forward to what lies ahead.

In the fifty years of their nationhood, the people of South Africa have built a strong economy founded upon a healthy agriculture and thriving and resilient industries. During my visit I have been able to see something of your mining industry, on which the prosperity of the country is so firmly based. I have seen your Iron and Steel Corporation and visited your Council of Scientific and Industrial Research at Pretoria. These two bodies, in their different ways, are symbols of a lively, forward-looking and expanding economy. I have seen the great city of Durban, with its wonderful port, and the skyscrapers of Johannesburg, standing where seventy years ago there was nothing but the open veldt. I have seen, too, the fine cities of Pretoria and Bloemfontein. This afternoon I hope to see something of your wine-growing industry, which so far I have only admired as a consumer.

No one could fail to be impressed with the immense material progress which has been achieved. That all this has been accomplished in so short a time is a striking testimony to the skill, energy and initiative of your people. We in Britain are proud of the contribution we have made to this remarkable achievement. Much of it has been financed by British capital. According to the recent survey made by the Union Government, nearly two-thirds of the overseas investment outstanding in the Union at the end of 1956 was British. That is after two staggering wars which have bled our economy white.

But that is not all. We have developed trade between us to our common advantage, and our economies are now largely interdependent. You export to us raw materials, food and gold. We, in return, send you our consumer goods or capital equipment. We take a third of all your exports and we supply a third of all your imports. This broad traditional pattern of investment and trade has been maintained in spite of the changes brought by the development of our two economies, and it gives me great encouragement to reflect that the economies of both our countries, while expanding rapidly, have yet remained interdependent and capable of sustaining one another. If you travel round this country by train you will travel on South African rails made by Iscor. If you prefer to fly you go in a British Viscount. Here is a true partnership, living proof of the interdependence between nations. Britain has always been your best customer and, as your new industries develop, we believe that we can be your best partners too.

In addition to building this strong economy within your own borders, you have also played your part as an independent nation in the world.

As a soldier in the First World War, and as a Minister in Sir Winston Churchill's Government in the Second, I know personally the value of the contribution which your forces made to victory in the cause of freedom. I know something, too, of the inspiration which General Smuts brought to us in Britain in our darkest hours. Again in the Korean crisis you played your full part. Thus, in the testing times of war or aggression, your statesmen and your soldiers have made their influence felt far beyond the African continent.

In the period of reconstruction, when Dr Malan was your Prime Minister, your resources greatly assisted the recovery of the sterling area. In the post-war world now, in the no less difficult tasks of peace, your leaders in industry, commerce and finance continue to be prominent in world affairs today. Your readiness to provide technical assistance to the less-developed parts of Africa is of immense help to the countries that receive it. It is also a source of strength to your friends in the Commonwealth and elsewhere in the western world. You are collaborating in the work of the Commission for Technical Co-operation in Africa south of the Sahara, and now in the United Nations Economic Commission for Africa. Your Minister of External Affairs intends to visit Ghana later this year. All this proves your determination, as the most advanced industrial country of the continent, to play your part in the new Africa of today.

Sir, as I have travelled around the Union I have found everywhere, as I expected, a deep preoccupation with what is happening in the rest of the African continent. I understand and sympathise with your interests in these events and your anxiety about them. Ever since the break-up of the Roman Empire, one of the constant facts of political life in Europe has been the emergence of independent nations. They have come into existence over the centuries in different forms, different kinds of government, but all have been inspired by a deep, keen feeling of nationalism, which has grown as the nations have grown.

In the 20th century, and especially since the end of the war, the processes that gave birth to the nation states of Europe have been repeated all over the world. We have seen the awakening of national consciousness in peoples who have for centuries lived in dependence upon some other power. Fifteen years ago this movement spread through Asia. Many countries there, of different races and civilisations, pressed their claim to an independent national life.

Today the same thing is happening in Africa, and the most striking of all the impressions I have formed since I left London a month ago is of the strength of this African national consciousness. In different places it takes different forms, but it is happening everywhere.

The wind of change is blowing through this continent, and whether we like it or not, this growth of national consciousness is a political fact. We must all accept it as a fact, and our national policies must take account of it.

Of course, you understand this better than anyone. You are sprung from Europe, the home of nationalism, and here in Africa you have yourselves created a free nation. A new nation. Indeed in the history of our times, yours will be recorded as the first of the African nationalisms, and this tide of national consciousness, which is now rising in Africa, is a fact for which both you and we and the other nations of the western world are ultimately responsible. For its causes are to be found in the achievements of western civilisation, in the pushing forwards of the frontiers of knowledge, the applying of science to the service of human needs, in the expanding of food production, in the speeding and multiplying of the means of communication, and perhaps above all and more than anything else in the spread of education.

As I have said, the growth of national consciousness in Africa is a political fact, and we must accept it as such. That means, I would judge, that we've got to come to terms with it. I sincerely believe that if we cannot do so we may imperil the precarious balance between the East and West on which the peace of the world depends.

The world today is divided into three main groups. First there are what we call the 'Western Powers'. You in South Africa and we in Britain belong to this group, together with our friends and allies in other parts of the Commonwealth. In the United States of America and in Europe we call it the 'Free World'. Secondly there are the communists – Russia and her satellites in Europe and China whose population will rise by the end of the next ten years to the staggering total of 800 million. Thirdly, there are those parts of the world whose people are at present uncommitted either to communism or to our Western ideas. In this context we think first of Asia and then of Africa.

As I see it, the great issue in this second half of the 20th century is whether the uncommitted peoples of Asia and Africa will swing to the East or to the West. Will they be drawn into the communist camp? Or will the great experiments in self-government that are now being made in Asia and Africa, especially within the Commonwealth, prove

so successful, and by their example so compelling, that the balance will come down in favour of freedom and order and justice?

The struggle is joined, and it is a struggle for the minds of men. What is now on trial is much more than our military strength or our diplomatic and administrative skill. It is our way of life. The uncommitted nations want to see before they choose.

What can we show them to help them choose right? Each of the independent members of the Commonwealth must answer that question for itself. It is a basic principle of our modern Commonwealth that we respect each other's sovereignty in matters of internal policy. At the same time we must recognise that in this shrinking world, in which we live today, the internal policies of one nation may have effects outside it. We may sometimes be tempted to say to each other, 'Mind your own business,' but in these days I would myself expand the old saying so that it runs: 'Mind your own business, but mind how it affects my business, too.'

Let me be very frank with you, my friends. What Governments and Parliaments in the United Kingdom have done since the war in according independence to India, Pakistan, Ceylon, Malaya, and Ghana, and what they will do for Nigeria and other countries now nearing independence, all this, though we take full responsibility for it, we do in the belief that it is the only way to establish the future of the Commonwealth and of the Free World on sound foundations.

All this, of course, is also of deep and close concern to you for nothing we do in this small world can be done in a corner or remain hidden. What we do today in West, Central and East Africa becomes known tomorrow to everyone in the Union, whatever his language, colour or traditions. Let me assure you, in all friendliness, that we are well aware of this and that we have acted, and will act, with full knowledge of the responsibility we have to all our friends.

Nevertheless, I am sure you will agree that in our own areas of responsibility we must each do what we think right. What we think right derives from a long experience both of failure and success in the management of our own affairs. We have tried to learn and apply the lessons of our judgement of right and wrong. Our justice is rooted in the same soil as yours – in Christianity and in the rule of law as the basis of a free society. This experience of our own explains why it has been our aim in the countries for which we have borne responsibility, not only to raise the material standards of living, but also to create a society which respects the rights of individuals, a society in which men are given the opportunity to grow to their full stature – and that must in our view include the opportunity to have an increasing share in political power and responsibility, a society in which individual merit, and individual merit alone, is the criterion for a man's advancement, whether political or economic.

Finally, in countries inhabited by several different races it has been our aim to find means by which the community can become more of a community, and fellowship can be fostered between its various parts. The problem is by no means confined to Africa. Nor is it a problem of a European minority. In Malaya, for instance, though there are Indian and European minorities, Malays and Chinese make up the great bulk of the population, and the Chinese are not much fewer in number than the Malays. Yet these two people must learn to live together in harmony and unity and the strength of Malaya as a nation will depend on the different contributions which the two races can make.

The attitude of the United Kingdom towards this problem was clearly expressed by the Foreign Secretary, Mr Selwyn Lloyd, speaking at the United Nations General Assembly on 17 September 1959. These were his words:

In those territories where different races or tribes live side by side, the task is to ensure that all the people may enjoy security and freedom and the chance to contribute as individuals to the progress and wellbeing of these countries. We reject the idea of any inherent superiority of one race over another. Our policy therefore is non-racial. It offers a future in which Africans, Europeans, Asians, the peoples of the Pacific, and others with whom we are concerned, will all play their full part as citizens in the countries where they live, and in which feelings of race will be submerged in loyalty to the new nations.

I have thought you would wish me to state plainly, and with full candour, the policy for which we in Britain stand. It may well be that in trying to do our duty as we see it, we shall sometimes make difficulties for you. If this proves to be so we shall regret it. But I know that, even so, you would not ask us to flinch from doing our duty.

You, too, will do your duty as you see it. I am well aware of the peculiar nature of the problems with which you are faced here in the Union of South Africa. I know the differences between your situation and that of most of the other states in Africa. We have here some three million people of European origin. This country is their home. It has been their home for many generations. They have no other. The same is true of Europeans in Central and East Africa. In most other African states, those who have come from Europe have come to work, to contribute their skills, perhaps to teach, but not to make a home.

The problem to which you, as members of the Union Parliament, have to address yourselves are very different from those which face the Parliaments of countries with homogenous populations. They are complicated and baffling problems. It would be surprising if your interpretation of your

duty did not sometimes produce very different results from ours in terms of Government policies and actions.

As a fellow member of the Commonwealth, it is our earnest desire to give South Africa our support and encouragement, but I hope you won't mind my saying frankly that there are some aspects of your policies which make it impossible for us to do this without being false to our own deep convictions about the political destinies of free men, to which in our own territories we are trying to give effect. I think we ought, as friends, to face together, without seeking to apportion credit or blame, the fact that in the world of today this difference of outlook lies between us.

I said I was speaking as a friend. I can also claim to be speaking as a relation, for we Scots can claim family connections with both the great European sections of your population, not only with the English-speaking people but with the Afrikaans-speaking as well. This is a point which hardly needs emphasis in Cape Town, where you can see every day the statue of that great Scotsman, Andrew Murray. His work in the Dutch Reformed Church in the Cape, and the work of his son in the Orange Free State, was among Afrikaans-speaking people. There has always been a very close connection between the Church of Scotland and the Church of the Netherlands. The Synod of Dort plays the same great part in the history of both. Many aspirants to the

Ministry of Scotland, especially in the 17th and 18th centuries, went to pursue their theological studies in the Netherlands. Scotland can claim to have repaid the debt in South Africa. I am thinking particularly of the Scots in the Orange Free State. Not only the younger Andrew Murray, but also the Robertsons, the Frasers, the McDonalds – families which have been called the Free State clans, who became burghers of the old Free State and whose descendants still play their part there.

But though I count myself a Scot, my mother was an American, and the United States provides a valuable illustration of one of the main points which I am trying to make in my remarks today. Its population, like yours, is of different strains, and over the years most of those who have gone to North America have gone there in order to escape conditions in Europe which they found intolerable. The Pilgrim Fathers were fleeing from persecution as Puritans, and the Marylanders from persecution as Roman Catholics. Throughout the 19th century a stream of immigrants flowed across the Atlantic to escape from the poverty in their homelands, and in the 20th century the United States have provided asylum for the victims of political oppression in Europe.

Thus for the majority of its inhabitants America has been a place of refuge, or a place to which people went because they wanted to get away from Europe. It is not surprising, therefore, that for many years a main objective of American statesmen, supported by the American public, was to isolate themselves from Europe, and with their great material strength, and the vast resources open to them, this might have seemed an attractive and practicable course. Nevertheless in the two World Wars of this century they have found themselves unable to stand aside. Twice, their manpower in arms has streamed back across the Atlantic to shed blood in those European struggles from which their ancestors thought they would escape by emigrating to the New World; and when the second war was over, they were forced to recognise that in the small world of today isolationism is out of date and offers no assurance of security.

The fact is that in this modern world no country, not even the greatest, can live for itself alone. Nearly two thousand years ago, when the whole of the civilised world was comprised within the confines of the Roman Empire, St Paul proclaimed one of the greatest truths of history – we are all members one of another. During this 20th century, that eternal truth has taken on a new and exciting significance. It has always been impossible for the individual man to live in isolation from his fellows, in the home, the tribe, the village, or the city. Today it is impossible for nations to live in isolation from one another. What Dr John Donne said of individual men three hundred years ago is true today of my country, your country, and all the countries of the world:

*Any man's death diminishes me, because I
am involved in Mankind. And therefore
never send to know for whom the bell tolls;
it tolls for thee.*

All nations now are interdependent, one
upon the other, and this is generally realised
throughout the Western World. I hope in due
course the countries of communism will
recognise it too.

It was certainly with that thought in
mind that I took the decision to visit Moscow
about this time last year. Russia has been
isolationist in her time and still has
tendencies that way, but the fact remains that
we must live in the same world with Russia,
and we must find a way of doing so. I believe
that the initiative which we took last year has
had some success, although grave difficulties
may arise. Nevertheless, I think nothing but
good can come out of its extending contacts
between individuals, contacts in trade, and
from the exchange of visitors.

I certainly do not believe in refusing to
trade with people because you may happen to
dislike the way they manage their internal
affairs at home. Boycotts will never get you
anywhere, and may I say in parenthesis that I
deprecate the attempts that are being made
today in Britain to organise the consumer
boycott of South African goods. It has never
been the practice, as far as I know, of any
Government of the United Kingdom, of
whatever complexion, to undertake or
support campaigns of this kind designed to
influence the internal politics of another
Commonwealth country, and my colleagues
in the United Kingdom deplore this proposed
boycott and regard it as undesirable from
every point of view. It can only have serious
effects on Commonwealth relations, on
trade, and lead to the ultimate detriment of
others than those against whom it is aimed.

I said I was speaking of the
interdependence of nations. The members of
the Commonwealth feel particularly strongly
the value of interdependence. They are as
independent as any nation in this shrinking
world can be, but they have voluntarily
agreed to work together. They recognise that
there may be – and must be – differences in
their institutions, in their internal policies,
and their membership does not imply the
wish to express a judgement on these matters,
or the need to impose a stifling uniformity. It
is, I think, a help that there has never been a
question of any rigid constitution for the
Commonwealth. Perhaps this is because we
have got on well enough in the United
Kingdom without a written constitution
and tend to look suspiciously at them.
Whether that is so or not, it is clear that a
rigid constitutional framework for the
Commonwealth will not work. At the first of
the stresses and strains which are inevitable in
this period of history, cracks will appear in
the framework and the whole structure will
crumble. It is the flexibility of our
Commonwealth institutions which gives
them their strength.

Mr President, Mr Speaker, Honourable Ministers, Ladies and Gentlemen, I fear I have kept you a long time. I much welcome the opportunity to speak to this great audience. In conclusion, may I say this? I have spoken frankly about the differences between our two countries in their approach to one of the great current problems with which each has to deal within its own sphere of responsibility. These differences are well known. They are matters of public knowledge, indeed of public controversy, and I should have been less than honest if by remaining silent on them I had seemed to imply that they did not exist. But differences on one subject, important though it is, need not and should not impair our capacity to co-operate with one another in furthering the many practical interests which we share in common.

The independent members of the Commonwealth do not always agree on every subject. It is not a condition of their association that they should do so. On the contrary, the strength of our Commonwealth lies largely in the fact that it is a free association of independent sovereign states, each responsible for ordering its own affairs but co-operating in the pursuit of common aims and purposes in world affairs. Moreover these differences may be transitory. In time they may be resolved. Our duty is to see them in perspective against the background of our long association. Of this at any rate I am certain – those of us who, by grace of the electorate, are temporarily in charge of affairs in your country and mine, we fleeting transient phantoms on the great stage of history, we have no right to sweep aside on this account the friendship that exists between our countries, for that is the legacy of history. It is not ours alone to deal with as we wish. To adapt a famous phrase, it belongs to those who are living, but it also belongs to those who are dead and to those who are yet unborn. We must face the differences, but let us try to see beyond them down the long vista of the future.

I hope – indeed, I am confident – that in another fifty years we shall look back on the differences that exist between us now as matters of historical interest, for as time passes and one generation yields to another, human problems change and fade. Let us remember these truths. Let us resolve to build, not to destroy, and let us remember always that weakness comes from division, strength from unity.

JOHN F. KENNEDY

INAUGURAL ADDRESS

The United States Capitol, Washington, D.C.,
20 January 1961

Seventy-three days after his narrow victory over Richard
Nixon in the 1960 presidential election, John F. Kennedy
took the oath of office, and began an inaugural address
that is frequently cited as one of the finest. The new
President began crafting the speech two months earlier,
soliciting opinions and suggestions from friends and
advisors. In the end, Kennedy incorporated two
quotations from the Bible – 'undo the heavy burdens…
and to let the oppressed go free' (Isaiah 58:6) and
'rejoicing in hope, patient in tribulation' (Romans 12:12);
otherwise the words are his own.

VICE PRESIDENT JOHNSON, Mr Speaker, Mr Chief
Justice, President Eisenhower, Vice President
Nixon, President Truman, reverend clergy, fellow
citizens: We observe today not a victory of party, but a
celebration of freedom – symbolizing an end, as well as a
beginning – signifying renewal, as well as change. For I
have sworn before you and Almighty God the same
solemn oath our forebears prescribed nearly a century and
three-quarters ago.

The world is very different now. For man holds in his
mortal hands the power to abolish all forms of human
poverty and all forms of human life. And yet the same
revolutionary beliefs for which our forebears fought are
still at issue around the globe – the belief that the rights of
man come not from the generosity of the state, but from
the hand of God.

We dare not forget today that we are the heirs of that

first revolution. Let the word go forth from this time and place, to friend and foe alike, that the torch has been passed to a new generation of Americans – born in this century, tempered by war, disciplined by a hard and bitter peace, proud of our ancient heritage – and unwilling to witness or permit the slow undoing of those human rights to which this nation has always been committed, and to which we are committed today at home and around the world.

Let every nation know, whether it wishes us well or ill, that we shall pay any price, bear any burden, meet any hardship, support any friend, oppose any foe, to assure the survival and the success of liberty.

This much we pledge – and more.

To those old allies whose cultural and spiritual origins we share, we pledge the loyalty of faithful friends. United, there is little we cannot do in a host of co-operative ventures. Divided, there is little we can do – for we dare not meet a powerful challenge at odds and split asunder.

To those new states whom we welcome to the ranks of the free, we pledge our word that one form of colonial control shall not have passed away merely to be replaced by a far more iron tyranny. We shall not always expect to find them supporting our view. But we shall always hope to find them strongly supporting their own freedom – and to remember that, in the past, those who foolishly sought power by riding the back of the tiger ended up inside.

To those peoples in the huts and villages across the globe, struggling to break the bonds of mass misery, we pledge our best efforts to help them help themselves, for whatever period is required – not because the communists may be doing it, not because we seek their votes, but because it is right. If a free society cannot help the many who are poor, it cannot save the few who are rich.

To our sister republics south of our border, we offer a special pledge – to convert our good words into good deeds, in a new alliance for progress – to assist free men and free governments in casting off the chains of poverty. But this peaceful revolution of hope cannot become the prey of hostile powers. Let all our neighbors know that we shall join with them to oppose aggression or subversion anywhere in the Americas. And let every other power know that this hemisphere intends to remain the master of its own house.

To that world assembly of sovereign states, the United Nations, our last best hope in an age where the instruments of war have far outpaced the instruments of peace, we renew our pledge of support to prevent it from becoming merely a forum for invective, to strengthen its shield of the new and the weak, and to enlarge the area in which its writ may run.

Finally, to those nations who would make themselves our adversary, we offer not a pledge but a request: that both sides begin anew the quest for peace, before the dark powers of destruction, unleashed by science, engulf all humanity in planned or accidental self-destruction.

We dare not tempt them with weakness. For only when our arms are sufficient beyond doubt can we be certain beyond doubt that they will never be employed.

But neither can two great and powerful groups of nations take comfort from our present course – both sides overburdened by the cost of modern weapons, both rightly alarmed by the steady spread of the deadly atom, yet both racing to alter that uncertain balance of terror that stays the hand of mankind's final war.

So let us begin anew, remembering on both sides that civility is not a sign of weakness, and sincerity is always subject to proof. Let us never negotiate out of fear. But let us never fear to negotiate.

Let both sides explore what problems unite us instead of belaboring those problems which divide us.

Let both sides, for the first time, formulate serious and precise proposals for the inspection and control of arms, and bring the absolute power to destroy other nations under the absolute control of all nations.

Let both sides seek to invoke the wonders of science instead of its terrors. Together let us explore the stars, conquer the deserts, eradicate disease, tap the ocean depths, and encourage the arts and commerce.

Let both sides unite to heed, in all corners of the earth, the command of Isaiah to – 'undo the heavy burdens... and let the oppressed go free.'

And if a beachhead of co-operation may push back the jungle of suspicion, let both sides join in creating a new endeavor – not a new balance of power, but a new world of law – where the strong are just, and the weak secure, and the peace preserved.

All this will not be finished in the first one hundred days. Nor will it be finished in the first one thousand days, nor in the life of this Administration, nor even perhaps in our lifetime on this planet. But let us begin.

In your hands, my fellow citizens, more than mine, will rest the final success or failure of our course. Since this country was founded, each generation of Americans has been summoned to give testimony to its national loyalty. The graves of young Americans who answered the call to service surround the globe.

Now the trumpet summons us again – not as a call to bear arms, though arms we need; not as a call to battle, though embattled we are – but a call to bear the burden of a long twilight struggle, year in and year out, 'rejoicing in hope, patient in tribulation', a struggle against the common enemies of man: tyranny, poverty, disease, and war itself.

Can we forge against these enemies a grand and global alliance, North and South, East and West, that can assure a more fruitful life for all mankind? Will you join in that historic effort?

In the long history of the world, only a few generations have been granted the role of defending freedom in its hour of maximum danger. I do not shrink from this responsibility – I welcome it. I do not believe that any of us would exchange places with any other people or any other generation. The energy, the faith, the devotion which we bring to this endeavor will light our country and all who serve it. And the glow from that fire can truly light the world.

And so, my fellow Americans: ask not what your country can do for you; ask what you can do for your country.

My fellow citizens of the world: ask not what America will do for you, but what together we can do for the freedom of man.

Finally, whether you are citizens of America or citizens of the world, ask of us here the same high standards of strength and sacrifice which we ask of you. With a good conscience our only sure reward, with history the final judge of our deeds, let us go forth to lead the land we love, asking His blessing and His help, but knowing that here on earth God's work must truly be our own.

A photograph of John F. Kennedy taken during the 22 months he served as President of the United States.

JOHN F. KENNEDY

'ICH BIN EIN BERLINER'
The Rathaus Schöneberg, West Berlin, West Germany,
26 June 1963

As the American President, Kennedy visited Berlin at a
time when the city was divided by the infamous Berlin
Wall. West Berlin existed within Communist East
Germany, geographically cut off from the Federal
Republic of Germany to which it belonged. One of the
most defiant of the Cold War, Kennedy's speech was
addressed as much to the East as to the West.

In his opening remarks Kennedy mentions Berlin's
Mayor (Willy Brandt, future Chancellor of West
Germany), the West German Chancellor (Konrad
Adenauer) and General Lucius Clay, who from 1947
until 1949 had served as military governor of Berlin's
American zone.

I AM PROUD TO COME TO THIS CITY as the guest of your
distinguished Mayor, who has symbolized throughout
the world the fighting spirit of West Berlin. And I am
proud to visit the Federal Republic with your distinguished
Chancellor, who for so many years has committed
Germany to democracy and freedom and progress, and to
come here in the company of my fellow American, General
Clay, who has been in this city during its great moments of
crisis and will come again if ever needed.

Two thousand years ago the proudest boast was *'civis
Romanus sum'* ['I am a Roman citizen']. Today, in the world
of freedom, the proudest boast is *'Ich bin ein Berliner'* ['I am
a Berliner'].

I appreciate my interpreter translating my German.

There are many people in the world who really don't

understand, or say they don't, what is the great issue between the free world and the communist world.

Let them come to Berlin.

There are some who say that communism is the wave of the future.

Let them come to Berlin.

And there are some who say, in Europe and elsewhere, we can work with the communists.

Let them come to Berlin.

And there are even a few who say that it is true that communism is an evil system, but it permits us to make economic progress.

Lasst sie nach Berlin kommen. Let them come to Berlin.

Freedom has many difficulties and democracy is not perfect, but we have never had to put a wall up to keep our people in, to prevent them from leaving us. I want to say, on behalf of my countrymen, who live many miles away on the other side of the Atlantic, who are far distant from you, that they take the greatest pride that they have been able to share with you, even from a distance, the story of the last eighteen years. I know of no town, no city, that has been besieged for eighteen years that still lives with the vitality and the force, and the hope and the determination of the city of West Berlin. While the wall is the most obvious and vivid demonstration of the failures of the communist system, for all the world to see, we take no satisfaction in it, for it is, as your Mayor has said, an offence not only against history but an offence against humanity, separating families, dividing husbands and wives and brothers and sisters, and dividing a people who wish to be joined together.

What is true of this city is true of Germany: real, lasting peace in Europe can never be assured as long as one German out of four is denied the elementary right of free men, and that is to make a free choice. In eighteen years of peace and good faith, this generation of Germans has earned the right to be free, including the right to unite their families and their nation in lasting peace, with goodwill to all people.

You live in a defended island of freedom, but your life is part of the main. So let me ask you as I close, to lift your eyes beyond the dangers of today, to the hopes of tomorrow, beyond the freedom merely of this city of Berlin, or your country of Germany, to the advance of freedom everywhere, beyond the wall to the day of peace with justice, beyond yourselves and ourselves to all mankind.

Freedom is indivisible, and when one man is enslaved, all are not free. When all are free, then we can look forward to that day when this city will be joined as one and this country and this great continent of Europe in a peaceful and hopeful globe. When that day finally comes, as it will, the people of West Berlin can take sober satisfaction in the fact that they were in the front lines for almost two decades.

All free men, wherever they may live, are citizens of Berlin, and therefore, as a free man, I take pride in the words *'Ich bin ein Berliner.'*

MARTIN LUTHER KING, JR

'I HAVE A DREAM'
The Lincoln Memorial, Washington, D.C., 28 August 1963

Given the position of this speech – often described as the greatest in American history – it is easy to overlook its place as part of a much larger event, known as the March on Washington for Jobs and Freedom. In fact, King was the last of nine speakers to address the assembled crowd of between two and three hundred thousand. The purpose of the March was a matter of debate, even among those who had organized the event. Some considered the gathering as a means of showing support for President John F. Kennedy's recently introduced Civil Rights bill, while others saw a chance to protest that the proposed legislation had not gone far enough. King himself viewed the event as an opportunity to raise issues beyond those covered in the bill; indeed the Reverend makes no mention of the measure in his speech.

As the Civil Rights Act of 1964, the legislation was passed by the House and the Senate and was signed into law some seven months after Kennedy's assassination.

I AM HAPPY TO JOIN WITH YOU TODAY in what will go down in history as the greatest demonstration for freedom in the history of our nation.

Five score years ago, a great American, in whose symbolic shadow we stand today, signed the Emancipation Proclamation. This momentous decree came as a great beacon light of hope to millions of Negro slaves who had been seared in the flames of withering injustice. It came as a joyous daybreak to end the long night of their captivity.

But one hundred years later, the Negro still is not free. One hundred years later, the life of the Negro is still sadly crippled by the manacles of segregation and the chains of discrimination. One hundred years later, the Negro lives on a lonely island of poverty in the midst of a vast ocean of material prosperity. One hundred years later, the Negro is still languished in the corners of American society and finds himself an exile in his own land. And so we've come here today to dramatize a shameful condition.

In a sense we've come to our nation's capital to cash a check. When the architects of our republic wrote the magnificent words of the Constitution and the Declaration of Independence, they were signing a promissory note to which every American was to fall heir. This note was a promise that all men, yes, black men as well as white men, would be guaranteed the 'unalienable Rights' of 'Life, Liberty and the pursuit of Happiness'. It is obvious today that America has defaulted on this promissory note, insofar as her citizens of color are concerned. Instead of honoring this sacred obligation, America has given the Negro people a bad check, a check which has come back marked 'insufficient funds'.

But we refuse to believe that the bank of justice is bankrupt. We refuse to believe that there are insufficient funds in the great vaults of opportunity of this nation. And so, we've come to cash this check, a check that will give us upon demand the riches of freedom and the security of justice.

We have also come to this hallowed spot to remind America of the fierce urgency of 'Now'. This is no time to engage in the luxury of cooling off or to take the tranquilizing drug of gradualism. Now is the time to make real the promises of democracy. Now is the time to rise from the dark and desolate valley of segregation to the sunlit path of racial justice. Now is the time to lift our nation from the quicksands of racial injustice to the solid rock of brotherhood. Now is the time to make justice a reality for all of God's children.

It would be fatal for the nation to overlook the urgency of the moment. This sweltering summer of the Negro's legitimate discontent will not pass until there is an invigorating autumn of freedom and equality. Nineteen sixty-three is not an end, but a beginning. And those who hope that the Negro needed to blow off steam and will now be content, will have a rude awakening if the nation returns to business as usual. And there will be neither rest nor tranquility in America until the Negro is granted his citizenship rights. The whirlwinds of revolt will continue to shake the foundations of our nation until the bright day of justice emerges.

But there is something that I must say to my people, who stand on the warm threshold which leads into the palace of justice. In the process of gaining our rightful place, we must not be guilty of wrongful deeds. Let us not seek to satisfy our thirst for freedom by drinking from the cup of bitterness and hatred. We must forever conduct our struggle on the high plane of dignity and discipline. We must not allow our creative protest to degenerate into physical violence. Again and again, we must rise to the majestic heights of meeting physical force with soul force.

The marvelous new militancy which has engulfed the Negro community must not lead us to a distrust of all white people, for many of our white brothers, as evidenced by their presence here today, have come to realize that their destiny is tied up with our destiny. And they have come to realize that their freedom is inextricably bound to our freedom.

We cannot walk alone.

And as we walk, we must make the pledge that we shall always march ahead.

We cannot turn back.

There are those who are asking the devotees of civil rights, 'When will you be satisfied?' We can never be satisfied as long as the Negro is the victim of the unspeakable horrors of police brutality. We can never be satisfied as long as our bodies, heavy with the fatigue of travel, cannot gain lodging in the motels of the highways and the hotels of the cities. We cannot be satisfied as long as the Negro's basic mobility is from a smaller ghetto to a larger one. We can never be satisfied as long as our children are stripped of their selfhood and robbed of their dignity by a sign stating: 'For Whites Only.' We cannot be satisfied as long as a Negro in Mississippi cannot vote and a Negro in New York believes he has nothing for which to vote. No, no, we are not satisfied, and we will not be satisfied

until 'justice rolls down like waters, and righteousness like a mighty stream.'

I am not unmindful that some of you have come here out of great trials and tribulations. Some of you have come fresh from narrow jail cells. And some of you have come from areas where your quest for freedom left you battered by the storms of persecution and staggered by the winds of police brutality. You have been the veterans of creative suffering. Continue to work with the faith that unearned suffering is redemptive. Go back to Mississippi, go back to Alabama, go back to South Carolina, go back to Georgia, go back to Louisiana, go back to the slums and ghettos of our northern cities, knowing that somehow this situation can and will be changed.

Let us not wallow in the valley of despair, I say to you today, my friends.

And so even though we face the difficulties of today and tomorrow, I still have a dream. It is a dream deeply rooted in the American dream.

I have a dream that one day this nation will rise up and live out the true meaning of its creed: 'We hold these truths to be self-evident, that all men are created equal.'

I have a dream that one day, on the red hills of Georgia, the sons of former slaves and the sons of former slave owners will be able to sit down together at the table of brotherhood.

I have a dream that one day even the state of Mississippi, a state sweltering with the heat of injustice, sweltering with the heat of oppression, will be transformed into an oasis of freedom and justice.

I have a dream that my four little children will one day live in a nation where they will not be judged by the color of their skin but by the content of their character.

I have a dream today!

I have a dream that one day, down in Alabama, with its vicious racists, with its Governor having his lips dripping with the words of 'interposition' and 'nullification' – one day right there in Alabama little black boys and black girls will be able to join hands with little white boys and white girls as sisters and brothers.

I have a dream today!

I have a dream that one day every valley shall be exalted, and every hill and mountain shall be made low, the rough places will be made plain, and the crooked places will be made straight; 'and the glory of the Lord shall be revealed and all flesh shall see it together.'

This is our hope, and this is the faith that I go back to the South with.

With this faith, we will be able to hew out of the mountain of despair a stone of hope. With this faith, we will be able to transform the jangling discords of our nation into a beautiful symphony of brotherhood. With this faith, we will be able to work together, to pray together, to struggle together, to go to jail together, to stand up for freedom together, knowing that we will be free one day.

This will be the day – this will be the day

Reverend Martin Luther King, Jr in 1964.

when all of God's children will be able to sing with new meaning:

'My country 'tis of thee, sweet land of liberty, of thee I sing.

Land where my fathers died, land of the Pilgrim's pride.

From every mountainside, let freedom ring!'

121

Participants in the March on Washington for Jobs and Freedom.

And if America is to be a great nation, this must become true. And so let freedom ring from the prodigious hilltops of New Hampshire.

Let freedom ring from the mighty mountains of New York.

Let freedom ring from the heightening Alleghenies of Pennsylvania.

Let freedom ring from the snow-capped Rockies of Colorado.

Let freedom ring from the curvaceous slopes of California.

But not only that, let freedom ring from Stone Mountain of Georgia.

Let freedom ring from Lookout Mountain of Tennessee.

Let freedom ring from every hill and molehill of Mississippi.

From every mountainside, let freedom ring.

And when this happens, when we allow freedom to ring, when we let it ring from every village and every hamlet, from every state and every city, we will be able to speed up that day when all of God's children, black men and white men, Jews and Gentiles, Protestants and Catholics, will be able to join hands and sing in the words of the old Negro spiritual:

'Free at last! Free at last!

Thank God Almighty, we are free at last!'

122

MARTIN LUTHER KING, JR

'I'VE BEEN TO THE MOUNTAINTOP'
Mason Temple, Memphis, Tennessee, 3 April 1968

During the spring of 1968, Martin Luther King was working in support of striking African-American sanitation workers in Memphis. He arrived in the city on 3 April, the same day of a gathering at Mason Temple, the headquarters of the Church of God in Christ. King had not planned on attending, but felt obliged to venture out after being told that the audience of three thousand would not leave until they had heard him speak.

In his impromptu speech, King focused on past accomplishments in civil rights, as well as goals and strategies for the future. As he drew close to the end of his speech he recalled the 1958 attempt on his life, in which he was stabbed by an African-American domestic named Izola Ware Curry in New York City. The Reverend referred to more recent threats, including a bomb threat, which had delayed the departure of his flight to Memphis. The conclusion is at once celebratory and premonitory, with King contemplating his own mortality. He was assassinated the next day.

THANK YOU VERY KINDLY, my friends. As I listened to Ralph Abernathy and his eloquent and generous introduction and then thought about myself, I wondered who he was talking about. It's always good to have your closest friend and associate to say something good about you. And Ralph Abernathy is the best friend that I have in the world. I'm delighted to see each of you here tonight in spite of a storm warning. You reveal that you are determined to go on anyhow.

Something is happening in Memphis; something is happening in our world. And you know, if I were standing at the beginning of time, with the possibility of taking a kind of general and panoramic view of the whole of human history up to now, and the Almighty said to me, 'Martin Luther King, which age would you like to live in?' I would take my mental flight by Egypt and I would watch God's children in their magnificent trek from the dark dungeons of Egypt through, or rather across the Red Sea, through the wilderness on toward the Promised Land. And in spite of its magnificence, I wouldn't stop there.

I would move on by Greece and take my mind to Mount Olympus. And I would see Plato, Aristotle, Socrates, Euripides and Aristophanes assembled around the Parthenon. And I would watch them around the Parthenon as they discussed the great and eternal issues of reality. But I wouldn't stop there.

I would go on, even to the great heyday of the Roman Empire. And I would see developments around there, through various emperors and leaders. But I wouldn't stop there.

I would even come up to the day of the Renaissance, and get a quick picture of all that the Renaissance did for the cultural and aesthetic life of man. But I wouldn't stop there.

I would even go by the way that the man for whom I am named had his habitat. And I would watch Martin Luther as he tacked his ninety-five theses on the door at the church of Wittenberg. But I wouldn't stop there.

I would come on up even to 1863, and watch a vacillating President by the name of Abraham Lincoln finally come to the conclusion that he had to sign the Emancipation Proclamation. But I wouldn't stop there.

I would even come up to the early thirties, and see a man grappling with the problems of the bankruptcy of his nation. And come with an eloquent cry that: 'we have nothing to fear but fear itself'. But I wouldn't stop there.

Strangely enough, I would turn to the Almighty, and say, 'If you allow me to live just a few years in the second half of the 20th century, I will be happy.'

Now that's a strange statement to make, because the world is all messed up. The nation is sick. Trouble is in the land; confusion all around. That's a strange statement. But I know, somehow, that only when it is dark enough can you see the stars. And I see God working in this period of the 20th century in a way that men, in some strange way, are responding.

Something is happening in our world. The masses of people are rising up. And wherever they are assembled today, whether they are in Johannesburg, South Africa; Nairobi, Kenya; Accra, Ghana; New York City; Atlanta, Georgia; Jackson, Mississippi; or Memphis, Tennessee – the cry is always the same: 'We want to be free.'

And another reason that I'm happy to live in this period is that we have been forced to a point where we are going to have to grapple with the problems that men have been trying to grapple with through history, but the demands didn't force them to do it. Survival demands that we grapple with them. Men, for years now, have been talking about war and peace. But now, no longer can they just talk about it. It is no longer a choice between violence and non-violence in this world; it's non-violence or non-existence. That is where we are today.

And also in the human rights revolution, if something isn't done, and done in a hurry, to bring the colored peoples of the world out of their long years of poverty, their long years of hurt and neglect, the whole world is doomed. Now, I'm just happy that God has allowed me to live in this period to see what is unfolding. And I'm happy that He's allowed me to be in Memphis. I can remember when Negroes were just going around as Ralph has said, so often, scratching where they didn't itch, and laughing when they were not tickled. But that day is all over. We mean business now, and we are determined to gain our rightful place in God's world.

And that's all this whole thing is about. We aren't engaged in any negative protest and in any negative arguments with anybody. We are saying that we are determined to be men. We are determined to be people. We are saying that we are God's children. And that

we are God's children, we don't have to live like we are forced to live.

Now, what does all of this mean in this great period of history? It means that we've got to stay together. We've got to stay together and maintain unity. You know, whenever Pharaoh wanted to prolong the period of slavery in Egypt, he had a favorite, favorite formula for doing it. What was that? He kept the slaves fighting among themselves. But whenever the slaves get together, something happens in Pharaoh's court, and he cannot hold the slaves in slavery. When the slaves get together, that's the beginning of getting out of slavery. Now let us maintain unity.

Secondly, let us keep the issues where they are. The issue is injustice. The issue is the refusal of Memphis to be fair and honest in its dealings with its public servants, who happen to be sanitation workers. Now, we've got to keep attention on that. That's always the problem with a little violence. You know what happened the other day, and the press dealt only with the window-breaking. I read the articles. They very seldom got around to mentioning the fact that 1,300 sanitation workers are on strike, and that Memphis is not being fair to them, and that Mayor Loeb is in dire need of a doctor. They didn't get around to that.

Now we're going to march again, and we've got to march again, in order to put the issue where it is supposed to be – and force everybody to see that there are 1,300 of God's children here suffering, sometimes going hungry, going through dark and dreary nights wondering how this thing is going to come out. That's the issue. And we've got to say to the nation: 'We know how it's coming out'. For when people get caught up with that which is right and they are willing to sacrifice for it, there is no stopping point short of victory.

We aren't going to let any mace stop us. We are masters in our non-violent movement in disarming police forces; they don't know what to do. I've seen them so often. I remember in Birmingham, Alabama, when we were in that majestic struggle there, we would move out of the 16th Street Baptist Church day after day; by the hundreds we would move out. And Bull Connor would tell them to send the dogs forth, and they did come; but we just went before the dogs singing: 'Ain't gonna let nobody turn me around.'

Bull Connor next would say: 'Turn the fire hoses on.' And as I said to you the other night, Bull Connor didn't know history. He knew a kind of physics that somehow didn't relate to the trans-physics that we knew about. And that was the fact that there was a certain kind of fire that no water could put out. And we went before the fire hoses; we had known water. If we were Baptist or some other denominations, we had been immersed. If we were Methodist, and some others, we had been sprinkled, but we knew water. That couldn't stop us.

And we just went on before the dogs and we would look at them; and we'd go on before the water hoses and we would look at it, and we'd just go on singing: 'Over my head I see freedom in the air.' And then we would be thrown in the paddy wagons, and sometimes we were stacked in there like sardines in a can. And they would throw us in, and old Bull would say: 'Take 'em off' – and they did. And we would just go in the paddy wagon singing 'We Shall Overcome'. And every now and then we'd get in jail, and we'd see the jailers looking through the windows being moved by our prayers, and being moved by our words and our songs. And there was a power there which Bull Connor couldn't adjust to; and so we ended up transforming Bull into a steer, and we won our struggle in Birmingham. Now we've got to go on in Memphis just like that. I call upon you to be with us when we go out Monday.

Now about injunctions: we have an injunction and we're going into court tomorrow morning to fight this illegal, unconstitutional injunction. All we say to America is: 'Be true to what you said on paper.' If I lived in China or even Russia, or any totalitarian country, maybe I could understand some of these illegal injunctions. Maybe I could understand the denial of certain basic First Amendment privileges, because they hadn't committed themselves to that over there. But somewhere I read of the freedom of assembly. Somewhere I read of the freedom of speech. Somewhere I read of the freedom of press. Somewhere I read that the greatness of America is the right to protest for right. And so just as I say, we aren't going to let dogs or water hoses turn us around, we aren't going to let any injunction turn us around. We are going on.

We need all of you. And you know what's beautiful to me is to see all of these ministers of the Gospel. It's a marvelous picture. Who is it that is supposed to articulate the longings and aspirations of the people more than the preacher? Somehow the preacher must have a kind of fire shut up in his bones. And whenever injustice is around he must tell it. Somehow the preacher must be an Amos, and saith: 'When God speaks who can but prophesy?' Again with Amos: 'Let justice roll down like waters and righteousness like a mighty stream.' Somehow the preacher must say with Jesus: 'The Spirit of the Lord is upon me, because he hath anointed me, and he's anointed me to deal with the problems of the poor.'

And I want to commend the preachers, under the leadership of these noble men: James Lawson, one who has been in this struggle for many years; he's been to jail for struggling; he's been kicked out of Vanderbilt University for this struggling, but he's still going on, fighting for the rights of his people. Reverend Ralph Jackson, Billy Kiles, I could just go right on down the list, but time will not permit. But I want to thank all of them. And I want you to thank them, because so often, preachers aren't concerned about anything but themselves. And I'm always happy to see a relevant ministry.

It's all right to talk about long white robes over yonder, in all of its symbolism, but ultimately people want some suits and dresses and shoes to wear down here! It's all right to talk about streets flowing with milk and honey, but God has commanded us to be concerned about the slums down here, and his children who can't eat three square meals a day. It's all right to talk about the new Jerusalem, but one day, God's preacher must talk about the new New York, the new Atlanta, the new Philadelphia, the new Los Angeles, the new Memphis, Tennessee. This is what we have to do.

Now the other thing we'll have to do is this: always anchor our external direct action with the power of economic withdrawal. Now, we are poor people. Individually, we are poor when you compare us with white society in America. We are poor. Never stop and forget that collectively – that means all of us together – collectively we are richer than all the nations in the world, with the exception of nine. Did you ever think about that? After you leave the United States, Soviet Russia, Great Britain, West Germany, France, and I could name the others, the American Negro collectively is richer than most nations of the world. We have an annual income of more than thirty billion dollars a year, which is more than all of the exports of the United States, and more than the national budget of

Canada. Did you know that? That's power right there, if we know how to pool it.

We don't have to argue with anybody. We don't have to curse and go around acting bad with our words. We don't need any bricks and bottles. We don't need any Molotov cocktails. We just need to go around to these stores, and to these massive industries in our country, and say: 'God sent us by here, to say to you that you're not treating his children right. And we've come by here to ask you to make the first item on your agenda fair treatment, where God's children are concerned. Now, if you are not prepared to do that, we do have an agenda that we must follow. And our agenda calls for withdrawing economic support from you.'

And so, as a result of this, we are asking you tonight, to go out and tell your neighbors not to buy Coca-Cola in Memphis. Go by and tell them not to buy Sealtest milk. Tell them not to buy – what is the other bread? – Wonder Bread. And what is the other bread company, Jesse? Tell them not to buy Hart's bread. As Jesse Jackson has said, up to now, only the garbage men have been feeling pain; now we must kind of redistribute the pain. We are choosing these companies because they haven't been fair in their hiring policies; and we are choosing them because they can begin the process of saying they are going to support the needs and the rights of these men who are on strike. And then they can move on town – downtown – and tell Mayor Loeb to do what is right.

But not only that, we've got to strengthen black institutions. I call upon you to take your money out of the banks downtown and deposit your money in Tri-State Bank. We want a 'bank-in' movement in Memphis. Go by the savings and loan association. I'm not asking you something that we don't do ourselves at SCLC. Judge Hooks and others will tell you that we have an account here in the savings and loan association from the Southern Christian Leadership Conference. We are telling you to follow what we are doing. Put your money there. You have six or seven black insurance companies here in the city of Memphis. Take out your insurance there. We want to have an 'insurance-in'.

Now these are some practical things that we can do. We begin the process of building a greater economic base. And at the same time, we are putting pressure where it really hurts. I ask you to follow through here.

Now, let me say as I move to my conclusion, that we've got to give ourselves to this struggle until the end. Nothing would be more tragic than to stop at this point in Memphis. We've got to see it through. And when we have our march, you need to be there. If it means leaving work, if it means leaving school, be there. Be concerned about your brother. You may not be on strike, but either we go up together, or we go down together.

Let us develop a kind of dangerous unselfishness. One day a man came to Jesus, and he wanted to raise some questions about some vital matters of life. At points, he wanted to trick Jesus, and show him that he knew a little more than Jesus knew and throw him off base. Now that question could have easily ended up in a philosophical and theological debate, but Jesus immediately pulled that question from midair, and placed it on a dangerous curve between Jerusalem and Jericho. And he talked about a certain man, who fell among thieves. You remember that a Levite and a priest passed by on the other side. They didn't stop to help him. And finally a man of another race came by. He got down from his beast, decided not to be compassionate by proxy. But he got down with him, administered first aid, and helped the man in need. Jesus ended up saying, this was the good man, this was the great man, because he had the capacity to project the 'I' into the 'thou', and to be concerned about his brother.

Now you know, we use our imagination a great deal to try to determine why the priest and the Levite didn't stop. At times, we say they were busy going to a church meeting, an ecclesiastical gathering, and they had to get on down to Jerusalem so they wouldn't be late for their meeting. At other times we would speculate that there was a religious law that: 'One who was engaged in religious ceremonials was not to touch a human body twenty-four hours before the ceremony.' And every now and then we begin to wonder whether maybe they were not going down to

Jerusalem, or down to Jericho rather, to organize a 'Jericho Road Improvement Association'. That's a possibility. Maybe they felt that it was better to deal with the problem from the causal root, rather than to get bogged down with an individual effect.

But I'm going to tell you what my imagination tells me. It's possible that those men were afraid. You see, the Jericho road is a dangerous road. I remember when Mrs King and I were first in Jerusalem. We rented a car and drove from Jerusalem down to Jericho. And as soon as we got on that road, I said to my wife: 'I can see why Jesus used this as the setting for his parable.' It's a winding, meandering road. It's really conducive for ambushing. You start out in Jerusalem, which is about 1,200 miles – or rather 1,200 feet above sea level – and by the time you get down to Jericho, fifteen or twenty minutes later, you're about 2,200 feet below sea level. That's a dangerous road. In the days of Jesus it came to be known as the 'Bloody Pass'. And you know, it's possible that the priest and the Levite looked over that man on the ground and wondered if the robbers were still around. Or it's possible that they felt that the man on the ground was merely faking and he was acting like he had been robbed and hurt, in order to seize them over there, lure them there for quick and easy seizure. And so the first question that the priest asked – the first question that the Levite asked – was: 'If I stop to help this man, what will happen to me?' But then the Good Samaritan came by and he

129

reversed the question: 'If I do not stop to help this man, what will happen to him?'

That's the question before you tonight. Not: 'If I stop to help the sanitation workers, what will happen to my job?' Not: 'If I stop to help the sanitation workers what will happen to all of the hours that I usually spend in my office every day and every week as a pastor?' The question is not: 'If I stop to help this man in need, what will happen to me?' The question is: 'If I do not stop to help the sanitation workers, what will happen to them?' That's the question.

Let us rise up tonight with a greater readiness. Let us stand with a greater determination. And let us move on in these powerful days, these days of challenge, to make America what it ought to be. We have an opportunity to make America a better nation. And I want to thank God, once more, for allowing me to be here with you.

You know, several years ago, I was in New York City autographing the first book that I had written. And while sitting there autographing books, a demented black woman came up. The only question I heard from her was: 'Are you Martin Luther King?' And I was looking down writing, and I said: 'Yes.' And the next minute I felt something beating on my chest. Before I knew it, I had been stabbed by this demented woman. I was rushed to Harlem Hospital. It was a dark Saturday afternoon. And that blade had gone through, and the X-rays revealed that the tip of the blade was on the edge of my aorta, the main artery. And once that's punctured, you're drowned in your own blood, that's the end of you.

It came out in the *New York Times* the next morning, that if I had merely sneezed, I would have died. Well, about four days later, they allowed me – after the operation, after my chest had been opened, and the blade had been taken out – to move around in the wheelchair in the hospital. They allowed me to read some of the mail that came in, and from all over the states and the world, kind letters came in. I read a few, but one of them I will never forget. I had received one from the President and the Vice President. I've forgotten what those telegrams said. I'd received a visit and a letter from the Governor of New York, but I've forgotten what that letter said. But there was another letter that came from a little girl, a young girl who was a student at the White Plains High School. And I looked at that letter, and I'll never forget it. It said simply: 'Dear Doctor King, I am a ninth-grade student at the White Plains High School.' And she said:

'While it should not matter, I would like to mention that I'm a white girl. I read in the paper of your misfortune and of your suffering. And I read that if you had sneezed, you would have died. And I'm simply writing you to say that I'm so happy that you didn't sneeze.'

And I want to say tonight – I want to say tonight that I too am happy that I didn't sneeze. Because if I had sneezed, I wouldn't have been around here in 1960, when students all over the South started sitting-in at lunch counters. And I knew that as they were sitting-in, they were really standing up for the best in the American dream, and taking the whole nation back to those great wells of democracy, which were dug deep by the Founding Fathers in the Declaration of Independence and the Constitution.

If I had sneezed, I wouldn't have been around here in 1961, when we decided to take a ride for freedom and ended segregation in inter-state travel.

If I had sneezed, I wouldn't have been around here in 1962, when Negroes in Albany, Georgia, decided to straighten their backs up. And whenever men and women straighten their backs up, they are going somewhere, because a man can't ride your back unless it is bent.

If I had sneezed I wouldn't have been here in 1963, when the black people of Birmingham, Alabama, aroused the conscience of this nation, and brought into being the Civil Rights bill.

If I had sneezed, I wouldn't have had a chance later that year, in August, to try to tell America about a dream that I had had.

If I had sneezed, I wouldn't have been down in Selma, Alabama, to see the great movement there.

If I had sneezed, I wouldn't have been in Memphis to see a community rally around those brothers and sisters who are suffering.

I'm so happy that I didn't sneeze.

And they were telling me – now, it doesn't matter, now. It really doesn't matter what happens now. I left Atlanta this morning, and as we got started on the plane, there were six of us. The pilot said over the public address system: 'We are sorry for the delay, but we have Doctor Martin Luther King on the plane. And to be sure that all of the bags were checked, and to be sure that nothing would be wrong with the plane, we had to check out everything carefully. And we've had the plane protected and guarded all night.'

And then I got into Memphis, and some began to say the threats, or talk about, the threats that were out. What would happen to me from some of our sick white brothers?

Well, I don't know what will happen now. We've got some difficult days ahead. But it really doesn't matter with me now, because I've been to the mountaintop.

And I don't mind.

Like anybody, I would like to live a long life. Longevity has its place but I'm not concerned about that now. I just want to do God's will. And He's allowed me to go up to the mountain. And I've looked over. And I've seen the Promised Land. I may not get there with you. But I want you to know tonight, that we, as a people, will get to the Promised Land!

And so I'm happy tonight, I'm not worried about anything; I'm not fearing any man. Mine eyes have seen the glory of the coming of the Lord!

131

ROBERT F. KENNEDY

ON THE ASSASSINATION OF MARTIN LUTHER KING, JR
Indianapolis, Indiana, 4 April 1968

On 4 April 1968, Robert F. Kennedy was in the early days of his campaign for the Democratic nomination for President. He had spoken at the University of Notre Dame and Ball State University, and was travelling to his final event for the day – a speech that was to take place before a largely African-American crowd in Indianapolis' inner city – when he was told of the assassination of Martin Luther King, Jr. Ignoring the advice of the police to cancel his appearance, Kennedy mounted a flatbed truck and gave news of King's death to the crowd of over one thousand.

The speech marked the only occasion upon which Robert Kennedy spoke publicly about the assassination of his brother, John F. Kennedy. Two months after making this speech in Indianapolis, Robert himself was assassinated in Los Angeles.

The signs that Kennedy asked to be lowered read: 'RFK for President'.

LADIES AND GENTLEMEN, I'm only going to talk to you just for a minute or so this evening, because I have some very sad news for all of you.

Could you lower those signs, please.

I have some very sad news for all of you, and I think sad news for all of our fellow citizens, and people who love peace all over the world, and that is that Martin Luther King was shot and was killed tonight in Memphis, Tennessee.

Martin Luther King dedicated his life to love and to justice between fellow human beings. He died in the cause of that effort. In this difficult day, in this difficult time for the United States, it's perhaps well to ask what kind of a nation we are and what direction we want to move in.

For those of you who are black – considering the evidence evidently is that there were white people who were responsible – you can be filled with bitterness, and with hatred, and a desire for revenge.

We can move in that direction as a country, in greater polarization – black people amongst blacks, and white amongst whites – filled with hatred toward one another. Or we can make an effort, as Martin Luther King did, to understand and to comprehend, and replace that violence, that stain of bloodshed that has spread across our land, with an effort to understand, compassion and love.

For those of you who are black and are tempted to be filled with hatred and mistrust of the injustice of such an act, against all white people, I would only say that I can also feel in my own heart the same kind of feeling. I had a member of my family killed, but he was killed by a white man. But we have to make an effort in the United States, we have to make an effort to understand, to get beyond or go beyond these rather difficult times.

My favorite poet was Aeschylus and he once wrote:

Even in our sleep, pain which cannot forget
falls drop by drop upon the heart,
until, in our own despair,
against our will,

comes wisdom
through the awful grace of God.

What we need in the United States is not division; what we need in the United States is not hatred; what we need in the United States is not violence and lawlessness, but is love and wisdom, and compassion toward one another, and a feeling of justice toward those who still suffer within our country, whether they be white or whether they be black.

So I ask you tonight to return home, to say a prayer for the family of Martin Luther King – yeah, that's true – but more importantly to say a prayer for our own country, which all of us love – a prayer for understanding and that compassion of which I spoke.

We can do well in this country. We will have difficult times. We've had difficult times in the past, and we will have difficult times in the future. It is not the end of violence; it is not the end of lawlessness; and it's not the end of disorder.

But the vast majority of white people and the vast majority of black people in this country want to live together, want to improve the quality of our life, and want justice for all human beings that abide in our land.

We dedicate ourselves to what the Greeks wrote so many years ago: 'to tame the savageness of man and make gentle the life of this world'. Let us dedicate ourselves to that, and say a prayer for our country and for our people.

Thank you very much.

RICHARD NIXON

Resignation Speech

The White House, Washington, D.C., 8 August 1974

The Watergate scandal was in its third year, when
Richard Nixon became the first and only American
president to resign from office. The reason given, a belief
that he no longer has a 'strong enough political base in
the Congress', is but a faint reflection of the challenges
facing his presidency. He had lost the support of all but a
handful in his party, and the previous month, the House
Judiciary Committee had prepared articles of
impeachment. While at this distance, resignation might
appear inevitable, in the early days of August 1974 it was
anything but certain. Indeed, the day before this speech,
the front page of *The Washington Post*, the very
newspaper that had broken the Watergate story, carried
the headline: 'Nixon Says He Won't Resign'. As Nixon
was agonizing over whether or not to resign, his
speechwriter Ray Price was working on two addresses:
the first, presented here, in which the President would
announce his resignation; and a second which would
have had Nixon saying that he would stay on for the good
of the nation.

   The speech did little to redeem Nixon's stature in the
eyes of the American public; indeed it was considered
condescending, unapologetic and obfuscating. Even his
successor, Gerald Ford, was critical, believing that Nixon
had offered not one note of contrition.

GOOD EVENING. This is the 37th time I have
spoken to you from this office, where so many
decisions have been made that shaped the
history of this nation. Each time I have done so to discuss

with you some matter that I believe affected the national interest.

In all the decisions I have made in my public life, I have always tried to do what was best for the nation. Throughout the long and difficult period of Watergate, I have felt it was my duty to persevere, to make every possible effort to complete the term of office to which you elected me.

In the past few days, however, it has become evident to me that I no longer have a strong enough political base in the Congress to justify continuing that effort. As long as there was such a base, I felt strongly that it was necessary to see the constitutional process through to its conclusion, that to do otherwise would be unfaithful to the spirit of that deliberately difficult process and a dangerously destabilizing precedent for the future.

But with the disappearance of that base, I now believe that the constitutional purpose has been served, and there is no longer a need for the process to be prolonged.

I would have preferred to carry through to the finish whatever the personal agony it would have involved, and my family unanimously urged me to do so. But the interest of the nation must always come before any personal considerations.

From the discussions I have had with Congressional and other leaders, I have concluded that because of the Watergate matter I might not have the support of the Congress that I would consider necessary to back the very difficult decisions and carry out

the duties of this office in the way the interests of the nation would require.

I have never been a quitter. To leave office before my term is completed is abhorrent to every instinct in my body. But as President, I must put the interest of America first.

America needs a full-time President and a full-time Congress, particularly at this time with problems we face at home and abroad.

To continue to fight through the months ahead for my personal vindication would almost totally absorb the time and attention of both the President and the Congress in a period when our entire focus should be on the great issues of peace abroad and prosperity without inflation at home.

Therefore, I shall resign the Presidency effective at noon tomorrow. Vice President Ford will be sworn in as President at that hour in this office.

As I recall the high hopes for America with which we began this second term, I feel a great sadness that I will not be here in this office working on your behalf to achieve those hopes in the next two and a half years. But in turning over direction of the Government to Vice President Ford, I know, as I told the nation when I nominated him for that office ten months ago, that the leadership of America will be in good hands.

In passing this office to the Vice President, I also do so with the profound sense of the weight of responsibility that will fall on his shoulders tomorrow and, therefore, of the understanding, the patience, the co-operation he will need from all Americans.

As he assumes that responsibility, he will deserve the help and the support of all of us. As we look to the future, the first essential is to begin healing the wounds of this nation, to put the bitterness and divisions of the recent past behind us, and to rediscover those shared ideals that lie at the heart of our strength and unity as a great and as a free people.

By taking this action, I hope that I will have hastened the start of that process of healing which is so desperately needed in America.

I regret deeply any injuries that may have been done in the course of the events that led to this decision. I would say only that if some of my judgments were wrong, and some were wrong, they were made in what I believed at the time to be the best interest of the nation.

To those who have stood with me during these past difficult months, to my family, my friends, to many others who joined in supporting my cause because they believed it was right, I will be eternally grateful for your support.

And to those who have not felt able to give me your support, let me say I leave with no bitterness toward those who have opposed me, because all of us, in the final analysis, have been concerned with the good of the country, however our judgments might differ.

So, let us all now join together in affirming that common commitment and in helping our new President succeed for the benefit of all Americans.

I shall leave this office with regret at not completing my term, but with gratitude for the privilege of serving as your President for the past five and a half years. These years have been a momentous time in the history of our nation and the world. They have been a time of achievement in which we can all be proud, achievements that represent the shared efforts of the Administration, the Congress, and the people.

But the challenges ahead are equally great, and they, too, will require the support and the efforts of the Congress and the people working in co-operation with the new Administration.

We have ended America's longest war, but in the work of securing a lasting peace in the world, the goals ahead are even more far-reaching and more difficult. We must complete a structure of peace so that it will be said of this generation – our generation – of Americans, by the people of all nations, not only that we ended one war but that we prevented future wars.

We have unlocked the doors that for a quarter of a century stood between the United States and the People's Republic of China. We must now ensure that the one quarter of the world's people who live in the People's Republic of China will be and remain not our enemies but our friends.

In the Middle East, one hundred million people in the Arab countries, many of

Richard Nixon during the first term of his presidency; he would not complete the second.

limiting, but reducing and finally destroying these terrible weapons, so that they cannot destroy civilization, and so that the threat of nuclear war will no longer hang over the world and the people.

We have opened a new relationship with the Soviet Union. We must continue to develop and expand that new relationship so that the two strongest nations of the world will live together in co-operation rather than confrontation.

Around the world, in Asia, in Africa, in Latin America, in the Middle East, there are millions of people who live in terrible poverty, even starvation. We must keep as our goal, turning away from production for war and expanding production for peace so that people everywhere on this earth can at last look forward in their children's time, if not in our own time, to having the necessities for a decent life.

Here in America, we are fortunate that most of our people have not only the blessings of liberty but also the means to live full and good and, by the world's standards, even abundant lives. We must press on, however, toward a goal of not only more and better jobs but of full opportunity for every American, and of what we are striving so hard right now to achieve, prosperity without inflation.

For more than a quarter of a century in public life, I have shared in the turbulent history of this era. I have fought for what I believed in. I have tried to the best of my

whom have considered us their enemy for nearly twenty years, now look on us as their friends. We must continue to build on that friendship so that peace can settle at last over the Middle East and so that the cradle of civilization will not become its grave.

Together with the Soviet Union, we have made the crucial breakthroughs that have begun the process of limiting nuclear arms. But we must set as our goal not just ability to discharge those duties and meet those responsibilities that were entrusted to me. Sometimes I have succeeded and sometimes I have failed, but always I have taken heart from what Theodore Roosevelt once said about the man in the arena: 'whose face is marred by dust and sweat and blood, who strives valiantly, who errs and comes short again and again because there is not effort without error and shortcoming, but who does actually strive to do the deed, who knows the great enthusiasms, the great devotions, who spends himself in a worthy cause, who at the best knows in the end the triumphs of high achievements, and who at the worst, if he fails, at least fails while daring greatly.'

I pledge to you tonight that as long as I have a breath of life in my body, I shall continue in that spirit. I shall continue to work for the great causes to which I have been dedicated throughout my years as a Congressman, a Senator, a Vice President, and President, the cause of peace – not just for America but among all nations – prosperity, justice and opportunity for all of our people.

There is one cause above all to which I have been devoted and to which I shall always be devoted for as long as I live.

When I first took the oath of office as President five and a half years ago, I made this sacred commitment, to: 'consecrate my office, my energies, and all the wisdom I can summon to the cause of peace among nations.'

I have done my very best in all the days since to be true to that pledge. As a result of these efforts, I am confident that the world is a safer place today, not only for the people of America but for the people of all nations, and that all of our children have a better chance than before of living in peace rather than dying in war.

This, more than anything, is what I hoped to achieve when I sought the presidency. This, more than anything, is what I hope will be my legacy to you, to our country, as I leave the presidency.

To have served in this office is to have felt a very personal sense of kinship with each and every American. In leaving it, I do so with this prayer: May God's grace be with you in all the days ahead.

PIERRE ELLIOTT TRUDEAU

AGAINST CAPITAL PUNISHMENT

The House of Commons, Ottawa, 15 June 1976

Pierre Elliott Trudeau held 'Reason before passion' as his personal motto. This speech, delivered in support of his government's bill to abolish capital punishment, is an example of his conviction. Trudeau's legislation was passed by a margin of 131 to 124, drawing votes from the governing Liberals, as well as opposition parties.

I AM SURE THAT VERY FEW OF US consciously contemplated, when we decided to run for public office, that we would find ourselves playing a decisive role in the resolution of a question as awesome as that of life and death. Yet, here we are, with all our individual limitations, required by the office we hold to make a decision on as profoundly important an issue as has ever divided Canadians.

It is not open to anyone among us to take refuge in the comforting illusion that we are debating nothing more than an abstract theory of criminal justice, and that it will be the Cabinet's sole responsibility to decide the actual fate of individual murderers, if this bill is defeated.

I want to make it very clear that, if a majority of honorable members vote against abolition, some people are going to be hanged. Their death would be a direct consequence of the negative decision made by this House on this bill.

I say that, Mr Speaker, not from any desire to be morbid or melodramatic, nor from any desire to try to absolve the Cabinet, in advance, of its share of responsibility for the taking of human life in the future, if

this bill is defeated. I say it in order to impress upon the House as strongly as I can that what we will actually be deciding, when we vote on this bill, is not merely how the law of the land will be written, but also whether some human beings will live or die.

At this moment, eleven men are being held in Canadian prisons under sentence of death for the murder of policemen or prison officials. Some have exhausted their rights appeal, others have not. Therefore, while it is impossible to pre-judge how Cabinet will treat any individual case, when the time comes to decide whether to invoke the royal prerogative of mercy and commute a death sentence to life imprisonment, it is inevitable that the defeat of this bill would eventually place the hangman's noose around some person's neck.

To make that quite clear: if this bill is defeated, some people will certainly hang.

While members are free to vote as they wish, those who vote against the bill, for whatever reason, cannot escape their personal share of responsibility for the hangings which will take place if the bill is defeated.

It is in that context, Mr Speaker, that I wish to place my remarks on the issue before us.

Any discussion of capital punishment must begin with the identification of its intended purpose, which is clearly the security of society, the protection of innocent people against the ultimate criminal violence. It is not that goal which divides us. It is the goal we all share. What divides us is the question of appropriateness of state execution of murderers, as a means of achieving that goal.

It is clear that the protection of innocent people against assaults on their lives and liberty is one of the highest duties of the state. It is equally clear that this duty requires aggressive and effective prevention, prosecution and punishment of criminal violence.

It is essential that people have confidence in the law, essential that they have confidence in the ability of the legal process to protect them against the lawless. Reinforcing that vital sense of confidence and security is the primary aim of Bill C-83, the companion piece to the bill we are now debating.

Longer mandatory sentences, and tightening of parole regulations in relation to convicted murderers, will give society the assurance it needs that those who have unlawfully taken the life of another will be removed from our midst for a very long time. Other provisions are designed to restrict the availability of guns, the most common murder weapons, and to strengthen the ability of our police forces to prevent and solve crimes. There is every reason to believe that such measures will effectively inhibit criminal activity, whereas capital punishment offers no such assurance. That is why the time has come for Parliament to decide whether we should remove capital punishment from the Criminal Code.

The crux of the question before us is whether execution is an effective and therefore justifiable weapon for the state to use in order to deter potential murderers.

There are those who sincerely believe that no man or group of men ever have the right to end a human life. They believe that life is a divine gift, which only God has the right to take away. I am not one of those who share that belief.

Our law, from its earliest beginnings, has always recognized the right of an individual to kill another when there exist reasonable grounds for believing that killing an aggressor is necessary to the protection of one's own life or that of another.

Moral philosophers and theologians have recognized for many centuries the right of a country to defend itself in a just war, even when defence involves the killing of enemies.

So the question before us is not whether execution by the state is justified per se. The question is whether state execution is an effective deterrent to murder, and therefore a justifiable act of collective self-defence.

The deterrent effect of capital punishment is at the very core of the issue, and since one's moral view of the justification of capital punishment is entirely determined by one's judgement of its deterrent effect, the proper focus of this debate is factual data and logical induction, not moral philosophy. In that sense, the issue before us must be resolved – by a practical rather than a moral judgement.

I know there are those who say that execution is justified because it prevents a murderer from ever again committing the same crime. It certainly does. But if you rely on that reasoning, you are killing a man not because his death may deter others from following in his footsteps, but because of what he might possibly do at some future time. To justify such preventive execution, there would have to be some reasonable grounds for believing that a convicted murderer, if released into society, would murder again. In fact, the probability lies strongly in the other direction.

We know of only four people who have been found guilty of murder by a Canadian court, and convicted of murder a second time. In order to be absolutely sure that no murderer would murder again, we would have to take the lives of all persons convicted of either first- or second-degree murder, even though the probability is that an infinitesimal percentage of them would ever murder again, if allowed to live. That's an unacceptably high price to pay in human lives for a sense of security insignificantly greater than we have now.

I might ask those who would execute a person to prevent a future murder, how they could logically avoid advocating the execution of mentally ill people who are found to have homicidal tendencies?

Well, you may say, let's execute the murderer for the crime he has committed. Let's take a life for a life. Let's remove a savage animal from the human race.

I do not deny that society has the right to punish a criminal, and the right to make the punishment fit the crime, but to kill a man for punishment alone is an act of

141

revenge. Nothing else. Some would prefer to call it 'retribution', because that word has a nicer sound. But the meaning is the same.

Are we, as a society, so lacking in respect for ourselves, so lacking in hope for human betterment, so socially bankrupt that we are ready to accept state vengeance as our penal philosophy?

Individuals who strike back at the murderer of a loved one, and kill him in a frenzy of passionate grief, have sometimes been excused by the courts because they were thought to have temporarily lost control of their reason. I have received letters from the parents and relatives of victims demanding the death penalty for the murderer, and have been deeply sympathetic to the suffering of those who have suffered such a tragic and cruel loss of a loved one. But the state cannot claim the excuse of blind grief or unreasoning passion when long after the provocative act, and after calm and deliberate consideration, it kills a man.

My primary concern here is not compassion for the murderer. My concern is for the society which adopts vengeance as an acceptable motive for its collective behaviour. If we make that choice, we will snuff out some of that boundless hope and confidence in ourselves and other people, which has marked our maturing as a free people. We will have chosen violence as a weapon against the violence we profess to abhor. Who is so confident that he knows for sure that such an official endorsement of violence will not

harden the society we were elected to improve; will not pervade gradually many different relationships in our society? Who is so confident that he knows for sure that acceptance of state violence will not lead to the greater social acceptance of lesser forms of violence among our people?

Vengeance and violence damage and destroy those who adopt them, and lessen respect for the dignity and rights of others among those who condone them.

There is only one other possible justification for capital punishment – the one we started with – the belief that execution of murderers will protect society by acting as a deterrent to the commission of murder by other people.

There are some who adopt an experimental approach to the question of deterrence, like a scientist experimenting with different combinations of chemicals in the search for a new healing drug.

Let's try it, they say, and see if it works. If it does, we'll keep it. If it doesn't, we can always stop using it. Let's not slam the door, they say, on a possibly effective weapon against murder, on some specious philosophical grounds. There are innocent lives at stake. If capital punishment prevents just one murder, they say, it will be adequately justified.

That's compelling rhetoric, but it contains a fatal flaw, namely that we would be experimenting with human lives. Respect for human life is absolutely vital for the rights and freedom we all enjoy. Even the life of the most hardened criminal must be accorded some degree of respect in a free society. If we take that life without proven purpose, without proven necessity, then we weaken dangerously one of the fundamental principles which allow us to live together in peace, harmony and mutual respect. That is why free peoples have always insisted that the onus is on the person who would interfere with another's life or liberty to prove that such interference is necessary for the common good.

Strictly speaking, therefore, it is not up to me, as an abolitionist, to prove that the execution of murderers will not prevent other murders. It is up to the advocates of capital punishment to prove that it will. If they cannot, their case must fail. Otherwise, this debate turns into a guessing game, and the lives of human beings become so many chips on the poker table. That's not good enough. I don't want to hear your guesses about the deterrent value of capital punishment. I don't want to hear about gut feelings. I want proof. Not absolute proof. Not even proof beyond a reasonable doubt. A preponderance of evidence will do. A preponderance of available evidence, showing that executions are likely to deter other murderers, would serve as an adequate justification for the act, an adequate guarantee that a human life was not being taken capriciously.

Show me the evidence that capital punishment anywhere, at any time, has deterred other people from committing murder. My own reading of the speeches made here on this issue since the first week of May, together with the Solicitor-General's daily monitoring of the debate, have indicated that no such evidence has been placed before the House.

The evidence does not exist, neither in the Canadian experience nor in the experience of any other jurisdiction. At best, the statistics are inconclusive. They prove nothing. There is no evidence proving that the use or non-use of capital punishment has had any effect whatsoever on murder rates anywhere in the world.

I must confess I cannot understand why anyone would agree to kill a man without the least shred of assurance that his death would accomplish any worthwhile social purpose. If penalties applied by the State against law-breakers cannot be justified for their rehabilitative, punitive or deterrent value, they cannot be justified at all – not in a civilized society. Capital punishment fails on all three counts. To retain it in the Criminal Code of Canada would be to abandon reason in favour of vengeance – to abandon hope and confidence in favour of despairing acceptance of our inability to cope with violent crime except with violence.

It is because I have an enduring confidence in mankind, and confidence in society's ability to protect itself without taking human life, that I am eager to support this bill and vote for the abolition of capital punishment.

MARGARET THATCHER

'THE LADY'S NOT FOR TURNING'
Conservative Party Conference, Brighton, 10 October 1980

This speech, delivered seventeen months after she'd led
the Conservatives to power in the 1979 general election,
captures well the determination that earned the British
Prime Minister, Margaret Thatcher, the epithet 'Iron
Lady'. In the face of growing public unrest, falling poll
numbers, and growing doubts within her own party, she
stands firm in her resolve. Thatcher drew some strength
from reports of the acrimonious Labour Party
conference, referred to as a 'strange assembly', which had
taken place at Blackpool the previous week.

As recorded here, Thatcher's speech was interrupted
briefly after two protestors, who had been marching
under the banner 'Right to Work', managed to gain
entrance to the hall. More than half a million people had
joined the ranks of the unemployed under the
Conservatives. The number of unemployed would peak
in 1983, at over three million.

M R CHAIRMAN, ladies and gentlemen: Most of
my cabinet colleagues have started off their
speeches of reply by paying very well-deserved
tributes to their junior ministers. At Number 10 I have no
junior ministers. There's just Denis and me, but I couldn't
do without him.

I am, however, very fortunate in having a marvellous
deputy who is wonderful in all places, at all times, in all
things – Willie Whitelaw.

At our party conference last year, I said that the task
on which the government was engaged – to change the
national attitude of mind – was the most challenging to

face any British Administration since the war. Now, challenge is exhilarating, and this week we Conservatives have been taking stock, discussing the achievements, the set-backs, the work that lies ahead as we enter our second parliamentary year. As you've said Mr Chairman, our debates have been stimulating and our criticisms been constructive. This week has demonstrated that we are a party united in purpose, strategy and resolve.

And we actually like one another.

When I am asked for a detailed forecast of what will happen in the coming months or years, I remember Sam Goldwyn's advice: 'Never prophesy, especially about the future.'

[Interruption from the floor: 'Tories out! Tories out! We want jobs!']

Nevertheless… Never mind, it's wet outside. I expect they wanted to come in.

You can't blame them; it's always better where the Tories are. And you – and perhaps they – will be looking to me this afternoon, for an indication of how the government sees the task before us and why we're tackling it the way we are. Before I begin let me get one point out of the way.

This week at Brighton, we have heard a good deal about last week at Blackpool. I'll have a little more to say about that strange assembly later, but for the moment I want to say just this: because of what happened at that conference, there has been, behind all our deliberations this week, a heightened awareness that now, more than ever, our Conservative government must succeed. We just must. Because there's even more at stake than some had realized.

There are many things to be done to set this nation on the road to recovery, and I don't mean economic recovery alone, but a new independence of spirit and a zest for achievement.

It's sometimes said that because of our past we, as a people, expect too much and set our sights too high. Mr Chairman, that's not the way I see it. Rather it seems to me that throughout my life in politics, our ambitions have steadily shrunk. And our response to disappointment hasn't been to lengthen our stride but to shorten the distance to be covered. But with confidence in ourselves and in our future, what a nation we could be.

In the first seventeen months, this government has laid the foundations for recovery. We've undertaken a heavy load of legislation, a load we don't intend to repeat because we don't share the socialist fantasy that achievement is measured by the number of laws you pass. But, you know, there was a formidable barricade of obstacles that we had to sweep aside. For a start, in his first budget, Geoffrey Howe began to restore incentives to stimulate the abilities and inventive genius of our people. Prosperity comes not from grand conferences of economists, but by countless acts of personal self-confidence and self-reliance.

Also, under Geoffrey's leadership, Britain has repaid $3,600,000,000 of international debt, debt which had been run up by our predecessors. And we paid quite a lot of it before it was due. In the last twelve months, Geoffrey has abolished exchange controls, over which British governments have dithered for decades. Our great enterprises are now free to seek opportunities overseas; and this will help to secure our living standards long after North Sea oil has run out. This government thinks about the future.

As you know, we've made the first crucial changes in trade union law, to remove the worst abuses of the closed shop, to restrict picketing to the place of work of the parties in dispute, and to encourage secret ballots. Jim Prior has carried all these measures through with the support of the vast majority of trade union members.

Keith Joseph, David Howell, John Nott and Norman Fowler have begun to break down the monopoly powers of nationalisation. Thanks to them, British Aerospace will soon be open to private investment. The monopoly of the Post Office and British Telecommunications is being diminished. The barriers to private generation of electricity for sale have been lifted. For the first time, nationalised industries and public utilities can be investigated by the Monopolies Commission – a long overdue reform.

Free competition in road passenger transport promises travellers a better deal. Michael Heseltine has given to millions – yes, millions – of council tenants the right to buy their own homes.

It was Anthony Eden who chose for us the goal of 'a property-owning democracy'. But for all the time that I've been in public affairs, that has been beyond the reach of so many, who were denied the right to the most basic ownership of all – the homes in which they live. They wanted to buy. Many of them could afford to buy. But they happened to live under the jurisdiction of a socialist council, which would not sell and did not believe in the independence that comes with ownership. Now Michael Heseltine has given them a chance to turn a dream into reality. And all this, Mr Chairman, and a lot more, in seventeen months. The Left continues to refer with relish to the death of capitalism. Well, if this is the death of capitalism, I must say it's quite a way to go.

But, Mr Chairman, all this will avail us little unless we achieve our prime economic objective – the defeat of inflation. Inflation destroys nations and societies as surely as invading armies do. It's the parent of unemployment; and it's the unseen robber of those who've saved.

No policy which puts at risk the defeat of inflation – however great its short-term attraction – can be right. But Mr Chairman, our policy for the defeat of inflation is, in fact, traditional. It existed long before Sterling M3 embellished the *Bank of England Quarterly Bulletin,* or 'monetarism' became a convenient term of political invective.

But you know, some people talk as if control of the money supply was a revolutionary policy. Yet it was an essential condition for the recovery of much of continental Europe. Those countries knew what was required for economic stability, because previously, they'd lived through rampant inflation; they knew it led to suitcase money, to massive unemployment, indeed to the breakdown of society itself. They determined never to go that way again. And today, after many years of monetary self-discipline, they have stable, prosperous economies better able than ours to withstand the buffeting of world recession.

So at international conferences to discuss economic affairs, many of my fellow heads of government find our policies not strange, unusual or revolutionary, but normal, sound and honest. And that's what they are.

Their only question to me is this: 'Has Britain the courage and resolve to sustain the discipline for long enough to break through to success?'

Yes, Mr Chairman, we have, and we shall. This government is determined to stay with the policy and see it through to its conclusion. And that is what marks this administration as one of the truly radical ministries of post-war Britain. Inflation is falling and should continue to fall.

Meanwhile, Mr Chairman, we're not heedless of the hardships and worries that accompany the conquest of inflation; and foremost among these is unemployment. Today, our country has more than two million unemployed. Now you can try to soften that figure a dozen ways. You can point out – and

it's quite legitimate to do so – that two million today doesn't mean what it meant in the thirties; that the percentage of unemployment is much less now than it was then. You can add that today many more married women go out to work. You can stress that because of the high birth rate in the early 1960s, there is an unusually large number of school-leavers this year looking for work, and that the same will be true for the next two years. You can emphasise that about a quarter of a million people find new jobs each month and therefore go off the employment register. And you can recall that there are now nearly twenty-five million people in jobs compared with only about eighteen million in the 1930s. You can point out that the Labour Party conveniently overlooks the fact that, of the two million unemployed for which they blame us, nearly a million and a half were bequeathed by their government.

But when all that's been said, the fact remains that the level of unemployment in our country today is a human tragedy. Let me make it clear beyond doubt, I'm profoundly concerned about unemployment. Human dignity and self-respect are undermined when men and women are condemned to idleness. The waste of a country's most precious assets – the talent and energy of its people – makes it the bounden duty of government to seek a real and lasting cure.

If I could press a button and genuinely solve the unemployment problem, do you think that I would not press that button this instant? Does anyone imagine that there is the smallest political gain in letting this level of unemployment continue, or that there is some obscure economic religion which demands this level of unemployment as part of its grisly ritual? Mr Chairman, this government is pursuing the only policy which gives any hope of bringing our people back to real and lasting employment. Indeed it's no coincidence that those countries, of which I spoke earlier, which have had lower rates of inflation have also had lower levels of unemployment.

Now, I know, Mr Chairman, that there's another real worry affecting many of our people. Although they accept that our policies are right, they feel deeply that the burden of carrying them out is falling much more heavily on the private than on the public sector. They say that the public sector is enjoying the advantages but the private sector's taking the knocks, and at the same time maintaining those in the public sector on better pay and pensions than they themselves enjoy.

I must tell you that I share this concern and understand the resentment. And that is why I and my colleagues say that to add to public spending takes away the very money and resources that industry needs to stay in business, let alone to expand. That higher public spending, far from curing unemployment, can be the very vehicle that loses jobs and causes bankruptcies in trade and commerce. That's why we warned local authorities that since rates are frequently the

biggest tax that industry now pays, increases in them can cripple local businesses. Councils must, therefore, learn to cut costs in the same way that companies have to.

That's why I stress that if those who work in public authorities take for themselves large pay increases, they leave less to be spent on equipment and new buildings. And that, in turn, deprives the private sector of the orders it needs, especially some of those industries in the hard-pressed regions. So those in the public sector have a duty to those in the private sector not to take out so much in pay that they cause others unemployment. That's why we point out that every time high wage settlements in nationalised monopolies lead to higher charges for telephones, electricity, coal and water, they can drive companies out of business and cost other people their jobs.

If spending money like water was the answer to our country's problems, we would have no problems now. Because if ever a nation has spent, spent, and spent again, ours has, and today that dream is over. All that money has got us nowhere, but it still has to come from somewhere. And those who urge us to relax the squeeze, to spend yet more money indiscriminately in the belief that it will help the unemployed and the small businessman, are not being kind, or compassionate, or caring. They are not the friends of the unemployed or the small business. They are asking us to do again the very thing that caused the problems in the first place.

Now we've made this point repeatedly, indeed, Mr Chairman, I am accused of lecturing or preaching about them. I suppose it's a critic's way of saying 'Well, we know it's true but we've got to carp at something.' I don't care about that, but I do care about the future of free enterprise, the jobs and exports it provides and the independence it brings to our people.

Independence? Yes, but let us be clear what we mean by that. Independence doesn't mean contracting out of all relationships with others. A nation can be free but it won't stay free for long if it has no friends and no alliances. Above all, it won't stay free if it can't pay its own way in the world. And by the same token, an individual needs to be part of a community and to feel that he is part of it. There's more to this than the chance to earn a living for himself and his family, essential though that is.

Of course, our vision and our aims go far beyond the complex arguments of economics, but unless we get the economy right we shall deny our people the opportunity to share that vision and to see beyond the narrow horizons of economic necessity. Without a healthy economy we can't have a healthy society; and without a healthy society the economy won't stay healthy for long.

Mr Chairman, but it isn't the state that creates a healthy society. For when the state grows too powerful, people feel that they count for less and less. The state drains society, not only of its wealth but of initiative, of

energy, the will to improve and innovate, as well as to preserve what is best. But our aim is to let people feel that they count for more and more. If we can't trust the deepest instincts of our people we shouldn't be in politics at all.

And, Mr Chairman, some aspects of our present society really do offend those instincts. Decent people do want to do a proper job at work, not to be restrained or intimidated from giving value for money. They believe that honesty should be respected, not derided. They see crime and violence as a threat, not just to society, but to their own orderly way of life. They want to be allowed to bring up their children in these beliefs, without the fear that their efforts will be daily frustrated in the name of progress or free expression. Indeed, that's what family life is all about. There isn't a generation gap in a happy and united family. People yearn to be able to rely on some generally accepted standards. Without them you haven't got a society at all, you have purposeless anarchy. A healthy society isn't created by its institutions, either. Great schools and universities don't make a great nation any more than great armies do, because only a great nation can create and involve great institutions of learning, of healing, of scientific advance. And a great nation is the voluntary creation of its people – a people composed of men and women whose pride in themselves is founded on the knowledge of what they can give to a community of which they, in turn, can be proud.

If our people feel that they are part of a

great nation and they are prepared to will the means to keep it great, then a great nation we shall be, and shall remain. So, Mr Chairman, what could stop us from achieving this? What, then, stands in our way – the prospect of another winter of discontent? I suppose it might. But I prefer to believe that certain lessons have been learned from experience, that we are coming slowly, painfully, to an autumn of understanding. And I hope it will be followed by a winter of common sense. If it isn't, we shall not be diverted from our course.

To those waiting with bated breath for that favourite media catchphrase, the 'U-turn', I have only one thing to say: 'You turn if you want to. The lady's not for turning.' And I say that not only to you but to our friends overseas as well, and also to those who are not our friends.

In foreign affairs, we've pursued our national interest robustly while remaining alive to the needs and interests of others. We have acted where our predecessors dithered; and here may I pay tribute to Lord Carrington. When I think of our much-travelled Foreign Secretary, I'm reminded of the advertisement – you know the one I mean – about 'The peer that refreshes those foreign parts that other peers can't reach.'

It seems I got that right.

Long before we came into office, and therefore long before the invasion of Afghanistan, I was pointing to the threat from the East. I was accused of scaremongering. But events have more than justified my words.

Soviet Marxism is ideologically, politically and morally bankrupt. But militarily the Soviet Union is a powerful and growing threat.

Yet it was Mr Kosygin who said: 'No peace-loving country, no person of integrity, should remain indifferent when an aggressor holds human life and world opinion in insolent contempt.' We agree. The British government is not indifferent to the occupation of Afghanistan. We will not allow it to be forgotten. For unless and until the Soviet troops are withdrawn, other nations are bound to wonder which of them may be next. Of course, there are those who say that by speaking out we are complicating East–West relations, that we are endangering détente. But the real danger would lie in keeping silent. Détente is indivisible and it is a two-way process.

The Soviet Union can't conduct wars by proxy in Southeast Asia and in Africa, foment trouble in the Middle East and the Caribbean, invade neighbouring countries, and still expect to conduct business as usual. Unless détente is pursued by both sides it can be pursued by neither, and it's a delusion to suppose otherwise. That's the message we shall be delivering loud and clear at the meetings of the European Security Conference in Madrid, in the weeks immediately ahead.

But we shall also be reminding the other participants in Madrid that the Helsinki Accord was supposed to promote the freer movement of people and ideas. The Soviet government's response so far has been a campaign of repression worse than any since Stalin's day. It had been hoped that Helsinki would open gates across Europe. In fact, the guards today are better armed and the walls are no lower. But behind those walls the human spirit is unvanquished. And the workers of Poland, in their millions, have signalled their determination to participate in the shaping of their destiny. We salute them.

Marxists claim that the capitalist system is in crisis. The Polish workers have shown that it's the communist system that is in crisis. The Polish people should be left to work out their own future without external interference.

Mr Chairman, at every party conference, and every November in Parliament, we used to face difficult decisions over Rhodesia and over sanctions. But no longer. Since we last met, the success at Lancaster House, and thereafter in Salisbury – a success won in the face of all the odds, a success that has created new respect for Britain – has given fresh hope to those grappling with the terrible problems of southern Africa. It's given the Commonwealth new strength and unity. And now it's for the new nation, Zimbabwe, to build her own future with the support of all those who believe that democracy has a place in Africa, and we wish her well.

We showed over Rhodesia that the hallmarks of Tory policy are, as they always have been, realism and resolve. Not for us the disastrous fantasies of unilateral disarmament, of withdrawal from NATO, of abandoning Northern Ireland. The irresponsibility of the Left on defence increases as the dangers which we face loom larger. And we for our part, under Francis Pym's brilliant leadership, have chosen a defence policy which potential foes will respect.

We are acquiring, with the co-operation of the United States government, the Trident missile system. This will ensure the credibility of our strategic deterrent until the end of the century and beyond; and it was very important for the reputation of Britain abroad that we should keep our independent nuclear deterrent, as well as for our citizens here.

We've agreed to the stationing of cruise missiles in this country. The unilateralists object, but the recent willingness of the Soviet government to open a new round of arms control negotiations shows, in fact, the wisdom of our firmness. We intend to maintain and, where possible, to improve our conventional forces so as to pull our weight in the Alliance. We've no wish to seek a free ride at the expense of our allies. We'll play our full part.

In Europe, we've shown that it is possible to combine a vigorous defence of our own interests with a deep commitment to the idea and to the ideals of the Community.

Mr Chairman, the last government was well aware that Britain's budget contribution was grossly unfair. They failed to do anything about it. We negotiated a satisfactory arrangement, which will give us and our partners time to tackle the underlying issues.

We've resolved the difficulties of New Zealand's lamb trade with the Community in a way which protects the interests of the farmers in New Zealand, while giving our own farmers and our own housewives an excellent deal, and Peter Walker deserves to be congratulated on his success. Now he's two-thirds on his way to success in making important progress towards agreement on a common fisheries policy. That's very important to our people, too; there are many, many people whose livelihoods depend on it.

Now, we face many other problems in the Community, but I'm confident that they too will yield to the firm, yet fair, approach which has already proved so much more effective than the previous government's five years of procrastination.

With each day, it becomes clearer that in the wider world we face darkening horizons, and the war between Iran and Iraq is the latest symptom of a deeper malady. Europe and North America are centres of stability in an increasingly anxious world. The Community and the Alliance are the guarantee to other countries that democracy and freedom of choice are still possible. They stand for order and the rule of law in an age when disorder and lawlessness are ever more widespread.

The British government intends to stand by both these great institutions – the Community and NATO. We will not betray them.

The restoration of Britain's place in the world and of the West's confidence in its own destiny are two aspects of the same process. No doubt there'll be unexpected twists in the road, but with wisdom and resolution we can reach our goal. I believe we'll show the wisdom, and you may be certain that we'll show the resolution.

Mr Chairman, in his warm-hearted and generous speech, Peter Thorneycroft said that when people are called upon to lead great nations, they must look into the hearts and minds of the people whom they seek to govern. I would add, that those who seek to govern must in turn be willing to allow their hearts and minds to lie open to the people.

This afternoon, I've tried to set before you some of my most deeply held convictions and beliefs. This party, which I am privileged to serve, and this government, which I am proud to lead, are engaged in the massive task of restoring confidence and stability to our people.

I've always known that task was vital; since last week, it has become even more vital than ever. We close our conference in the aftermath of that sinister Utopia unveiled at Blackpool. Let Labour's Orwellian nightmare of the Left be the spur for us to dedicate, with a new urgency, our every ounce of energy and moral strength to rebuild the fortunes of this free nation.

If we were to fail, that freedom could be imperilled. So let us resist the blandishments of the faint-hearts; let us ignore the howls and threats of the extremists; let us stand together and do our duty, and we shall not fail.

RONALD REAGAN

'TEAR DOWN THIS WALL'

The Brandenburg Gate, West Berlin, West Germany,
12 June 1987

President Ronald Reagan's 1987 visit to Berlin was ostensibly to commemorate the 750th anniversary of the then-divided city. His address came twenty-four years after John F. Kennedy had delivered his famous 'Ich bin ein Berliner' speech, a fact noted in the opening remarks. Where Kennedy was met by an adoring crowd, Reagan's reception was somewhat mixed, as recognized in the conclusion of the speech.

CHANCELLOR KOHL, Governing Mayor Diepgen, Ladies and Gentlemen: Twenty-four years ago, President John F. Kennedy visited Berlin, speaking to the people of this city and the world at the City Hall. Well, since then two other presidents have come, each in his turn, to Berlin. And today I, myself, make my second visit to your city.

We come to Berlin, we American presidents, because it's our duty to speak, in this place, of freedom. But I must confess, we're drawn here by other things as well: by the feeling of history in this city, more than five hundred years older than our own nation; by the beauty of the Grunewald and the Tiergarten; most of all, by your courage and determination.

Perhaps the composer Paul Lincke understood something about American presidents. You see, like so many presidents before me, I come here today because wherever I go, whatever I do: *Ich hab noch einen Koffer in Berlin* [I still have a suitcase in Berlin].

Our gathering today is being broadcast throughout

Western Europe and North America. I understand that it is being seen and heard as well in the East. To those listening throughout Eastern Europe, I extend my warmest greetings and the goodwill of the American people. To those listening in East Berlin, a special word: although I cannot be with you, I address my remarks to you just as surely as to those standing here before me. For I join you, as I join your fellow countrymen in the West, in this firm, this unalterable belief: *Es gibt nur ein Berlin* [There is only one Berlin].

Behind me stands a wall that encircles the free sectors of this city, part of a vast system of barriers that divides the entire continent of Europe. From the Baltic south, those barriers cut across Germany in a gash of barbed wire, concrete, dog runs, and guard towers. Farther south, there may be no visible, no obvious wall but there remain armed guards and checkpoints all the same – still a restriction on the right to travel; still an instrument to impose upon ordinary men and women the will of a totalitarian state. Yet it is here, in Berlin, where the wall emerges most clearly; here, cutting across your city, where the news photo and the television screen have imprinted this brutal division of a continent upon the mind of the world. Standing before the Brandenburg Gate, every man is a German, separated from his fellow men. Every man is a Berliner, forced to look upon a scar.

President von Weizsacker has said: 'The German question is open as long as the Brandenburg Gate is closed.' Today, I say, as long as this gate is closed, as long as this scar of a wall is permitted to stand, it is not the German question alone that remains open, but the question of freedom for all mankind.

Yet I do not come here to lament. For I find in Berlin a message of hope, even in the shadow of this wall, a message of triumph.

In the season of spring in 1945, the people of Berlin emerged from their air-raid shelters to find devastation. Thousands of miles away, the people of the United States reached out to help, and in 1947 Secretary of State – as you've been told – George Marshall announced the creation of what would become known as the Marshall Plan.

Speaking precisely forty years ago this month, he said: 'Our policy is directed not against any country or doctrine, but against hunger, poverty, desperation, and chaos.'

In the Reichstag a few moments ago, I saw a display commemorating this fortieth anniversary of the Marshall Plan. I was struck by the sign on a burnt-out, gutted structure that was being rebuilt. I understand that Berliners of my own generation can remember seeing signs like it dotted throughout the western sectors of the city. The sign read simply: 'The Marshall Plan is helping here to strengthen the free world.' A strong, free world in the West, that dream became real. Japan rose from ruin to become an economic giant. Italy, France, Belgium – virtually every nation in Western Europe – saw political and economic rebirth; the

European Community was founded.

In West Germany and here in Berlin, there took place an economic miracle, the Wirtschaftswunder. Adenauer, Erhard, Reuter, and other leaders understood the practical importance of liberty; that just as truth can flourish only when the journalist is given freedom of speech, so prosperity can come about only when the farmer and businessman enjoy economic freedom. The German leaders reduced tariffs, expanded free trade, lowered taxes. From 1950 to 1960 alone, the standard of living in West Germany and Berlin doubled.

Where four decades ago there was rubble, today in West Berlin there is the greatest industrial output of any city in Germany: busy office blocks, fine homes and apartments, proud avenues, and the spreading lawns of parkland. Where a city's culture seemed to have been destroyed, today there are two great universities, orchestras and an opera, countless theatres and museums. Where there was want, today there's abundance: food, clothing, automobiles, the wonderful goods of the Ku'damm. From devastation, from utter ruin, you Berliners have, in freedom, rebuilt a city that once again ranks as one of the greatest on earth. The Soviets may have had other plans but my friends, there were a few things the Soviets didn't count on: *Berliner Herz, Berliner Humor, ja, und Berliner Schnauze* [Berliner heart, Berliner humor, yes, and Berliner lip].

In the 1950s, Khrushchev predicted:

'We will bury you.' But in the West today, we see a free world that has achieved a level of prosperity and wellbeing unprecedented in all human history. In the communist world, we see failure, technological backwardness, declining standards of health, even want of the most basic kind. Too little food – even today, the Soviet Union still cannot feed itself. After these four decades, then, there stands before the entire world one great and inescapable conclusion: Freedom leads to prosperity. Freedom replaces the ancient hatreds among the nations with comity and peace. Freedom is the victor.

And now, the Soviets themselves may, in a limited way, be coming to understand the importance of freedom. We hear much from Moscow about a new policy of reform and openness. Some political prisoners have been released. Certain foreign news broadcasts are no longer being jammed. Some economic enterprises have been permitted to operate with greater freedom from state control.

Are these the beginnings of profound changes in the Soviet state? Or are they token gestures, intended to raise false hopes in the West, or to strengthen the Soviet system without changing it? We welcome change and openness; for we believe that freedom and security go together, that the advance of human liberty can only strengthen the cause of world peace. There is one sign the Soviets can make that would be unmistakable, that would advance dramatically the cause of freedom and peace.

155

General Secretary Gorbachev, if you seek peace, if you seek prosperity for the Soviet Union and Eastern Europe, if you seek liberalization: Come here to this gate! Mr Gorbachev, open this gate! Mr Gorbachev, tear down this wall!

I understand the fear of war and the pain of division that afflict this continent, and I pledge to you my country's efforts to help overcome these burdens. To be sure, we in the West must resist Soviet expansion. So we must maintain defenses of unassailable strength. Yet we seek peace; so we must strive to reduce arms on both sides.

Beginning ten years ago, the Soviets challenged the Western alliance with a grave new threat, hundreds of new and more deadly SS-20 nuclear missiles, capable of striking every capital in Europe. The Western alliance responded by committing itself to a counter-deployment, unless the Soviets agreed to negotiate a better solution: namely, the elimination of such weapons on both sides. For many months, the Soviets refused to bargain in earnestness. As the Alliance, in turn, prepared to go forward with its counter-deployment, there were difficult days – days of protests like those during my 1982 visit to this city – and the Soviets later walked away from the table.

But through it all, the Alliance held firm. And I invite those who protested then – I invite those who protest today – to mark this fact: because we remained strong, the Soviets came back to the table. And because we remain strong today, we have within reach the possibility, not merely of limiting the growth of arms, but of eliminating, for the first time, an entire class of nuclear weapons from the face of the earth.

As I speak, NATO ministers are meeting in Iceland to review the progress of our proposals for eliminating these weapons. At the talks in Geneva, we have also proposed deep cuts in strategic offensive weapons, and the Western allies have likewise made far-reaching proposals to reduce the danger of conventional war and to place a total ban on chemical weapons.

While we pursue these arms reductions, I pledge to you that we will maintain the capacity to deter Soviet aggression at any level at which it might occur. And in co-operation with many of our allies, the United States is pursuing the Strategic Defense Initiative – research to base deterrence not on the threat of offensive retaliation, but on defenses that truly defend; on systems, in short, that will not target populations, but shield them. By these means, we seek to increase the safety of Europe and all the world. But we must remember a crucial fact: East and West do not mistrust each other because we are armed; we are armed because we mistrust each other. And our differences are not about weapons, but about liberty.

When President Kennedy spoke at the City Hall those twenty-four years ago, freedom was encircled, Berlin was under siege. And today, despite all the pressures upon this city, Berlin stands secure in its liberty, and freedom itself is transforming the globe. In the Philippines, in South and Central America, democracy has been given a rebirth. Throughout the Pacific, free markets are working miracle after miracle of economic growth. In the industrialized nations, a technological revolution is taking place, a revolution marked by rapid, dramatic advances in computers and telecommunications.

In Europe, only one nation and those it controls refuse to join the community of freedom. Yet in this age of redoubled economic growth, of information and innovation, the Soviet Union faces a choice: it must make fundamental changes, or it will become obsolete.

Today, thus, represents a moment of hope. We in the West stand ready to co-operate with the East to promote true openness, to break down barriers that separate people, to create a safe, freer world. And surely there is no better place than Berlin, the meeting place of East and West, to make a start.

Free people of Berlin, today, as in the past, the United States stands for the strict observance and full implementation of all parts of the Four-Power Agreement of 1971. Let us use this occasion, the 750th anniversary of this city, to usher in a new era, to seek a still fuller, richer life for the Berlin of the future. Together, let us maintain and develop the ties between the Federal Republic and the Western sectors of Berlin, which is permitted by the 1971 Agreement.

And I invite Mr Gorbachev: Let us work to bring the Eastern and Western parts of the city closer together, so that all the inhabitants of all Berlin can enjoy the benefits that come with life in one of the great cities of the world.

To open Berlin still further to all Europe, East and West, let us expand the vital air access to this city, finding ways of making commercial air service to Berlin more convenient, more comfortable, and more economical. We look to the day when West Berlin can become one of the chief aviation hubs in all central Europe.

With our French and British partners, the United States is prepared to help bring international meetings to Berlin. It would be only fitting for Berlin to serve as the site of United Nations meetings, or world conferences on human rights and arms control or other issues that call for international co-operation.

There is no better way to establish hope for the future than to enlighten young minds, and we would be honored to sponsor summer youth exchanges, cultural events, and other programs for young Berliners from the East. Our French and British friends, I'm certain, will do the same. And it's my hope that an authority can be found in East Berlin to sponsor visits from young people of the Western sectors.

One final proposal, one close to my heart: sport represents a source of enjoyment and ennoblement, and you may have noted that the Republic of Korea – South Korea – has offered to permit certain events of the 1988

Olympics to take place in the North. International sports competitions of all kinds could take place in both parts of this city. And what better way to demonstrate to the world the openness of this city than to offer in some future year to hold the Olympic Games here in Berlin, East and West?

In these four decades, as I have said, you Berliners have built a great city. You've done so in spite of threats: the Soviet attempts to impose the East-mark; the blockade. Today the city thrives in spite of the challenges implicit in the very presence of this wall. What keeps you here? Certainly there's a great deal to be said for your fortitude, for your defiant courage. But I believe there's something deeper, something that involves Berlin's whole look and feel and way of life, not mere sentiment. No one could live long in Berlin without being completely disabused of illusions. Something instead, that has seen the difficulties of life in Berlin but chose to accept them, that continues to build this good and proud city in contrast to a surrounding totalitarian presence that refuses to release human energies or aspirations. Something that speaks with a powerful voice of affirmation, that says 'yes' to this city, 'yes' to the future, 'yes' to freedom. In a word, I would submit that what keeps you in Berlin is love; love both profound and abiding.

Perhaps this gets to the root of the matter, to the most fundamental distinction of all between East and West. The totalitarian world produces backwardness because it does such

violence to the spirit, thwarting the human impulse to create, to enjoy, to worship. The totalitarian world finds even symbols of love and of worship an affront. Years ago, before the East Germans began rebuilding their churches, they erected a secular structure: the television tower at Alexander Platz. Virtually ever since, the authorities have been working to correct what they view as the tower's one major flaw, treating the glass sphere at the top with paints and chemicals of every kind. Yet even today when the sun strikes that sphere – that sphere that towers over all Berlin – the light makes the sign of the cross. There in Berlin, like the city itself, symbols of love, symbols of worship, cannot be suppressed.

As I looked out a moment ago from the Reichstag, that embodiment of German unity, I noticed words crudely spray-painted upon the wall, perhaps by a young Berliner: 'This wall will fall. Beliefs become reality.' Yes, across Europe, this wall will fall. For it cannot withstand faith; it cannot withstand truth. The wall cannot withstand freedom.

And I would like, before I close, to say one word. I have read, and I have been questioned since I've been here about certain demonstrations against my coming. And I would like to say just one thing, and to those who demonstrate so. I wonder if they have ever asked themselves that if they should have the kind of government they apparently seek, no one would ever be able to do what they're doing again.

Thank you and God bless you all.

NELSON MANDELA

INAUGURAL ADDRESS

The Union Buildings, Pretoria, 10 May 1994

It is estimated that a billion viewers watched the
broadcast of Nelson Mandela's inauguration as the first
black State President of the Republic of South Africa.
The guest list featured some four thousand names,
among them Prince Philip, Fidel Castro and Chaim
Herzog. This stood in stark contrast with that of his
predecessor five years earlier: the inauguration of
F.W. de Klerk, a more modest affair, was not televised
internationally and had not one foreign dignitary
as witness.

YOUR MAJESTIES, Your Highnesses, Distinguished
Guests, Comrades and Friends: Today, all of us
do, by our presence here, and by our celebrations
in other parts of our country and the world, confer glory
and hope to newborn liberty.

Out of the experience of an extraordinary human
disaster that lasted too long, must be born a society of
which all humanity will be proud. Our daily deeds as
ordinary South Africans must produce an actual South
African reality that will reinforce humanity's belief in
justice, strengthen its confidence in the nobility of the
human soul and sustain all our hopes for a glorious life for
all. All this we owe both to ourselves and to the peoples of
the world who are so well represented here today.

To my compatriots, I have no hesitation in saying
that each one of us is as intimately attached to the soil of
this beautiful country as are the famous jacaranda trees of
Pretoria and the mimosa trees of the Bushveld. Each time
one of us touches the soil of this land, we feel a sense of

personal renewal. The national mood changes as the seasons change. We are moved by a sense of joy and exhilaration when the grass turns green and the flowers bloom.

That spiritual and physical oneness we all share with this common homeland explains the depth of the pain we all carried in our hearts as we saw our country tear itself apart in a terrible conflict, and as we saw it spurned, outlawed and isolated by the peoples of the world, precisely because it has become the universal base of the pernicious ideology and practice of racism and racial oppression.

We, the people of South Africa, feel fulfilled that humanity has taken us back into its bosom, that we, who were outlaws not so long ago, have today been given the rare privilege to be host to the nations of the world on our own soil.

We thank all our distinguished international guests for having come to take possession with the people of our country of what is, after all, a common victory for justice, for peace, for human dignity. We trust that you will continue to stand by us as we tackle the challenges of building peace, prosperity, non-sexism, non-racialism and democracy.

We deeply appreciate the role that the masses of our people and their political mass democratic, religious, women, youth, business, traditional and other leaders have played to bring about this conclusion. Not least among them is my Second Deputy President, the Honourable F.W. de Klerk.

We would also like to pay tribute to our security forces, in all their ranks, for the distinguished role they have played in securing our first democratic elections and the transition to democracy, from blood-thirsty forces which still refuse to see the light.

The time for the healing of the wounds has come.

The moment to bridge the chasms that divide us has come.

The time to build is upon us.

We have, at last, achieved our political emancipation. We pledge ourselves to liberate all our people from the continuing bondage of poverty, deprivation, suffering, gender and other discrimination.

We succeeded to take our last steps to freedom in conditions of relative peace. We commit ourselves to the construction of a complete, just and lasting peace.

We have triumphed in the effort to implant hope in the breasts of the millions of our people. We enter into a covenant that we shall build the society in which all South Africans, both black and white, will be able to walk tall, without any fear in their hearts, assured of their inalienable right to human dignity – a rainbow nation at peace with itself and the world.

As a token of its commitment to the renewal of our country, the new Interim Government of National Unity will, as a matter of urgency, address the issue of amnesty for various categories of our

Nelson Mandela after having won the presidency of the Republic of South Africa.

people who are currently serving terms of imprisonment.

We dedicate this day to all the heroes and heroines in this country and the rest of the world who sacrificed in many ways and surrendered their lives so that we could be free. Their dreams have become reality. Freedom is their reward.

We are both humbled and elevated by the honour and privilege that you, the people of South Africa, have bestowed on us, as the first President of a united, democratic, non-racial and non-sexist South Africa, to lead our country out of the valley of darkness.

We understand it still that there is no easy road to freedom.

We know it well that none of us acting alone can achieve success.

We must therefore act together as a united people, for national reconciliation, for nation building, for the birth of a new world.

Let there be justice for all.

Let there be peace for all.

Let there be work, bread, water and salt for all.

Let each know that for each the body, the mind and the soul have been freed to fulfil themselves. Never, never and never again shall it be that this beautiful land will again experience the oppression of one by another and suffer the indignity of being the skunk of the world.

Let freedom reign.

The sun shall never set on so glorious a human achievement!

God bless Africa!

Thank you.

POPE JOHN PAUL II

SPEECH AT YAD VASHEM

Hall of Remembrance, Yad Vashem, Israel, 23 March 2000

More than any other, Pope John Paul II worked to improve relations between the Jewish people and the Roman Catholic Church. He became the first pope to visit the Great Synagogue in Rome, the first to visit Auschwitz, and he oversaw the establishment of diplomatic communications with the State of Israel. John Paul II was in the last years of his pontificate when he made a pilgrimage to the Holy Land, during which he spoke to a small audience at Yad Vashem, Israel's official memorial to the Jewish victims of the Holocaust.

THE WORDS OF THE ANCIENT PSALM, rise from our hearts: 'I have become like a broken vessel. I hear the whispering of many – terror on every side – as they scheme together against me, as they plot to take my life. But I trust in you, O Lord: I say, "You are my God."'

In this place of memories, the mind and heart and soul feel an extreme need for silence. Silence in which to remember. Silence in which to try to make some sense of the memories which come flooding back. Silence because there are no words strong enough to deplore the terrible tragedy of the Shoah.

My own personal memories are of all that happened when the Nazis occupied Poland during the war. I remember my Jewish friends and neighbours, some of whom perished, while others survived. I have come to Yad Vashem to pay homage to the millions of Jewish people who, stripped of everything, especially of human dignity, were murdered in the Holocaust. More than half a century has passed, but the memories remain.

Here, as at Auschwitz and many other places in Europe, we are overcome by the echo of the heart-rending laments of so many. Men, women and children, cry out to us from the depths of the horror that they knew. How can we fail to heed their cry? No one can forget or ignore what happened. No one can diminish its scale.

We wish to remember. But we wish to remember for a purpose, namely to ensure that never again will evil prevail, as it did for the millions of innocent victims of Nazism.

How could man have such utter contempt for man? Because he had reached the point of contempt for God. Only a godless ideology could plan and carry out the extermination of a whole people.

The honour given to the 'Just Gentiles' by the state of Israel at Yad Vashem for having acted heroically to save Jews, sometimes to the point of giving their own lives, is a recognition that not even in the darkest hour is every light extinguished. That is why the Psalms and the entire Bible, though well aware of the human capacity for evil, also proclaims that evil will not have the last word.

Out of the depths of pain and sorrow, the believer's heart cries out: 'I trust in you, O Lord: I say, "You are my God." '

Jews and Christians share an immense spiritual patrimony, flowing from God's self-revelation. Our religious teachings and our spiritual experience demand that we overcome evil with good. We remember, but not with any desire for vengeance or as an incentive to hatred. For us, to remember is to pray for peace and justice, and to commit ourselves to their cause. Only a world at peace, with justice for all, can avoid repeating the mistakes and terrible crimes of the past.

As Bishop of Rome and successor of the Apostle Peter, I assure the Jewish people that the Catholic Church, motivated by the Gospel law of truth and love, and by no political considerations, is deeply saddened by the hatred, acts of persecution and displays of anti-Semitism directed against the Jews by Christians at any time and in any place.

The church rejects racism in any form, as a denial of the image of the Creator inherent in every human being.

In this place of solemn remembrance, I fervently pray that our sorrow for the tragedy which the Jewish people suffered in the 20th century will lead to a new relationship between Christians and Jews. Let us build a new future in which there will be no more anti-Jewish feeling among Christians or anti-Christian feeling among Jews, but rather the mutual respect required of those who adore the one Creator and Lord, and look to Abraham as our common father in faith.

The world must heed the warning that comes to us from the victims of the Holocaust, and from the testimony of the survivors. Here at Yad Vashem the memory lives on, and burns itself onto our souls. It makes us cry out: 'I hear the whispering of many – terror on every side – but I trust in you, O Lord: I say, "You are my God." '

GEORGE W. BUSH

ADDRESS TO CONGRESS FOLLOWING THE ATTACKS OF 9/11

The United States Capitol, Washington, D.C.,
20 September 2001

President George W. Bush's speech to Congress was not the first after the terrorist attacks of 11 September 2001; on the day itself he had made a televised broadcast from the White House and another followed on 14 September. Of the three, this speech is not only the most eloquent, but is also the most important, in that it provides the earliest statement as to the administration's response. Here Bush declares a 'war on terror'. Expanding on his statement – made in a previous speech – that terrorists attacked because the United States is 'freedom's home and defender', for the first time, he names al Qaeda and its leader Osama bin Laden, as the perpetrators of the attacks, a case put forward by the White House the previous week.

Early in the speech, Bush praises Todd Beamer, one of the passengers who apparently fought with the hijackers of United Airlines Flight 93. It is thought that the plane, which crashed in rural Pennsylvania, had been intended to strike the very building in which Bush made his address.

MR SPEAKER, Mr President Pro Tempore, members of Congress, and fellow Americans: In the normal course of events, presidents come to this chamber to report on the state of the Union. Tonight, no such report is needed. It has already been delivered by the American people.

We have seen it in the courage of passengers, who rushed terrorists to save others on the ground – passengers like an exceptional man named Todd Beamer. And would you please help me welcome his wife, Lisa Beamer, here tonight.

We have seen the state of our Union in the endurance of rescuers, working past exhaustion. We have seen the unfurling of flags, the lighting of candles, the giving of blood, the saying of prayers – in English, Hebrew, and Arabic. We have seen the decency of a loving and giving people who have made the grief of strangers their own.

My fellow citizens, for the last nine days, the entire world has seen for itself the state of our Union – and it is strong.

Tonight we are a country awakened to danger and called to defend freedom. Our grief has turned to anger, and anger to resolution. Whether we bring our enemies to justice, or bring justice to our enemies, justice will be done.

I thank the Congress for its leadership at such an important time. All of America was touched on the evening of the tragedy to see Republicans and Democrats joined together on the steps of this Capitol, singing 'God Bless America'. And you did more than sing; you acted, by delivering $40 billion to rebuild our communities and meet the needs of our military. Speaker Hastert, Minority Leader Gephardt, Majority Leader Daschle and Senator Lott, I thank you for your friendship, for your leadership, and for your service to our country. And on behalf of the American people, I thank the world for its outpouring of support. America will never forget the sounds of our National Anthem playing at Buckingham Palace, on the streets of Paris, and at Berlin's Brandenburg Gate.

We will not forget South Korean children gathering to pray outside our embassy in Seoul, or the prayers of sympathy offered at a mosque in Cairo. We will not forget moments of silence and days of mourning in Australia and Africa and Latin America. Nor will we forget the citizens of eighty other nations who died with our own: dozens of Pakistanis; more than 130 Israelis; more than 250 citizens of India; men and women from El Salvador, Iran, Mexico and Japan; and hundreds of British citizens. America has no truer friend than Great Britain. Once again, we are joined together in a great cause – so honored the British Prime Minister has crossed an ocean to show his unity of purpose with America. Thank you for coming, friend.

On September 11th, enemies of freedom committed an act of war against our country. Americans have known wars but for the past 136 years, they have been wars on foreign soil, except for one Sunday in 1941. Americans have known the casualties of war but not at the center of a great city on a peaceful morning. Americans have known surprise attacks but never before on thousands of civilians. All of this was brought upon us in a single day and night fell on a different world, a world where freedom itself is under attack.

Americans have many questions tonight. Americans are asking: 'Who attacked our country?' The evidence we have gathered all points to a collection of loosely affiliated terrorist organizations known as al Qaeda. They are some of the murderers indicted for bombing American embassies in Tanzania and Kenya, and responsible for bombing the USS *Cole*. Al Qaeda is to terror what the mafia is to crime. But its goal is not making money; its goal is remaking the world and imposing its radical beliefs on people everywhere.

The terrorists practice a fringe form of Islamic extremism that has been rejected by Muslim scholars and the vast majority of Muslim clerics; a fringe movement that perverts the peaceful teachings of Islam. The terrorists' directive commands them to kill Christians and Jews, to kill all Americans, and make no distinctions among military and civilians, including women and children. This group and its leader – a person named Osama bin Laden – are linked to many other organizations in different countries, including the Egyptian Islamic Jihad and the

Islamic Movement of Uzbekistan. There are thousands of these terrorists in more than sixty countries. They are recruited from their own nations and neighborhoods, and brought to camps in places like Afghanistan, where they are trained in the tactics of terror. They are sent back to their homes, or sent to hide in countries around the world, to plot evil and destruction.

The leadership of al Qaeda has great influence in Afghanistan and supports the Taliban regime in controlling most of that country. In Afghanistan, we see al Qaeda's vision for the world. Afghanistan's people have been brutalized; many are starving and many have fled. Women are not allowed to attend school. You can be jailed for owning a television. Religion can be practiced only as their leaders dictate. A man can be jailed in Afghanistan if his beard is not long enough.

The United States respects the people of Afghanistan. After all, we are currently its largest source of humanitarian aid. But we condemn the Taliban regime. It is not only repressing its own people, it is threatening people everywhere by sponsoring and sheltering and supplying terrorists. By aiding and abetting murder, the Taliban regime is committing murder.

And tonight, the United States of America makes the following demands on the Taliban: Deliver to United States authorities all the leaders of al Qaeda who hide in your land. Release all foreign nationals, including American citizens, you have unjustly imprisoned. Protect foreign journalists, diplomats and aid workers in your country. Close immediately and permanently every terrorist training camp in Afghanistan, and hand over every terrorist, and every person in their support structure, to appropriate authorities. Give the United States full access to terrorist training camps, so we can make sure they are no longer operating. These demands are not open to negotiation or discussion. The Taliban must act, and act immediately. They will hand over the terrorists, or they will share in their fate.

I also want to speak tonight directly to Muslims throughout the world. We respect your faith. It's practiced freely by many millions of Americans, and by millions more in countries that America counts as friends. Its teachings are good and peaceful, and those who commit evil in the name of Allah blaspheme the name of Allah. The terrorists are traitors to their own faith, trying, in effect, to hijack Islam itself. The enemy of America is not our many Muslim friends; it is not our many Arab friends. Our enemy is a radical network of terrorists, and every government that supports them.

Our war on terror begins with al Qaeda, but it does not end there. It will not end until every terrorist group of global reach has been found, stopped and defeated.

Americans are asking: 'Why do they hate us?' They hate what we see right here in this chamber, a democratically elected government. Their leaders are self-appointed.

They hate our freedoms: our freedom of religion; our freedom of speech; our freedom to vote, and assemble and disagree with each other. They want to overthrow existing governments in many Muslim countries, such as Egypt, Saudi Arabia and Jordan. They want to drive Israel out of the Middle East. They want to drive Christians and Jews out of vast regions of Asia and Africa. These terrorists kill not merely to end lives, but to disrupt and end a way of life. With every atrocity, they hope that America grows fearful, retreating from the world and forsaking our friends. They stand against us, because we stand in their way.

We are not deceived by their pretenses to piety. We have seen their kind before. They are the heirs of all the murderous ideologies of the 20th century. By sacrificing human life to serve their radical visions; by abandoning every value except the will to power, they follow in the path of fascism, Nazism and totalitarianism. And they will follow that path all the way, to where it ends: in history's unmarked grave of discarded lies. Americans are asking: 'How will we fight and win this war?' We will direct every resource at our command: every means of diplomacy; every tool of intelligence; every instrument of law enforcement; every financial influence; and every necessary weapon of war, to the disruption and to the defeat of the global terror network.

Now, this war will not be like the war against Iraq a decade ago, with a decisive

167

liberation of territory and a swift conclusion. It will not look like the air war above Kosovo two years ago, where no ground troops were used and not a single American was lost in combat. Our response involves far more than instant retaliation and isolated strikes. Americans should not expect one battle, but a lengthy campaign, unlike any other we have ever seen. It may include dramatic strikes, visible on TV, and covert operations, secret even in success. We will starve terrorists of funding, turn them one against another, drive them from place to place, until there is no refuge or no rest. And we will pursue nations that provide aid or safe haven to terrorism. Every nation, in every region, now has a decision to make. Either you are with us, or you are with the terrorists. From this day forward, any nation that continues to harbor or support terrorism will be regarded by the United States as a hostile regime.

Our nation has been put on notice: we're not immune from attack. We will take defensive measures against terrorism to protect Americans. Today, dozens of federal departments and agencies, as well as state and local governments, have responsibilities affecting homeland security. These efforts must be co-ordinated at the highest level. So tonight I announce the creation of a cabinet-level position reporting directly to me: the Office of Homeland Security. And tonight I also announce a distinguished American to lead this effort, to strengthen American security: a military veteran, an effective governor, a true patriot, a trusted friend, Pennsylvania's Tom Ridge. He will lead, oversee and co-ordinate a comprehensive national strategy to safeguard our country against terrorism, and respond to any attacks that may come.

These measures are essential. But the only way to defeat terrorism as a threat to our way of life is to stop it, eliminate it, and destroy it where it grows. Many will be involved in this effort, from FBI agents to intelligence operatives to the reservists we have called to active duty. All deserve our thanks, and all have our prayers. And tonight, a few miles from the damaged Pentagon, I have a message for our military: 'Be ready.' I've called the Armed Forces to alert, and there is a reason. The hour is coming when America will act, and you will make us proud.

This is not, however, just America's fight. And what is at stake is not just America's freedom. This is the world's fight. This is civilization's fight. This is the fight of all who believe in progress and pluralism, tolerance and freedom.

We ask every nation to join us. We will ask, and we will need, the help of police forces, intelligence services and banking systems around the world. The United States is grateful that many nations and many international organizations have already responded with sympathy and with support. Nations from Latin America, to Asia, to Africa, to Europe, to the Islamic world. Perhaps the NATO Charter reflects best the attitude of the world: 'An attack on one is an attack on all.' The civilized world is rallying to America's side. They understand that if this terror goes unpunished, their own cities, their own citizens may be next. Terror, unanswered, can not only bring down buildings, it can threaten the stability of legitimate governments. And you know what? We're not going to allow it.

Americans are asking: 'What is expected of us?' I ask you to live your lives, and hug your children. I know many citizens have fears tonight, and I ask you to be calm and resolute, even in the face of a continuing threat. I ask you to uphold the values of America, and remember why so many have come here. We are in a fight for our principles, and our first responsibility is to live by them. No one should be singled out for unfair treatment or unkind words because of their ethnic background or religious faith.

I ask you to continue to support the victims of this tragedy with your contributions. Those who want to give can go to a central source of information, libertyunites.org, to find the names of groups providing direct help in New York, Pennsylvania, and Virginia.

The thousands of FBI agents who are now at work in this investigation may need your co-operation, and I ask you to give it. I ask for your patience, with the delays and inconveniences that may accompany tighter security; and for your patience in what will be a long struggle. I ask your continued

participation and confidence in the American economy. Terrorists attacked a symbol of American prosperity. They did not touch its source. America is successful because of the hard work, and creativity, and enterprise of our people. These were the true strengths of our economy before September 11th, and they are our strengths today. And, finally, please continue praying for the victims of terror and their families; for those in uniform; and for our great country. Prayer has comforted us in sorrow, and will help strengthen us for the journey ahead.

Tonight I thank my fellow Americans for what you have already done and for what you will do. And ladies and gentlemen of the Congress, I thank you, their representatives, for what you have already done and for what we will do together. Tonight, we face new and sudden national challenges. We will come together to improve air safety: to dramatically expand the number of air marshals on domestic flights; and take new measures to prevent hijacking. We will come together to promote stability and keep our airlines flying with direct assistance during this emergency. We will come together to give law enforcement the additional tools it needs to track down terror here at home. We will come together to strengthen our intelligence capabilities: to know the plans of terrorists before they act; and find them before they strike. We will come together to take active steps that strengthen America's economy, and put our people back to work.

Tonight we welcome two leaders who embody the extraordinary spirit of all New Yorkers: Governor George Pataki, and Mayor Rudolph Giuliani. As a symbol of America's resolve, my administration will work with Congress and these two leaders, to show the world that we will rebuild New York City.

After all that has just passed – all the lives taken, and all the possibilities and hopes that died with them – it is natural to wonder if America's future is one of fear. Some speak of an age of terror. I know there are struggles ahead and dangers to face. But this country will define our times not be defined by them. As long as the United States of America is determined and strong, this will not be an age of terror; this will be an age of liberty, here and across the world.

Great harm has been done to us. We have suffered great loss. And in our grief and anger we have found our mission and our moment. Freedom and fear are at war. The advance of human freedom – the great achievement of our time and the great hope of every time – now depends on us. Our nation – this generation – will lift a dark threat of violence from our people and our future. We will rally the world to this cause by our efforts, by our courage. We will not tire, we will not falter and we will not fail.

It is my hope that in the months and years ahead, life will return almost to normal.

We'll go back to our lives and routines, and that is good. Even grief recedes with time and grace. But our resolve must not pass. Each of us will remember what happened that day, and to whom it happened. We'll remember the moment the news came: where we were and what we were doing. Some will remember an image of a fire, or a story of rescue. Some will carry memories of a face and a voice gone forever.

And I will carry this: it is the police shield of a man named George Howard, who died at the World Trade Center trying to save others. It was given to me by his mom, Arlene, as a proud memorial to her son. This is my reminder of lives that ended and a task that does not end. I will not forget this wound to our country or those who inflicted it. I will not yield; I will not rest; I will not relent in waging this struggle for freedom and security for the American people. The course of this conflict is not known, yet its outcome is certain. Freedom and fear, justice and cruelty, have always been at war, and we know that God is not neutral between them.

Fellow citizens, we'll meet violence with patient justice, assured of the rightness of our cause and confident of the victories to come. In all that lies before us, may God grant us wisdom, and may He watch over the United States of America.

Thank you.

AL GORE

AFTER HURRICANE KATRINA

Moscone Center, San Francisco, 9 September 2005

On the opening morning of the 2005 National Sierra
Club Convention, former presidential candidate Al Gore
spoke before an audience of over two thousand. Eleven
days had passed since Hurricane Katrina had struck the
Gulf Coast and devastated the city of New Orleans.
Although the full extent of the damage was not yet
known, it was clear that it was the most costly natural
disaster in American history.

In his speech, Gore mentions and quotes several
people, including George W. Bush, Abraham Lincoln
and the muckraking novelist Upton Sinclair, but it is
Winston Churchill from whom he draws the most. He
quotes the British statesman twice, repeating Churchill's
reproach of Prime Minister Stanley Baldwin in 1936;
then his 1938 warning to Neville Chamberlain about the
effects of the Munich Agreement.

Carl Pope, to whom Gore refers to only by his first
name, is the Executive Director of the Sierra Club.

I KNOW THAT YOU are deeply concerned, as I am, about
the direction in which our country has been moving.
About the erosion of social capital. About the lack of
respect for a very basic principle, and that is that we, as
Americans, have to put ourselves and our ability to seek
out the truth because we know it will make us free. And
then on the basis of truth, as we share it to the best of our
abilities with one another, we act to try to form a more
perfect union and provide for the general welfare and
make this country worthy of the principles upon which it
was founded.

My heart is heavy for another reason today, and many have mentioned this, but I want to tell you personally that my heart is heavy because of the suffering that the people of the Gulf Coast have been enduring. The losses that they've suffered in Louisiana, Mississippi, Alabama, New Orleans in particular, but other cities as well, and rural areas. We are here thinking of them, thinking as well of the many brave men and women who have exceeded the limits of exhaustion as they do their duty in responding to this crisis, to the families of those responders and the families of the victims.

When I received the invitation that you generously extended for me to come and speak to you, I did not at first accept, because I was trying to resolve a scheduling conflict. The fifty State Insurance Commissioners were meeting in New Orleans, and asked me to speak about global warming and hurricanes. I was supposed to be there today and tomorrow morning. And of course, as we all watch this tragedy unfold, we had a lot of different thoughts and feelings. But then all those feelings were mixed in with puzzlement at why there was no immediate response, why there was not an adequate plan in place. We are now told that this is not a time to point fingers, even as some of those saying 'don't point fingers' are themselves pointing fingers at the victims of the tragedy, who did not – many of whom could not – evacuate the city of New Orleans, because they didn't have automobiles, and they did not have adequate public transportation.

We're told this is not a time to hold our national government accountable because there are more important matters that confront us. This is not an either/or choice. They are linked together. As our nation belatedly finds effective ways to help those who have been so hard hit by Hurricane Katrina, it is important that we learn the right lessons of what has happened, lest we are spoon-fed the wrong lessons from what happened. If we do not absorb the right lessons, we are – in the historian's phrase – doomed to repeat the mistakes that have already been made. All of us know that our nation – all of us, the United States of America – failed the people of New Orleans and the Gulf Coast when this hurricane was approaching them, and when it struck. When the corpses of American citizens are floating in toxic floodwaters five days after a hurricane strikes, it is time not only to respond directly to the victims of the catastrophe, but to hold the processes of our nation accountable, and the leaders of our nation accountable, for the failures that have taken place.

The Bible in which I believe, in my own faith tradition, says: 'Where there is no vision, the people perish.'

Four years ago in August of 2001, President Bush received a dire warning: 'Al Qaeda determined to attack inside the US.' No meetings were called, no alarms were sounded, no one was brought together to say:

'What else do we know about this imminent threat? What can we do to prepare our nation for what we have been warned is about to take place?' If there had been preparations, they would have found a lot of information collected by the FBI, and CIA and NSA, including the names of most of the terrorists who flew those planes into the WTC and the Pentagon and the field in Pennsylvania. The warnings of FBI field offices that there were suspicious characters getting flight training without expressing any curiosity about the part of the training that has to do with landing. They would have found directors of FBI field offices in a state of agitation about the fact that there was no plan in place and no effective response. Instead, it was vacation time, not a time for preparation or protecting the American people.

Four years later, there were dire warnings, three days before Hurricane Katrina hit New Orleans, that if it followed the path it was then on, the levees would break and the city of New Orleans would drown, and thousands of people would be at risk. It was once again vacation time. And the preparations were not made, the plans were not laid, the response then was not forthcoming.

In the early days of the unfolding catastrophe, the President compared our ongoing efforts in Iraq to World War II and victory over Japan. Let me cite one difference between those two historical events: When imperial Japan attacked us at Pearl Harbor,

Franklin Roosevelt did not invade Indonesia.

I personally believe that the very fact that there has been no accountability for the horrendous misjudgments and outright falsehoods that laid the basis for this horrible tragedy that we have ongoing in Iraq, the fact that there was no accountability for those mistakes, misjudgments and dissembling, is one of the principal reasons why there was no fear of being held accountable for a cavalier, lackluster, mistaken, inadequate response to the onrushing tragedy that was clearly visible – for those who were watching television, for those who were reading the news – what happened was not only knowable, it was known in advance, in great and painstaking detail. They did tabletop planning exercises, they identified exactly what the scientific evidence showed would take place. Where there is no vision, the people perish.

It's not only that there is no vision; it's that there has been a misguided vision. One of the principle philosophical guides for this administration has been the man who said famously that he wants to render the government of the United States so weak and helpless that you can drown it in a bathtub. There were warnings three years ago from the last director in the Clinton-Gore Administration of FEMA [the US Federal Emergency Management Agency], that FEMA was being rendered weak and helpless, unable to respond in the event of a catastrophe. The budget was cut, the resources sent elsewhere.

173

Carl [Pope] said he was embarrassed. The word is a tricky word. What did you feel after the invasion of Iraq when you saw American soldiers holding dog leashes attached to helpless prisoners? (99 per cent of whom, by the way, were innocent of any connection to violence against our troops, much less terrorism). Innocent prisoners who were being tortured in our name – what did you feel? I don't know the words. I don't know the words, but I want you to draw a line connecting the feelings you had when you saw the visual images providing evidence that our soldiers – acting in our name, with our authority – were torturing helpless people and that it was a matter of policy. Now, they pointed fingers at the privates and corporals that were in charge, but I want you to draw a line between the emotions that you felt when you absorbed that news, and the emotions that you felt over the last ten days, when you saw those corpses in the water, when you saw people without food, water, medicine – our fellow citizens left helpless. And of course in both cases the story is complex and many factors are involved, but I want you draw a line connecting the feelings that you had then and now. And I want you to draw another line, connecting those responsible for both of those unbelievable tragedies that embarrassed our nation in the eyes of the world.

There are scientific warnings now of another onrushing catastrophe. We were warned of an imminent attack by al Qaeda; we didn't respond. We were warned the levees would break in New Orleans; we didn't respond. Now, the scientific community is warning us that the average hurricane will continue to get stronger because of global warming. A scientist at MIT has published a study well before this tragedy, showing that since the 1970s, hurricanes in both the Atlantic and the Pacific have increased in duration, and in intensity, by about 50 per cent. The newscasters told us, after Hurricane Katrina went over the southern tip of Florida, that there was a particular danger for the Gulf Coast of the hurricanes becoming much stronger because it was passing over unusually warm waters in the gulf. The waters in the gulf have been unusually warm. The oceans generally have been getting warmer. And the pattern is exactly consistent with what scientists have predicted for twenty years. Two thousand scientists, in a hundred countries, engaged in the most elaborate, well-organized scientific collaboration in the history of humankind, have produced long-since a consensus that we will face a string of terrible catastrophes unless we act to prepare ourselves and deal with the underlying causes of global warming. It is important to learn the lessons of what happens when scientific evidence and clear authoritative warnings are ignored, in order to induce our leaders not to do it again, and not to ignore the scientists again, and not to leave us unprotected in the face of those threats that are facing us right now.

The President says that he is not sure that

global warming is a real threat. He says that he is not ready to do anything meaningful to prepare us for a threat that he's not certain is real. He tells us that he believes the science of global warming is in dispute. This is the same President who said last week: 'Nobody could have predicted that the levees would break.' It's important to establish accountability in order to make our democracy work. And the uncertainty and lack of resolution; the willful misunderstanding of what the scientific community is saying; the preference for what a few supporters in the coal and oil industry – far from all, but a few – want him to do, ignore the science. That is a serious problem. The President talked about the analogies to World War II; let me give another analogy to World War II.

Winston Churchill, when the storm was gathering on continental Europe, provided warnings of what was at stake. And he said this about the government then in power in England – which wasn't sure that the threat was real – he said: 'They go on in strange paradox, decided only to be undecided, resolved to be irresolute, adamant for drift, solid for fluidity, all powerful to be impotent.' He continued, 'The era of procrastination, of half measures, of soothing and baffling expedience of delays, is coming to a close. In its place we are entering a period of consequences.'

Ladies and gentlemen, the warnings about global warming have been extremely clear for a long time. We are facing a global climate crisis. It is deepening. We are entering a period of consequences. Churchill also said this, and he directed it at the people of his country who were looking for any way to avoid having to really confront the threat that he was warning of and asking them to prepare for. He said that he understood why there was a natural desire to deny the reality of the situation and to search for vain hope that it wasn't really as serious as some claimed it was. He said they should know the truth. And after the appeasement by Neville Chamberlain, he said: 'This is only the beginning of the reckoning. This only the first sip, the first foretaste, of a bitter cup which will be proffered to us year by year – unless by a supreme recovery of moral health and martial vigour, we rise again and take our stand for freedom.'

It is time now for us to recover our moral health in America and stand again to rise for freedom, demand accountability for poor decisions, missed judgments, lack of planning, lack of preparation, and willful denial of the obvious truth about serious and imminent threats that are facing the American people.

Abraham Lincoln said, 'The occasion is piled high with difficulty and we must rise with the occasion. As our case is new, we must think anew and act anew. We must disenthrall ourselves and then we shall save our country.'

We must disenthrall ourselves with the sound-and-light show that has diverted the attentions of our great democracy from the important issues and challenges of our day. We must disenthrall ourselves from the Michael Jackson trial, and the Aruba search, and the latest sequential obsession with celebrity trials, or whatever relative triviality dominates the awesomeness of democracy instead of making room for us as free American citizens to talk with one another about our true situation, and then save our country. We must resist those wrong lessons.

Some are now saying, including in the current administration, that the pitiful response by government proves that we cannot ever rely on the Government. They have, in the past, proposed more unilateral power for themselves as the solution for a catastrophe of their own creation, and we should not acquiesce in allowing them to investigate themselves, and giving them more power to abuse and misuse, the way they have so recently done. The fact that an administration can't manage its own way out of a horse show doesn't mean that all government programs should be abolished. FEMA worked extremely well during the previous administration.

A hundred years ago, Upton Sinclair wrote: 'It is difficult to get a man to understand something when his salary depends upon him not understanding.' Here's what I think we here understand about Hurricane Katrina and global warming. Yes, it is true that no single hurricane can be blamed on global warming. Hurricanes have

come for a long time, and will continue to come in the future. Yes, it is true that the science does not definitively tell us that global warming increases the frequency of hurricanes – because yes, it is true there is a multi-decadal cycle, twenty to forty years that profoundly affects the number of hurricanes that come in any single hurricane season. But it is also true that the science is extremely clear now; that warmer oceans make the average hurricane stronger, not only makes the winds stronger, but dramatically increases the moisture from the oceans evaporating into the storm – thus magnifying its destructive power – [which] makes the duration, as well as the intensity of the hurricane, stronger.

Last year we had a lot of hurricanes. Last year, Japan set an all-time record for typhoons: ten, the previous record was seven. Last year the science textbooks had to be rewritten. They said: 'It's impossible to have a hurricane in the south Atlantic.' We had the first one last year, in Brazil. We had an all-time record last year for tornadoes in the United States – 1,717 – largely because hurricanes spawned tornadoes. Last year, we had record temperatures in many cities. This year 200 cities in the Western United States broke all-time records. Tucson tied its all-time record for consecutive days above 100 degrees; Reno, thirty-nine days consecutively above 100 degrees.

The scientists are telling us that what the science tells them is that this – unless we act quickly and dramatically – that this, in

Churchill's phrase, is only the first sip of a bitter cup which will be proffered to us year by year, until there is a supreme recovery of moral health. We have to rise with this occasion. We have to connect the dots. When the Superfund sites aren't cleaned up, we get a toxic gumbo in a flood. When there is not adequate public transportation for the poor, it is difficult to evacuate a city. When there is no ability to give medical care to poor people, it's difficult to get hospitals to take refugees in the middle of a crisis. When the wetlands are turned over to the developers, then the storm surges from the ocean threaten the coastal cities more. When there is no effort to restrain the global warming pollution gasses, then global warming gets worse, with all of the consequences that the scientific community has warned us about.

My friends, the truth is that our circumstances are not only new; they are completely different than they have ever been in all of human history. The relationship between humankind and the earth has been utterly transformed in the last hundred years. We have quadrupled the population of our planet. The population in many ways is a success story. The demographic transition has been occurring more quickly than was hoped for, but the reality of our new relationship with the planet brings with it a moral responsibility to accept our new circumstances and to deal with the consequences of the relationship we have with this planet. And it's not just population. By any means, the power

of the technologies now at our disposal vastly magnifies the average impact that individuals can have on the natural world. Multiply that by six and a half billion people, and then stir into that toxic mixture a mindset and an attitude that says its okay to ignore scientific evidence – that we don't have to take responsibility for the future consequences of present actions – and you get a collision between our civilization and the earth. The refugees that we have seen – I don't like that word when applied to American citizens in our own country, but the refugees that we have seen could well be the first sip of that bitter cup, because sea-level rise in countries around the world will mobilize millions of environmental refugees. The other problems are known to you, but here is what I want to close with:

This is a moral moment. This is not ultimately about any scientific debate or political dialogue. Ultimately it is about who we are as human beings. It is about our capacity to transcend our own limitations; to rise to this new occasion. To see with our hearts, as well as our heads, the unprecedented response that is now called for. To disenthrall ourselves; to shed the illusions that have been our accomplices in ignoring the warnings that were clearly given, and hearing the ones that are clearly given now.

Where there is no vision, the people perish. And Lincoln said, at another moment of supreme challenge, that the question facing the people of the United States of

America ultimately was whether or not this government, conceived in liberty, dedicated to freedom, of the people, by the people, and for the people – or any government so conceived – would perish from this earth.

There is another side to this moral challenge. Where there is vision, the people prosper and flourish, and the natural world recovers, and our communities recover. The good news is, we know what to do. The good news is, we have everything we need now to respond to the challenge of global warming. We have all the technologies we need, more are being developed, and as they become available and become more affordable when produced in scale, they will make it easier to respond. But we should not wait, we cannot wait, we must not wait, we have everything we need – save, perhaps, political will. And in our democracy, political will is a renewable resource.

I know that you are debating as an organization, and talking among yourselves about your own priorities. I would urge you to make global warming your priority. I would urge you to focus on a unified theme. I would urge you to work with other groups in ways that have not been done in the past, even though there have been Herculean efforts on your part and the part of others. I would urge you to make this a moral moment. To make this a moral cause.

There are those who would say that the problem is too big and we can't solve it. There are many people who go from denial to despair without pausing on the intermediate step of actually solving the problem. To those who say it's too big for us, I say that we have accepted and successfully met such challenges in the past. We declared our liberty, and then won it. We designed a country that respected and safeguarded the freedom of individuals. We freed the slaves. We gave women the right to vote. We took on Jim Crow and segregation. We cured great diseases. We have landed on the moon. We have won two wars in the Pacific and the Atlantic simultaneously. We brought down communism; we brought down apartheid. We have even solved a global environmental crisis before – the hole in the stratospheric ozone layer – because we had leadership; and because we had vision; and because people who exercise moral authority in their local communities empowered our nation's government 'of the people, by the people and for the people' to take ethical actions, even thought they were difficult. This is another such time. This is your moment. This is the time for those who see and understand, and care and are willing to work, to say this time, the warnings will not be ignored. This time, we will prepare. This time, we will rise to the occasion. And we will prevail.

Thank you. Good luck to you, God bless you.

KEVIN RUDD

APOLOGY TO ABORIGINAL PEOPLES
Parliament House, Canberra, 13 February 2008

During Australia's 2007 federal election campaign, opposition party leader Kevin Rudd pledged that, if elected, he would issue an apology for the abuses suffered by the country's indigenous people. Calls for just such an apology had been made for well over a decade, and had grown considerably after the 1997 'Bringing Them Home' report was tabled in Parliament. However, Prime Minister John Howard, believing that contemporary Australia should not be held responsible for the actions and policies of previous governments, had chosen instead to issue a statement of regret. Howard also argued that any form of apology could lead to significant claims for compensation.

After Rudd's victory, he gave the apology priority; as 'Government business, motion No. 1', it was the first act of his new government. Though his words were well received, some believed that they should have been accompanied by an offer of financial compensation.

In April, 'From Little Things Big Things Grow', a protest song that sampled Rudd's speech, reached the fourth spot on Australia's singles chart. Profits from the song were dedicated to Aboriginal charities.

MR SPEAKER, I move that: Today we honour the Indigenous peoples of this land, the oldest continuing cultures in human history.

We reflect on their past mistreatment.

We reflect in particular on the mistreatment of those who were Stolen Generations – this blemished chapter in our national history.

The time has now come for the nation to turn a new page in Australia's history by righting the wrongs of the past and so moving forward with confidence to the future.

We apologize for the laws and policies of successive Parliaments and governments that have inflicted profound grief, suffering and loss on these our fellow Australians.

We apologize especially for the removal of Aboriginal and Torres Strait Islander children from their families, their communities and their country.

For the pain, suffering and hurt of these Stolen Generations, their descendants and for their families left behind, we say sorry.

To the mothers and the fathers, the brothers and the sisters, for the breaking up of families and communities, we say sorry. And for the indignity and degradation thus inflicted on a proud people and a proud culture, we say sorry.

We the Parliament of Australia respectfully request that this apology be received in the spirit in which it is offered, as part of the healing of the nation.

For the future we take heart; resolving that this new page in the history of our great continent can now be written. We today take this first step by acknowledging the past and laying claim to a future that embraces all Australians. A future where this Parliament resolves that the injustices of the past must never, never happen again.

A future where we harness the determination of all Australians, Indigenous and non-Indigenous, to close the gap that lies between us in life expectancy, educational achievement and economic opportunity.

A future where we embrace the possibility of new solutions to enduring problems where old approaches have failed. A future based on mutual respect, mutual resolve and mutual responsibility.

A future where all Australians, whatever their origins, are truly equal partners, with equal opportunities and with an equal stake in shaping the next chapter in the history of this great country, Australia.

Mr Speaker, there comes a time in the history of nations when their peoples must become fully reconciled to their past if they are to go forward with confidence to embrace their future. Our nation, Australia, has reached such a time, and that is why the Parliament is today here assembled. To deal with this unfinished business of the nation, to remove a great stain from the nation's soul and in a true spirit of reconciliation to open a new chapter in the history of this great land, Australia.

Mr Speaker, last year I made a commitment to the Australian people that if we formed the next Government of the Commonwealth we would in Parliament say 'sorry' to the Stolen Generations. Mr Speaker, today I honour that commitment. I said we would do so early in the life of the new Parliament. Mr Speaker, again today I honour that commitment, by doing so at the commencement of this, the 42nd Parliament of the Commonwealth. Because the time has come, well and truly come, for all peoples of our great country, for all citizens of our great Commonwealth, for all Australians, those who are Indigenous and those who are not, to come together to reconcile and together build a new future for our nation.

Some have asked: 'Why apologize?' Let me begin to answer by telling the Parliament just a little of one person's story: an elegant, eloquent and wonderful woman in her eighties, full of life, full of funny stories, despite what has happened in her life's journey; a woman who has travelled a long way to be with us today; a member of the Stolen Generation, who shared some of her story with me when I called around to see her just a few days ago.

Nanna Nungala Fejo, as she prefers to be called, was born in the late 1920s. She remembers her earliest childhood days living with her family and her community in a bush camp just outside Tennant Creek. She remembers the love and the warmth and the kinship of those days long ago, including traditional dancing around the campfire at night. She loved the dancing. She remembers once getting into strife when, as a four-year-old girl, she insisted on dancing with the male tribal elders, rather than just sitting and watching the men, as the girls were supposed to do.

But then, some time around 1932, when she was about four, she remembers the coming of the welfare men. Her family had feared that day and had dug holes in the creek bank where the children could run and hide. What they hadn't expected was that the white welfare men didn't come alone. They brought a truck, they brought two white men and an aboriginal stockman on horseback, cracking his stockwhip. The kids were found; they ran for their mothers screaming, but they couldn't get away. They were herded and piled onto the back of the truck. Tears flowing, her mum tried clinging to the sides of the truck as her children were taken away to The Bungalow in Alice, all in the name of protection.

A few years later government policy changed. Now the children would be handed over to the missions, to be cared for by the churches. But which church would care for them? The kids were simply told to line up in three lines. Nanna Fijo and her sisters stood in the middle line, her older brother and cousin on her left. Those on her left were told that they had become Catholics; those in the middle, Methodists; and those on the right, Church of England. That's how the complex questions of post-Reformation theology were resolved in the Australian Outback in the 1930s. It was as crude as that. She and her sister were sent to a Methodist mission on Goulburn Island, and then Croker Island. Her Catholic brother was sent to work at a cattle station, and her cousin to a Catholic mission. Nanna Fijo's family had been broken up for a second time. She stayed at the mission until after the war, when she was allowed to leave for a pre-arranged job as a domestic in Darwin. She was 16. Nanna Fijo never saw her mum again. After she left the mission, her brother let her know that her mum had died years before, a broken woman fretting for the children that had literally been ripped away from her.

I asked Nanna Fejo what she would have me say today about her story. She thought for a few moments, then said that what I should say today is that all mothers are important, and she added: 'Families – keeping them together is very important. It's a good thing that you are surrounded by love and that love is passed down the generations. That's what gives you happiness.'

As I left later on Nanna Fejo took one of my staff aside, wanting to make sure that I wasn't too hard on the Aboriginal stockman who'd hunted those kids down all those years ago. The stockman had found her again decades later, this time himself to say: 'Sorry'. And remarkably, extraordinarily, she had forgiven him.

Nanna Fijo's is just one story. There are thousands, tens of thousands of them: stories of forced separation of Aboriginal and Torres Strait Islander children from their mums and dads over the better part of a century. Some of these stories are graphically told in 'Bringing Them Home', the report commissioned in 1995 by Prime Minister Keating, and received in 1997 by Prime Minister Howard. There is something terribly primal about these first-hand accounts. The pain is searing; it screams from the pages. The hurt, the humiliation, the degradation and the sheer brutality of the act of physically separating a mother from her children, is a deep assault on our senses, and our most elemental humanity. These stories cry out to be heard. They cry out for an apology.

Instead from the nation's Parliament there has been a stony and stubborn and deafening silence for more than a decade. A view that somehow we, the Parliament, should suspend our most basic instincts of what is right, and what is wrong; a view that instead, we should look for any pretext to push this great wrong to one side, to leave it languishing with the historians, the academics and the cultural warriors, as if the Stolen Generations are little more than an interesting sociological phenomenon. But the Stolen Generations are not intellectual curiosities. They are human beings: human beings who have been damaged deeply by the decisions of parliaments and governments. But as of today, the time for denial, the time for delay, is at last come to an end.

Mr Speaker, the nation is demanding of its political leadership to take us forward. Mr Speaker, decency, human decency, universal human decency, demands that the nation now steps forward to right an historical wrong, and that is what we are doing in this place today. But should there still be doubts as to why we must now act, let the Parliament reflect for a moment on the following facts. That between 1910 and 1970, between 10 and 30 per cent of Indigenous children were taken from their mothers and fathers. That, as a result, up to

50,000 children were forcibly taken from their families. That this was the product of the deliberate, calculated policies of the state, as reflected in the explicit powers given to them under statute. That this policy was taken to such extremes by some in administrative authority, that the forced extractions of children of so-called 'mixed lineage' were seen as part of broader policy of dealing with 'the problem of the Aboriginal population'.

One of the most notorious examples of this approach was from the Northern Territory Protector of Natives who stated, and I quote: 'Generally by the fifth, and invariably by the sixth generation, all native characteristics of the Australian Aborigine are eradicated. The problem of our half-castes,' – to quote the Protector – 'will quickly be eliminated by the complete disappearance of the black race and the swift submergence of their progeny in the white'. The West Australian Protector of Natives expressed not dissimilar views, expounding them at length in Canberra 1937, at the first National Conference on Indigenous Affairs that brought together the Commonwealth and State Protectors of Natives. These are uncomfortable things to be brought out into the light. They are not pleasant. They are profoundly disturbing. But we must acknowledge these facts if we are to deal once and for all with the argument that the policy of generic, forced separation was somehow well motivated, justified by its historical context, and as a result, unworthy of any apology today.

Then we come to the argument of inter-generational responsibility, also used by some to argue against giving an apology today. But let us remember the fact that the forced removal of children was happening as late as the early 1970s. The 1970s is not exactly a point in remote antiquity. There are still serving members of this Parliament who were first elected to this place in the early 1970s. It is well within the adult memory span of many of us. The uncomfortable truth for us all is that the parliaments of the nation, individually and collectively, enacted statutes and delegated authority under those statutes that made the forced removal of children on racial grounds fully lawful.

There is a further reason for an apology, as well. It is that reconciliation is, in fact, an expression of a core value of our nation, and that value is a 'fair go for all'. There is a deep and abiding belief in the Australian community that for the Stolen Generations there was no 'fair go' at all. And there is a pretty basic Aussie belief that says it is time to put right this most outrageous of wrongs. It is for these reasons, Mr Speaker, quite apart from concerns of fundamental human decency, that the governments and parliaments of this nation must make this apology. Because, put simply, the laws that our parliaments enacted made the Stolen Generations possible. We, the parliaments of the nation, are ultimately responsible, not those who gave effect to our laws. The problem lay with the laws themselves. As has

183

been said of settler societies elsewhere, we are the bearers of many blessings from our ancestors, and therefore we must also be the bearer of their burdens as well.

Therefore, for our people, the course of action is clear, and that is to deal now with what has become one of the darkest chapters in Australia's history. In doing so, we are doing more than contending with the facts, the evidence, and the often rancorous public debate. In doing so, we are also wrestling with our own soul. This is not, as some would argue, a 'black armband' view of history. It's just the truth; the cold, confronting, uncomfortable truth; facing it, dealing with it, moving on from it. And until we fully confront that truth, there will always be a shadow hanging over us and our future as a fully united and fully reconciled people. It's time to reconcile. It's time to recognize the injustices of the past. It's time to say 'sorry'. It's time to move forward together.

To the Stolen Generations I say the following:

As Prime Minister of Australia, I am sorry.
On behalf of the Government of Australia, I am sorry.
On behalf of the Parliament of Australia, I am sorry.
And I offer you this apology without qualification.

We apologize for the hurt, the pain and the suffering we the Parliament have caused you by the laws that previous Parliaments have enacted. We apologize for the indignity, the degradation and the humiliation these laws embodied. We offer this apology to the mothers, the fathers, the brothers, the sisters, the families and the communities whose lives were ripped apart by the actions of successive governments, under successive parliaments.

In making this apology, I would also like to speak personally to the members of the Stolen Generation and their families: those here today, so many of you; to those listening today across the nation, from Yindamoo in the central west of the Northern Territory, to Yabara in north Queensland and to Pitjantjatjara in South Australia.

I know that in offering this apology on behalf of the Government and the Parliament there is nothing I can say today that can take away the pain you have suffered personally. Whatever words I speak today, I cannot undo that. Words alone are not that powerful; grief is a very personal thing.

I ask those non-Indigenous Australians listening today, who may not fully understand why what we are doing is so important, I ask those non-Indigenous Australians to imagine for a moment if this had happened to you. I say to Honourable Members here present: 'Imagine if this had happened to us. Imagine the crippling effect. Imagine how hard it would be to forgive.' But my proposal is this: If the apology we extend today is accepted in the spirit of reconciliation in which it is offered, we can today resolve together that

Kevin Rudd (right) with his eldest son, Nicholas, some months before becoming Prime Minister of Australia.

there be a new beginning for Australia. And it is to such a new beginning that I believe the nation is now calling us.

Australians are a passionate lot. We're also a very practical lot. For us symbolism is important, but unless the great symbolism of reconciliation is accompanied by an even greater substance, it is little more than a clanging gong. It's not sentiment that makes history; it's our actions that make history. Today's apology, however inadequate, is aimed at righting past wrongs. It is also aimed at building a bridge between Indigenous and non-Indigenous Australians; a bridge based on a real respect rather than a thinly veiled contempt. Our challenge for the future is now to cross that bridge, and in so doing embrace a new partnership between Indigenous and non-Indigenous Australians;

embracing, as part of that partnership, expanded Link-Up and other critical services to help the Stolen Generations to trace their families, if at all possible, and to provide dignity to their lives.

But the core of this partnership for the future is closing the gap between Indigenous and non-Indigenous Australians, on life expectancy, educational achievement and employment opportunities. This new partnership on closing the gap will set concrete targets for the future: within a decade to halve the widening gap in literacy, numeracy and employment outcomes and opportunities for Indigenous children; within a decade to halve the appalling gap in infant mortality rates between Indigenous and non-Indigenous children; and within a generation to close the appalling seventeen-year life gap between Indigenous and non-Indigenous when it comes to overall life expectancy.

The truth is a 'business as usual' approach towards Indigenous Australians is not working. Most old approaches are not working. We need a new beginning: a new beginning that contains real measures of policy success or policy failure; a new beginning, a new partnership, on closing the gap with sufficient flexibility, not to insist on a 'one size fits all' approach for each of the hundreds of remote and regional Indigenous communities across the country, but instead allowing flexible, tailored, local approaches to achieve commonly agreed national objectives that lie at the core of our proposed new partnership; and a new beginning that draws intelligently on the experiences of new policy settings across the nation.

However unless we, as a Parliament, set a destination for the nation, we have no clear point to guide our policy, our programmes or our purpose; no central organizing principle. So let us resolve today to begin with the little children – a fitting place to start on this day of apology for the Stolen Generations. Let us resolve, over the next five years, to have every Indigenous four-year-old in a remote Aboriginal community enrolled in and attending a proper early childhood education centre or opportunity, and engaged in proper pre-literacy and pre-numeracy programmes. Let us resolve to build new educational opportunities for these little ones, year by year, step by step, following the completion of their crucial pre-school year. Let us resolve to use this systematic approach to building future educational opportunities for Indigenous children, and providing proper primary and preventative healthcare for the same children. To begin the task of rolling back the obscenity that we find today in infant mortality rates in remote Indigenous communities, up to four times higher than in other communities.

None of this will be easy. Most of it will be hard – very hard. But none of it – none of it – is impossible, and all of it is achievable with clear goals, clear thinking, and by placing an absolute premium on respect, co-operation and mutual responsibility as the guiding principles of this new partnership on closing the gap. The mood of the nation is for reconciliation now between Indigenous and non-Indigenous Australians. The mood of the nation on Indigenous policy and politics is very simple. The nation is calling on us, the politicians, to move beyond our infantile bickering, our point-scoring and our mindlessly partisan politics, and elevate this one – at least this one – core area of national responsibility to a rare position beyond the partisan divide. Surely this is the spirit – the unfulfilled spirit – of the 1967 referendum? Surely at least, from this day forward, we should give it a go.

So let me take this one step further, and take what some may see as a piece of political posturing and make a practical proposal to the Opposition on this, the first full sitting day of the new Parliament. I said before the election the nation needed a kind of War Cabinet on parts of Indigenous policy, because the challenges are too great and the consequences too great to just allow it all to become a political football, as it has been so often in the past.

I therefore propose a joint policy commission to be led by the Leader of the Opposition and me, and with a mandate to develop and implement, to begin with, an effective housing strategy for remote communities over the next five years. It will be consistent with the Government's policy framework, a new partnership for closing the gap. If this commission operates well, I then propose that it work on the further task of constitutional recognition of the First Australians, consistent with the longstanding platform commitments of my Party, and the pre-election position of the Opposition. This will probably be desirable in any event, because unless such a proposition was absolutely bipartisan it would fail at a referendum. As I have said before, the time has come for new approaches to enduring problems, and working constructively together on such defined projects I believe would meet with the support of the nation. It's time for fresh ideas to fashion the nation's future.

Mr Speaker, today the Parliament has come together to right a great wrong. We have come together to deal with the past so that we might fully embrace the future. And we have had sufficient audacity of faith to advance a pathway to that future, with arms extended rather than with fists still clenched. So let us seize the day. Let it not become a moment of mere sentimental reflection. Let us take it with both hands and allow this day, this day of national reconciliation, to become one of those rare moments in which we might just be able to transform the way in which the nation thinks about itself. Whereby the injustice administered to these Stolen Generations in the name of these, our Parliaments, causes all of us to reappraise, at the deepest level of our beliefs, the real possibility of reconciliation writ large; reconciliation across all Indigenous Australia;

reconciliation across the entire history of the often bloody encounter between those who emerged from the Dreamtime a thousand generations ago and those who, like me, came across the seas only yesterday; reconciliation which opens up whole new possibilities for the future.

It is for the nation to bring the first two centuries of our settled history to a close, as we begin a new chapter. We embrace with pride, admiration and awe, these great and ancient cultures we are blessed – truly blessed – to have among us. Cultures that provide a unique, uninterrupted human thread linking our Australian continent to the most ancient prehistory of our planet. And growing from this new respect to see our Indigenous brothers and sisters with fresh eyes, with new eyes, and with our minds wide open as to how we might tackle together the great practical challenges that Indigenous Australia faces in the future.

So let us turn this page together, Indigenous and non-Indigenous Australians, Government and Opposition, Commonwealth and State, and write this new chapter in our nation's story together. First Australians, First Fleeters, and those who first took the Oath of Allegiance just a few weeks ago, let's grasp this opportunity to craft a new future for this great land, Australia.

Mr Speaker, I commend the motion to the House.

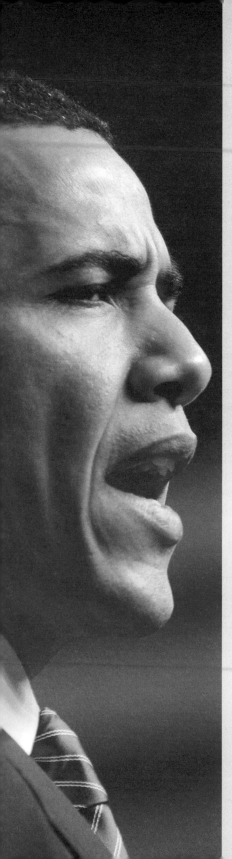

BARACK OBAMA

'A MORE PERFECT UNION'

National Constitution Center, Philadelphia, 18 March 2008

In March of 2008, less than midway through the Democratic primaries, media attention began to shift from the candidates' speeches toward the past sermons of Reverend Jeremiah Wright. Segments broadcast showed Wright expressing his beliefs that the United States supported state-sponsored terrorism; that the attack on Pearl Harbor was known in advance; and that the CIA had helped the South African government imprison Nelson Mandela. As the former pastor of the Trinity United Church of Christ in Chicago, which Obama attended, and as the man who had officiated at the candidate's wedding, Wright's remarks brought controversy to the candidacy. Obama moved to distance himself from Wright, using the storm to address the issues of race and inequality present in the United States.

He begins by quoting the United States Constitution, and refers to legal documents and events from America's past: the 19th- and 20th-century Jim Crow segregation laws; and *Brown v. Board of Education of Topeka*, in which the United States Supreme Court found that segregated public schools were 'inherently unequal'. More recent events include the 1995 trial of O.J. Simpson, and the devastation wrought by Hurricane Katrina in 2005. Obama also refers to a remark made by Geraldine Ferraro, a Hillary Clinton supporter, that had Obama been a white man 'he would not be in this position. And if he was a woman (of any color) he would not be in this position.'

Nearly forty minutes in length, Obama's speech was broadcast without interruption by most 24-hour news networks and led evening newscasts.

What follows is roughly two-thirds of his speech.

'WE THE PEOPLE, in order to form a more perfect union....' Two hundred and twenty-one years ago, in a hall that still stands across the street, a group of men gathered and, with these simple words, launched America's improbable experiment in democracy. Farmers and scholars, statesmen and patriots who had traveled across the ocean to escape tyranny and persecution finally made real their declaration of independence at a Philadelphia convention that lasted through the spring of 1787.

The document they produced was eventually signed, but ultimately unfinished. It was stained by this nation's original sin of slavery, a question that divided the colonies and brought the convention to a stalemate until the founders chose to allow the slave trade to continue for at least twenty more years, and to leave any final resolution to future generations.

Of course, the answer to the slavery question was already embedded within our Constitution; a Constitution that had at its very core the ideal of equal citizenship under the law; a Constitution that promised its people liberty, and justice, and a union that could be and should be perfected over time.

And yet words on a parchment would not be enough to deliver slaves from bondage, or provide men and women of every color and creed their full rights and obligations as citizens of the United States. What would be needed were Americans in successive generations who were willing to do their part

– through protests and struggles, on the streets and in the courts, through a civil war and civil disobedience, and always at great risk – to narrow that gap between the promise of our ideals and the reality of their time.

This was one of the tasks we set forth at the beginning of this presidential campaign: to continue the long march of those who came before us, a march for a more just, more equal, more free, more caring and more prosperous America. I chose to run for president at this moment in history because I believe deeply that we cannot solve the challenges of our time unless we solve them together; unless we perfect our union by understanding that we may have different stories, but we hold common hopes; that we may not look the same and may not have come from the same place, but we all want to move in the same direction: towards a better future for our children and our grandchildren.

This belief comes from my unyielding faith in the decency and generosity of the American people. But it also comes from my own story.

I am the son of a black man from Kenya and a white woman from Kansas. I was raised with the help of a white grandfather who survived a Depression to serve in Patton's Army during World War II, and a white grandmother who worked on a bomber assembly line at Fort Leavenworth while he was overseas. I've gone to some of the best schools in America and I've lived in one of the world's poorest nations. I am married to a black American who carries within her the blood of slaves and slave owners – an inheritance we pass on to our two precious daughters. I have brothers, sisters, nieces, nephews, uncles and cousins of every race and every hue scattered across three continents, and for as long as I live, I will never forget that in no other country on earth is my story even possible.

It's a story that hasn't made me the most conventional of candidates. But it is a story that has seared into my genetic makeup the idea that this nation is more than the sum of its parts – that out of many, we are truly one.

Throughout the first year of this campaign, against all predictions to the contrary, we saw how hungry the American people were for this message of unity. Despite the temptation to view my candidacy through a purely racial lens, we won commanding victories in states with some of the whitest populations in the country. In South Carolina, where the Confederate Flag still flies, we built a powerful coalition of African-Americans and white Americans.

This is not to say that race has not been an issue in this campaign. At various stages in the campaign, some commentators have deemed me either 'too black' or 'not black enough'. We saw racial tensions bubble to the surface during the week before the South Carolina primary. The press has scoured every single exit poll for the latest evidence of racial polarization, not just in terms of white and black, but black and brown as well.

And yet, it's only been in the last couple of weeks that the discussion of race in this campaign has taken a particularly divisive turn.

On one end of the spectrum, we've heard the implication that my candidacy is somehow an exercise in affirmative action; that it's based solely on the desire of wild and wide-eyed liberals to purchase racial reconciliation on the cheap. On the other end, we've heard my former pastor, Jeremiah Wright, use incendiary language to express views that have the potential not only to widen the racial divide, but views that denigrate both the greatness and the goodness of our nation, and that rightly offend white and black alike.

I have already condemned, in unequivocal terms, the statements of Reverend Wright that have caused such controversy, and in some cases pain. For some, nagging questions remain. Did I know him to be an occasionally fierce critic of American domestic and foreign policy? Of course. Did I ever hear him make remarks that could be considered controversial while I sat in the church? Yes. Did I strongly disagree with many of his political views? Absolutely – just as I'm sure many of you have heard remarks from your pastors, priests, or rabbis with which you strongly disagreed.

But the remarks that have caused this recent firestorm weren't simply controversial. They weren't simply a religious leader's efforts to speak out against perceived injustice. Instead, they expressed a profoundly distorted view of this country; a view that sees white racism as endemic, and that elevates what is wrong with America above all that we know is right with America; a view that sees the conflicts in the Middle East as rooted primarily in the actions of stalwart allies like Israel, instead of emanating from the perverse and hateful ideologies of radical Islam.

As such, Reverend Wright's comments were not only wrong but divisive. Divisive at a time when we need unity, racially charged at a time when we need to come together to solve a set of monumental problems: two wars, a terrorist threat, a falling economy, a chronic health care crisis, and potentially devastating climate change; problems that are neither black or white or Latino or Asian but, rather, problems that confront us all.

Given my background, my politics, and my professed values and ideals, there will no doubt be those for whom my statements of condemnation are not enough. Why associate myself with Reverend Wright in the first place, they may ask; why not join another church? And I confess that if all that I knew of Reverend Wright were the snippets of those sermons that have run in an endless loop on the television sets and YouTube, if Trinity United Church of Christ conformed to the caricatures being peddled by some commentators, there is no doubt that I would react in much the same way. But the truth is, that isn't all that I know of the man. The man I met more than twenty years ago is a man

who helped introduce me to my Christian faith, a man who spoke to me about our obligations to love one another; to care for the sick and lift up the poor. He is a man who served his country as a United States Marine, and who has studied and lectured at some of the finest universities and seminaries in the country, and who over thirty years has led a church that serves the community by doing God's work here on earth: by housing the homeless; ministering to the needy; providing day care services and scholarships and prison ministries; and reaching out to those suffering from HIV/AIDS.

I can no more disown him than I can disown the black community. I can no more disown him than I can disown my white grandmother: a woman who helped raise me; a woman who sacrificed again and again for me; a woman who loves me as much as she loves anything in this world; but a woman who once confessed her fear of black men who passed her by on the street, and who on more than one occasion has uttered racial or ethnic stereotypes that made me cringe. These people are part of me. And they are part of America, this country that I love.

Now, some will see this as an attempt to justify or excuse comments that are simply inexcusable. I can assure you it is not. And I suppose the politically safe thing to do would be to move on from this episode and just hope that it fades into the woodwork. We can dismiss Reverend Wright as a crank or a demagogue, just as some have dismissed

Geraldine Ferraro, in the aftermath of her recent statements, as harboring some deep-seated bias. But race is an issue that I believe this nation cannot afford to ignore right now. We would be making the same mistake that Reverend Wright made in his offending sermons about America; to simplify and stereotype and amplify the negative to the point that it distorts reality.

The fact is that the comments that have been made and the issues that have surfaced over the last few weeks, reflect the complexities of race in this country that we've never really worked through; a part of our union that we have not yet made perfect. And if we walk away now, if we simply retreat into our respective corners, we will never be able to come together and solve challenges like healthcare, or education, or the need to find good jobs for every American.

But I have asserted a firm conviction – a conviction rooted in my faith in God and my faith in the American people – that working together we can move beyond some of our old racial wounds and that, in fact, we have no choice. We have no choice, if we are to continue on the path of a more perfect union.

For the African-American community, that path means embracing the burdens of our past without becoming victims of our past. It means continuing to insist on a full measure of justice in every aspect of American life. But it also means binding our particular grievances – for better health care, and better schools, and better jobs – to the larger aspirations of all Americans: the white woman struggling to break the glass ceiling; the white man who's been laid off; the immigrant trying to feed his family. And it means also taking full responsibility for our own lives: by demanding more from our fathers; and spending more time with our children; and reading to them; and teaching them that while they may face challenges and discrimination in their own lives, they must never succumb to despair or cynicism. They must always believe that they can write their own destiny.

Ironically, this quintessentially American – and, yes, conservative – notion of self-help found frequent expression in Reverend Wright's sermons. But what my former pastor too often failed to understand is that embarking on a program of self-help also requires a belief that society can change. The profound mistake of Reverend Wright's sermons is not that he spoke about racism in our society. It's that he spoke as if our society was static; as if no progress had been made; as if this country – a country that has made it possible for one of its own members to run for the highest office in the land and build a coalition of white and black, Latino, Asian, rich, poor, young and old – is still irrevocably bound to a tragic past. What we know – what we have seen – is that America can change. That is true genius of this nation. What we have already achieved gives us hope – the audacity to hope – for what we can and must achieve tomorrow.

Barack Obama and his wife, Michelle, during his campaign for the presidency of the United States.

Now, in the white community, the path to a more perfect union means acknowledging that what ails the African-American community does not just exist in the minds of black people; that the legacy of discrimination and current incidents of discrimination – while less overt than in the past – that these things are real and must be addressed. Not just with words, but with deeds: by investing in our schools and our communities; by enforcing our civil rights laws and ensuring fairness in our criminal justice system; by providing this generation with ladders of opportunity that were unavailable for previous generations. It requires all Americans to realize that your dreams do not have to come at the expense of my dreams; that investing in the health, welfare, and education of black and brown and white children will ultimately help all of America prosper.

In the end, then, what is called for is nothing more, and nothing less, than what all the world's great religions demand: that we do unto others as we would have them do unto us. Let us be our brother's keeper, Scripture tells us. Let us be our sister's keeper. Let us find that common stake we all have in one another, and let our politics reflect that spirit as well.

For we have a choice in this country. We can accept a politics that breeds division, and conflict, and cynicism. We can tackle race only as spectacle, as we did in the O.J. trial; or in the wake of tragedy, as we did in the aftermath of Katrina; or as fodder for the nightly news. We can play Reverend Wright's sermons on every channel, every day, and talk about them from now until the election, and make the only question in this campaign whether or not the American people think that I somehow believe or sympathize with his most offensive words. We can pounce on some gaffe by a Hillary supporter as evidence that she's playing the race card, or we can speculate on whether white men will all flock to John McCain in the general election regardless of his policies.

We can do that. But if we do, I can tell you that in the next election, we'll be talking about some other distraction; and then another one; and then another one. And nothing will change. That is one option. Or, at this moment, in this election, we can come together and say: 'Not this time.'

This time, we want to talk about the crumbling schools that are stealing the future of black children, and white children, and Asian children, and Hispanic children, and Native American children. This time, we want to reject the cynicism that tells us that these kids can't learn; that those kids who don't look like us are somebody else's problem. The children of America are not 'those kids', they are 'our kids', and we will not let them fall behind in the 21st-century economy. Not this time.

This time, we want to talk about how the lines in the emergency room are filled with whites and blacks and Hispanics who do not have health care; who don't have the power on their own to overcome the special interests in Washington, but who can take them on if we do it together.

This time, we want to talk about the shuttered mills that once provided a decent life for men and women of every race; and the homes for sale that once belonged to Americans from every religion, every region, every walk of life. This time, we want to talk about the fact that the real problem is not that someone who doesn't look like you might take your job; it's that the corporation you work for will ship it overseas for nothing more than a profit.

This time, we want to talk about the men and women of every color and creed who serve together, and fight together, and bleed together under the same proud flag. We want to talk about how to bring them home from a war that should've never been authorized and should've never been waged; and we want to talk about how we'll show our patriotism by caring for them, and their families, and giving them the benefits that they have earned.

I would not be running for president if I didn't believe with all my heart that this is what the vast majority of Americans want for this country. This union may never be perfect, but generation after generation has shown that it can always be perfected. And today, whenever I find myself feeling doubtful or cynical about this possibility, what gives me the most hope is the next generation; the young people whose attitudes and beliefs and openness to change have already made history in this election.

There is one story in particular that I'd like to leave you with today; a story I told when I had the great honor of speaking on Doctor King's birthday at his home church, Ebenezer Baptist, in Atlanta.

There is a young, 23-year-old white woman named Ashley Baia, who organized for our campaign in Florence, South Carolina. She had been working to organize a mostly African-American community since the beginning of this campaign, and one day she was at a round-table discussion where everyone went around telling their story and why they were there. And Ashley said that when she was nine years old, her mother got cancer. And because she had to miss days of work, she was let go and lost her health care. They had to file for bankruptcy; and that's when Ashley decided that she had to do something to help her mom.

She knew that food was one of their most expensive costs, and so Ashley convinced her mother that what she really liked, and really wanted to eat more than anything else, was mustard and relish sandwiches, because that was the cheapest way to eat. That's the mind of a nine-year-old. She did this for a year, until her mom got better. And so Ashley told everyone at the round-table that the reason she had joined our campaign was so that she could help the millions of other children in the country who want and need to help their parents too. Now, Ashley might have made a different choice. Perhaps somebody told her along the way that the source of her mother's problems were blacks who were on welfare and too lazy to work, or Hispanics who were coming into the country illegally. But she didn't. She sought out allies in her fight against injustice.

Anyway, Ashley finishes her story and then goes around the room and asks everyone else why they're supporting the campaign. They all have different stories and different reasons. Many bring up a specific issue. And finally they come to this elderly black man, who's been sitting there quietly the entire time. And Ashley asks him why he's there. And he doesn't bring up a specific issue. He does not say: 'Health care' or 'the economy'. He does not say: 'Education' or 'the war'. He does not say that he was there because of Barack Obama. He simply says to everyone in the room: 'I am here because of Ashley.'

'I am here because of Ashley.'

By itself, that single moment of recognition between that young white girl and that old black man is not enough. It is not enough to give health care to the sick, or jobs to the jobless, or education to our children. But it is where we start. It is where our union grows stronger. And as so many generations have come to realize over the course of the 221 years since a band of patriots signed that document, right here in Philadelphia, that is where perfection begins.

BARACK OBAMA

ELECTION VICTORY SPEECH

Grant Park, Chicago, 4 November 2008

Twenty months after announcing his candidacy, nearly eight months after he'd delivered his 'A More Perfect Union' speech, Barack Obama was elected the first African-American president of the United States. The victory was a decisive one; the Democrat Obama garnered close to a seven-point majority of the popular vote and won 365 electoral votes to chief rival John McCain's 162. Following tradition, Obama paid tribute to his Republican opponent, and Sarah Palin, McCain's running mate. He also thanked supporters and family, making special mention of his maternal grandmother, Madelyn Dunham, who had died two days earlier. However, it was the inclusion of Ann Nixon Cooper, a name previously not mentioned in the campaign, which attracted the most attention. A centenarian, Cooper had spent much of her life working for the rights of African-Americans. Informed by Obama's campaign that she would be mentioned, she made a special effort to stay up late to listen to the speech.

H ELLO, CHICAGO. If there is anyone out there who still doubts that America is a place where all things are possible, who still wonders if the dream of our founders is alive in our time, who still questions the power of our democracy, tonight is your answer.

It's the answer told by lines that stretched around schools and churches in numbers this nation has never seen, by people who waited three hours and four hours, many for the first time in their lives, because they believed that this time must be different, that their voices could be that difference.

It's the answer spoken by young and old, rich and poor, Democrat and Republican, black, white, Hispanic, Asian, Native American, gay, straight, disabled and not disabled; Americans who sent a message to the world that we have never been just a collection of individuals or a collection of red states and blue states; we are, and always will be, the United States of America.

It's the answer that led those who've been told for so long, by so many, to be cynical and fearful and doubtful about what we can achieve, to put their hands on the arc of history and bend it once more toward the hope of a better day. It's been a long time coming, but tonight, because of what we did on this day, in this election, at this defining moment, change has come to America.

A little bit earlier this evening, I received an extraordinarily gracious call from Senator McCain. Senator McCain fought long and hard in this campaign; and he's fought even longer and harder for the country that he loves. He has endured sacrifices for America that most of us cannot begin to imagine. We are better off for the service rendered by this brave and selfless leader. I congratulate him; I congratulate Governor Palin for all that they've achieved and I look forward to working with them to renew this nation's promise in the months ahead.

I want to thank my partner in this journey: a man who campaigned from his heart; and spoke for the men and women he grew up with on the streets of Scranton; and rode with on the train home to Delaware; the Vice President-elect of the United States, Joe Biden.

And I would not be standing here tonight without the unyielding support of my best friend for the last sixteen years, the rock of our family, the love of my life, the nation's next first lady, Michelle Obama.

Sasha and Malia, I love you both more than you can imagine. And you have earned the new puppy that's coming with us to the White House.

And while she's no longer with us, I know my grandmother's watching, along with the family that made me who I am. I miss them tonight. I know that my debt to them is beyond measure.

To my sister Maya, my sister Alma, all my other brothers and sisters, thank you so much for all the support that you've given me. I am grateful to them.

And to my campaign manager, David Plouffe, the unsung hero of this campaign, who built the best – the best political campaign, I think, in the history of the United States of America.

To my chief strategist, David Axelrod, who's been a partner with me every step of the way.

To the best campaign team ever assembled in the history of politics: you made this happen, and I am forever grateful for what you've sacrificed to get it done.

But above all, I will never forget who this victory truly belongs to. It belongs to you. It belongs to you.

I was never the likeliest candidate for this office. We didn't start with much money or many endorsements. Our campaign was not hatched in the halls of Washington. It began in the backyards of Des Moines and the living rooms of Concord and the front porches of Charleston. It was built by working men and women who dug into what little savings they had to give five dollars, and ten dollars, and twenty dollars to the cause.

It grew strength from the young people who rejected the myth of their generation's apathy; who left their homes and their families for jobs that offered little pay and less sleep.

It drew strength from the not-so-young people who braved the bitter cold and scorching heat to knock on doors of perfect strangers; and from the millions of Americans who volunteered and organized, and proved that more than two centuries later a government of the people, by the people, and for the people has not perished from the earth.

This is your victory.

And I know you didn't do this just to win an election. And I know you didn't do it for me. You did it because you understand the enormity of the task that lies ahead. For even as we celebrate tonight, we know the challenges that tomorrow will bring are the greatest of our lifetime: two wars; a planet in peril; the worst financial crisis in a century.

Even as we stand here tonight, we know there are brave Americans waking up in the deserts of Iraq and the mountains of Afghanistan, to risk their lives for us.

There are mothers and fathers who will lie awake after the children fall asleep and wonder how they'll make the mortgage or pay their doctors' bills or save enough for their child's college education.

There's new energy to harness, new jobs to be created, new schools to build, and threats to meet, alliances to repair.

The road ahead will be long. Our climb will be steep. We may not get there in one year or even in one term. But, America, I have never been more hopeful than I am tonight that we will get there. I promise you, we as a people will get there.

There will be setbacks and false starts. There are many who won't agree with every decision or policy I make as President, and we know the government can't solve every problem. But I will always be honest with you about the challenges we face. I will listen to you, especially when we disagree. And, above all, I will ask you to join in the work of remaking this nation, the only way it's been done in America for 221 years – block by block, brick by brick, calloused hand by calloused hand.

What began twenty-one months ago in the depths of winter cannot end on this autumn night. This victory alone is not the change we seek; it is only the chance for us to make that change. And that cannot happen if we go back to the way things were. It can't happen without you, without a new spirit of service, a new spirit of sacrifice.

So let us summon a new spirit: of patriotism, of responsibility, where each of us resolves to pitch in and work harder, and look after not only ourselves but each other. Let us remember that, if this financial crisis taught us anything, it's that we cannot have a thriving Wall Street while Main Street suffers.

In this country, we rise or fall as one nation, as one people. Let's resist the temptation to fall back on the same partisanship and pettiness and immaturity that has poisoned our politics for so long.

Let's remember that it was a man from this state who first carried the banner of the Republican Party to the White House, a party founded on the values of self-reliance and individual liberty and national unity. Those are values that we all share. And while the Democratic Party has won a great victory tonight, we do so with a measure of humility and determination to heal the divides that have held back our progress.

As Lincoln said to a nation far more divided than ours: 'We are not enemies but friends.' Though passion may have strained, it must not break our bonds of affection.

To those Americans whose support I have yet to earn: I may not have won your vote tonight, but I hear your voices. I need your help. And I will be your President, too.

And to all those watching tonight from beyond our shores, from parliaments and palaces to those who are huddled around radios in the forgotten corners of the world: our stories are singular but our destiny is shared, and a new dawn of American leadership is at hand.

To those – to those who would tear the world down: We will defeat you. To those who seek peace and security: We support you. And to all those who have wondered if America's beacon still burns as bright: Tonight we proved once more that the true strength of our nation comes not from the might of our arms or the scale of our wealth, but from the enduring power of our ideals: democracy, liberty, opportunity and unyielding hope.

That's the true genius of America: that America can change. Our union can be perfected. What we've already achieved gives us hope for what we can and must achieve tomorrow.

This election had many firsts, and many stories that will be told for generations. But one that's on my mind tonight's about a woman who cast her ballot in Atlanta. She's a lot like the millions of others who stood in line to make their voice heard in this election, except for one thing, Ann Nixon Cooper is 106 years old.

She was born just a generation past slavery. A time when there were no cars on the road or planes in the sky; when someone like her couldn't vote for two reasons: because she was a woman and because of the color of her skin.

And tonight, I think about all that she's seen throughout her century in America: the heartache and the hope; the struggle and the progress; the times we were told that we can't, and the people who pressed on with that American creed: Yes we can.

At a time when women's voices were silenced and their hopes dismissed, she lived to see them stand up and speak out and reach for the ballot. Yes we can.

When there was despair in the dust bowl and depression across the land, she saw a nation conquer fear itself with a New Deal, new jobs, a new sense of common purpose. Yes we can.

When the bombs fell on our harbor and tyranny threatened the world, she was there to witness a generation rise to greatness and a democracy was saved. Yes we can.

She was there for the buses in Montgomery, the hoses in Birmingham, a bridge in Selma, and a preacher from Atlanta who told a people that: 'We shall overcome.' Yes we can.

A man touched down on the moon, a wall came down in Berlin, a world was connected by our own science and imagination.

And this year, in this election, she touched her finger to a screen, and cast her vote, because after 106 years in America, through the best of times and the darkest of hours, she knows how America can change. Yes we can.

America, we have come so far. We have seen so much but there is so much more to do. So tonight, let us ask ourselves: if our children should live to see the next century, if my daughters should be so lucky to live as long as Ann Nixon Cooper, what change will they see? What progress will we have made?

This is our chance to answer that call. This is our moment. This is our time, to put our people back to work and open doors of opportunity for our kids; to restore prosperity and promote the cause of peace; to reclaim the American dream and reaffirm that fundamental truth, that, out of many, we are one; that while we breathe, we hope. And where we are met with cynicism and doubts and those who tell us that we can't, we will respond with that timeless creed that sums up the spirit of a people: Yes, we can.

Thank you; God bless you. And may God bless the United States of America.

BIOGRAPHIES

SUSAN BROWNELL ANTHONY (1820–1906) was one of the foremost American civil rights leaders of the 19th century. Born in West Grove, Massachusetts, to an abolitionist couple, she was educated at a number of modest institutions and worked for several years in education. In 1848, she began working for women's rights and 21 years later founded the National Women's Suffrage Association with Elizabeth Cody Stanton. She died 14 years before American women obtained the right to vote in national elections.

GEORGE WALKER BUSH (1946–) was born into a wealthy political family in New Haven, Connecticut. His father, George H.W. Bush, was the 41st President of the United States (1989-93). After attending Yale University and the Harvard Business School, he worked in the oil industry. In 1994, he was elected Governor of Texas, a position he held for six years. He was declared the victor in the 2000 presidential election. His first term was marked by the attacks of 11 September 2001 and the invasions of Afghanistan and Iraq. In 2004, he was elected to a second term.

CHARLES I (1600–49), the son of James I, was the King of England, Scotland and Ireland from 1625 until 1649. The second king of the Stuart dynasty, his reign was marked by religious conflict, financial mismanagement and political struggle. England eventually descended into a period of civil war, during which Charles was tried and found guilty of treason. His subsequent execution ushered in the short-lived, republican Commonwealth of England.

WINSTON CHURCHILL, né **WINSTON SPENCER-CHURCHILL (1874–1965)**, was a British statesman, historian and writer, remembered for his service as Prime Minister of the United Kingdom during the Second World War. A son of privilege, he was born at Blenheim Palace in Oxfordshire. He studied at Harrow School and the Royal Military Academy, Sandhurst, and served with the army in India, the Sudan and South Africa. In 1900, Churchill was elected to the House of Commons as a Conservative, but four years later crossed the floor to join the Liberals. Over the next two decades, he held a number of important posts including Home Secretary, First Lord of the Admiralty and Secretary of State for War. In 1922, he failed re-election; and returned to the Conservative Party in 1924. With the beginning of the Second World War, Churchill was again appointed First Lord of the Admiralty. In 1940, he became Prime Minister of a coalition government until 1945, when he was defeated in the next general election. Re-elected in 1951, Churchill served one final term as Prime Minister until 1955, during which time he also received the Nobel Prize for Literature.

FREDERICK DOUGLASS, né **FREDERICK BAILEY (1818–95)**, was born into slavery in Talbot County, Maryland. In 1838, he escaped to freedom and within a few years began speaking as an anti-slavery lecturer in the United States, Canada and Great Britain. An accomplished writer and editor, he published several abolitionist newspapers, and composed several works of autobiography: *A Narrative of the Life of Frederick Douglass, an American Slave* (1845), *My Bondage and My Freedom* (1855) and *Life and Times of Frederick Douglass* (1881). He held a number of political offices after the American Civil War, and in 1872 was nominated as Equality Party running mate for Victoria Woodhall, the first woman to campaign for the presidency of the United States.

EDWARD VIII (1894–1972) was the second monarch of the House of Windsor. Born the son of the future King George V at White Lodge in Richmond, England, he was educated at the Royal Naval College at Osborne, Dartmouth Royal Naval College and Magdalen College, Oxford. At the death of his father in 1936, he succeeded to the throne, only to abdicate less than 11 months later, never having been crowned. As the Duke of Windsor, he lived much of the next 36 years with his wife in France. He died at his home in Paris and was buried at Frogmore, adjoining Windsor Castle.

ALBERT EINSTEIN (1878–1955), a theoretical physicist, is generally regarded as one of the greatest scientific minds of the 20th century. He was born in Ulm, Germany, and later gave up his citizenship in order to avoid military service. Einstein studied at the Swiss Federal Institute of Technology in Zürich, graduating in 1900 with a degree in physics. Unable to find employment in his chosen field, he worked for many years at the Federal Office for Intellectual Property in Berne. It was while working at the office that Einstein experienced what has been termed his 'Annus Mirabilis', during which he published four papers of continuing importance to modern physics. He later accepted positions at a number of academic institutions. Einstein received the 1921 Nobel Prize in Physics, and is best remembered for his Theory of Relativity.

ELIZABETH I (1533–1603) was the last monarch of the Tudor dynasty. The daughter of Henry VIII, she was declared illegitimate after the execution of her mother, Anne Boleyn. Elizabeth was later cut out of the succession by her half-brother Edward VI, but in 1558 succeeded to the throne after the death of her half-sister, Mary I. Her reign of 44 years coincided with the height of the English Renaissance and the great expansion of England's seafaring power, which included the 1588 defeat of the Spanish Armada.

MOHANDAS GANDHI (1869–1948), also known as Mahatma ('Great Soul'), was an Indian nationalist leader. He was born into a political family in Porbandar, in present-day Gujarat. He studied law at University College, London, and later practised in South Africa. There he became involved with the civil rights movement and adopted the policy of non-violent protest. Returning to India in 1915, he became a key figure in the struggle for Home Rule. He was assassinated within months of India's independence.

ALBERT GORE (1948–) is an environmental activist and was the 45th Vice President of the United States. He was born in Washington, D.C., the son of a Representative and later Congressman. Gore studied at Harvard University. In 1978, he was elected to Congress and six years later became a Senator. From 1993 to 2001, Gore served as Vice President under Bill Clinton. As the Democratic Party candidate for President in 2000, he lost a controversial election to George W. Bush. In 2007, *An Inconvenient Truth*, a documentary based on a lecture written and presented by Gore, received an Academy Award. Later that same year, he was awarded the Nobel Peace Prize.

PATRICK HENRY (1736–99) was a leader in the American Revolution, and later served two terms as Governor of Virginia. Born in Hanover County, Virginia, Henry was a failed businessman who turned to law and politics. In 1765, he was elected to Virginia's legislative body, the House of Burgesses, and eventually became one of the most radical proponents of the American Revolution.

JOHN PAUL II, né **KAROL JÓZEF WOJTYLA (1920–2005)**, was the 264th Pope of the Roman Catholic Church. As a young scholar he studied at Jagiellonian University in Krakow, until it was closed by Nazi occupation forces during the Second World War. He spent the conflict working at a variety of jobs while studying for the priesthood. Ordained in 1946, 12 years later he became the youngest bishop in Poland, He was elected Pope in 1978, after the death of John Paul I, and three years later survived an assassination attempt in Vatican City. Physically active, John Paul II travelled more extensively than any previous Pope, however the last 15 years of his pontificate were hampered by Parkinson's disease.

JOHN FITZGERALD KENNEDY (1917–63) was born in Brookline, Massachusetts, to a wealthy, political family. He was educated at Harvard University and graduated with a degree in International Affairs. After naval service in the Second World War, Kennedy was elected to Congress and, later, the Senate. In 1960, he defeated Richard Nixon to become the 35th President of the United States. Kennedy held the office from 20 January 1961 until his assassination in Dallas, Texas on 22 November 1963.

ROBERT FRANCIS KENNEDY (1925–68), a younger brother of John F. Kennedy, was born in Brookline, Massachusetts. Educated at Harvard University and the University of Virginia School of Law, Kennedy worked as a lawyer in the political sphere. After his brother was elected President, he was appointed Attorney General. In 1964, he resigned his position and ran successfully for the Senate. He was assassinated in Los Angeles, California, while campaigning to become the Democratic nominee for the presidency of the United States.

MARTIN LUTHER KING, JR (1929–68), a Baptist minister, was one of the foremost leaders in the American civil rights movement. Born **MICHAEL KING, JR**, his name was later changed by his father, a clergyman, in honour of the German Protestant reformer Martin Luther. King was an accomplished scholar; he entered Morehouse College at 15, and later studied at Crozier Theological Seminary and Boston University. As an activist, he first came to national attention as an organizer of the 1955 Montgomery Bus Boycott, and two years later was involved in the establishment of the Southern Christian Leadership Conference. At the age of 35, he became the youngest person to receive the Nobel Peace Prize. On 4 April 1968, he was assassinated in Memphis, Tennessee.

ABRAHAM LINCOLN (1809–65) was the 16th President of the United States. Famously born in a log cabin in Hardin County, Kentucky, he is thought to have had only 18 months of formal schooling. Lincoln entered politics in 1832 with an unsuccessful bid for a seat in the Illinois General Assembly. He was elected to the state legislature two years later and in 1846 won a seat in the House of Representatives. After one term, Lincoln left public office to practise law in Illinois. In 1854, after a five-year break, Lincoln re-entered the political arena, and in 1860 was elected as the Republican Party candidate for the presidency. His time in office was consumed by the American Civil War. Re-elected in 1864, he was assassinated less than a week after the war's end.

DAVID LLOYD GEORGE (1863–1945) was the last Liberal Prime Minister of the United Kingdom. Born in Manchester to Welsh parents, he was raised and educated in Wales. A solicitor, he was first elected to public office as an alderman and won a seat in the House of Commons the following year. He served in a number of important positions, including Chancellor of the Exchequer. Two years into the First World War, Lloyd George became Secretary of State for War. Critical of Liberal Prime Minister H.H. Asquith, with the aid of opposition parties, Lloyd George replaced him. In 1921, he oversaw the settlement that brought about the Irish Free State. The next year he was involved in a scandal over the sale of peerages, and resigned as Prime Minister. He remained a Member of Parliament until his death.

HAROLD MACMILLAN (1894–1986) was Prime Minister of the United Kingdom. Born in London, he studied at Oxford and served in the First World War. He was later employed by Macmillan Publishers, a company founded by his paternal grandfather. First elected to the House of Commons in 1924, Macmillan served in his first ministerial position during the Second World War. In 1957, with the resignation of Anthony Eden, Macmillan became Prime Minister. He himself resigned in 1963, after having been diagnosed incorrectly with having inoperable cancer. Macmillan retired from politics the following year and became chairman of his family's publishing house.

NELSON MANDELA (1918–) is the former President of South Africa. He was born in Mvezo, a small village in the district of Umtata; his father was village chief. Mandela began study at Fort Hare University, but was expelled due to his involvement in a student boycott over the institution's policies. Mandela completed his degree through a University of South Africa correspondence course, then studied law at the University of Witwatersrand. In 1943, he joined the African National Congress, an involvement that would ultimately lead to his being tried on charges of sabotage and treason. Mandela was convicted in 1964 and received a life sentence. Released in 1990, he worked to transform South Africa into a multi-racial democracy. He received the Nobel Peace Prize in 1993, and the following year was elected President of South Africa. Mandela retired from politics in 1999.

JAWAHARLAL NEHRU (1889–1964) was the first and longest-serving Prime Minister in India's history. He was born in Allahabad, a city now located in the state of Uttar Pradesh. The son of a wealthy barrister and politician, Nehru was educated in England at Harrow School and Trinity College, Cambridge. Influenced by his friend Mohandas Gandhi, he adopted the philosophies of non-violence and non-co-operation in working for Home Rule. The President of the Indian National Congress from an early age, he became Prime Minister upon Indian independence and held the position until his death at 74. He was the father of Indira Gandhi, and grandfather of Rajiv Gandhi, both of whom also served in the office of Prime Minister.

RICHARD NIXON (1913–94) was the 37th President of the United States. Born in Yorba Linda, California, he attended Whittier College and Duke University, and later served in the Second World War. Nixon's career in politics began in 1947, when he was elected to Congress. In 1950, he was elected to the Senate, and three years later became Vice President under Dwight D. Eisenhower. The 1960 Republican nominee for the presidency, he lost a close election to John F. Kennedy. In 1968, Nixon defeated George McGovern to become President. In 1974, embroiled in scandal involving political espionage, and facing almost certain impeachment, he resigned.

BARACK OBAMA (1961–) was elected 44th President of the United States in 2008. Born in Honolulu to a Kenyan father and Kansan mother, he was raised in Hawaii and Indonesia. Obama studied at Occidental College, Columbia University, and Harvard Law School, after which he worked in Chicago as a community organizer. He was elected to the Illinois Senate in 1996, and nine years later became a United States Senator, before becoming the first successful African-American candidate for the presidency.

EMMELINE PANKHURST, née **EMMELINE GOULDEN (1858–1928)**, was the foremost leader of the British suffragette movement. She was born in Manchester and educated at schools both in that city and in Paris. In the late 19th and early 20th centuries Pankhurst founded the Women's Franchise League and the Women's Social and Political Union, two organizations devoted to women's suffrage. Initially a socialist, Pankhurst recast her political beliefs and joined the Conservative Party after women received the vote.

PATRICK PEARSE (1879–1916) was one of the leaders in the 1916 Easter Rising. The son of an English father and Irish mother, he was born and received much of his education in Dublin. In 1901, Pearse earned a law degree from King's Inns and was called to the bar. Over time, his interest in the promotion of Irish culture – in evidence through his boyhood membership of the Gaelic League – grew increasingly political. In 1913, he joined the Irish Republican Brotherhood, dedicated to overthrowing British rule. Chosen as spokesman, it was Pearse who, on 24 April 1916, delivered the Proclamation of the Republic during the Easter Rising. He was executed by firing squad ten days later.

RONALD REAGAN (1911–2004) was the 40th President of the United States. Born in Tampico, Illinois, he attended nearby Eureka College. After graduation, Reagan pursued a career in broadcasting and film, eventually starring in a number of Hollywood movies, most notably *Knute Rockne, All American* and *The Killers*. Once a Democrat, in 1962 he joined the Republican Party and five years later became Governor of California. He became the American President in 1981, after defeating Jimmy Carter.

ELEANOR ROOSEVELT (1884–1962) was a civil rights advocate and First Lady of the United States. She was born into the wealthy New York City family and was educated in the United States and England. In 1905, she married Franklin Delano Roosevelt, her fifth cousin. As her husband's political career progressed, Eleanor Roosevelt became increasingly involved in public life. She served as a delegate to the United Nations General Assembly and was the first chairperson of the UN Human Rights Commission. Her last political appointment, to the National Advisory Committee for the Peace Corps, came under John F. Kennedy.

FRANKLIN DELANO ROOSEVELT (1882–1945) was the 32nd and longest-serving President of the United States. He was born in Hyde Park, New York, into one of the oldest and wealthiest families in the country. He studied at Harvard University, practised law, and in 1910 was elected to the New York State Senate. Ten years later, he was nominated as Vice President on a failed ticket with James N. Cox. In 1928, he was elected Governor of New York, and four years later defeated incumbent Herbert Hoover to become President of the United States. Re-elected three times,

Roosevelt served as President during the Depression and the Second World War. He died in office, less than five months before the war's conclusion.

KEVIN RUDD (1957–) was the 26th Prime Minister of Australia. Born in Nambour, Queensland, he joined the Australian Labor Party at the age of 15. Rudd studied Chinese history and language at the Australian National University in Canberra, and later worked for the Australian Department of Foreign Affairs, serving in embassies in Stockholm and Beijing. He entered the Federal Parliament after winning a seat in the 1998 election. He became leader of the Australian Labor Party in 2006, and defeated incumbent Prime Minister John Howard in the federal elections held the following year.

TECUMSEH (1768–1813), a Shawnee chief, was the greatest Native American leader of his time. Believed to have been born just outside the borders of present-day Xenia, Ohio, his early life was semi-nomadic; displacement having been caused by encroaching settlers. A proponent of a Native homeland, he fought against American expansionism and, in the War of 1812, allied his warriors with the British and Canadians. He was killed during the Battle of the Thames, fought in what is present-day Ontario.

MARGARET THATCHER (1925–) is the first woman to have served as Prime Minister of the United Kingdom. She was born in Grantham, Lincolnshire, and studied chemistry at Oxford. Thatcher worked as a research chemist, before becoming a barrister specializing in tax law. First elected to Parliament in 1958, she served as Secretary of State for Education and Science under Edward Heath. In 1975, Thatcher was elected leader of the Conservative Party and became Prime Minister four years later. Her 11 years in office were marked by economic liberalism, the Falklands War, and a hardened stance against the Soviet Union. The victor in three general elections, Thatcher's was the longest consecutive tenure in office since the early 19th century.

PIERRE ELLIOTT TRUDEAU (1919–2000) was one of the most influential Canadian politicians of the 20th century. Born into a wealthy Montreal family, he was educated at the Université de Montréal, Harvard University, the Institut d'Etudes Politiques de Paris and the London School of Economics. Trudeau worked as a lawyer, journalist and professor before entering politics. Elected to the Canadian House of Commons in 1965, he served as parliamentary secretary to Prime Minister Lester B. Pearson and, later, as Minister of Justice. In 1968, Trudeau became the 15th Prime Minister of Canada. With one eight-month interruption, he held the position until his retirement from politics in 1984.

SOJOURNER TRUTH, née **ISABELLA BAUMFREE (1797–1883)**, was an African-American abolitionist, pacifist and campaigner for women's rights. Born into slavery in Swartekill, New York, she had five different owners, and was forced into marriage with another slave before escaping to freedom in 1826. Truth worked several years as a domestic servant and began speaking publicly. As she was never taught to read or write, her memoir, *The Narrative of Sojourner Truth: A Northern Slave* (1850), was dictated to a friend.

WOODROW WILSON (1856–1924) was the 28th President of the United States and the recipient of the 1919 Nobel Peace Prize. The son of a Presbyterian clergyman, he was born in Staunton, Virginia. Though unable to read before the age of 12, Wilson became highly educated. He studied at Davidson College, Princeton University, the University of Virginia and Johns Hopkins University. After graduation, he pursued a career in the academic world, teaching at Bryn Mawr College, Wesleyan College and, finally, Princeton University, at which he would also serve as President. Wilson also practised law and was the author of several titles dealing with governance. In 1910, he became Governor of New Jersey and in 1912 was elected to the first of two terms as President of the United States. His last two years in office were marred by the effects of a debilitating stroke. The poor state of Wilson's health was kept secret until his death, just over three years after he'd left office.

JAMES WOLFE (1727–59) was a British Army officer born to a military family in Westerham, Kent. Although he saw service in the War of the Austrian Succession and the Jacobite Risings, he is best remembered for his accomplishments during the Seven Years' War against the French in Canada, which enabled the British to establish rule there. He was instrumental in the 1758 capture of the Fortress of Louisbourg. He died the following year at the Battle of the Plains of Abraham, his greatest victory.

BIBLIOGRAPHY

'An Account of the Proceedings on the Trial of Susan B. Anthony, on the Charge of Illegal Voting. Rochester, NY.' *Daily Democrat and Chronicle*, 1874.

'Australia Says "Sorry" to Aborigines for Mistreatment.' *The New York Times.* 13 February 2008.

'Barack Obama's Speech on Race.' *The New York Times.* 18 March 2008.

Beasley, Maurine H., Holly C. Shulman, and Henry R. Beasley. *The Eleanor Roosevelt Encyclopedia.* Westport, CT: Greenwood, 2001.

Bryan, William Jennings, editor-in-chief. *The World's Famous Orations.* New York; Funk & Wagnalls, 1906.

Busby, Brian. *Great Canadian Speeches: Words That Shaped a Nation.* London: Arcturus, 2008.

Churchill, Winston S. *Blood, Sweat and Tears: Speeches by the Right Honourable Winston S. Churchill, P.C., M.P.* Toronto: McClelland & Stewart, 1941.

Dallek, Robert. *An Unfinished Life: John F. Kennedy, 1917-1963.* Boston: Little, Brown, 2003.

Douglass, Frederick. *My Bondage and My Freedom.* Auburn, NY: Miller, Orton & Mulligan, 1855.

Dunleavy, Janet Eagleson and Gareth W. Dunleavy. *Douglas Hyde: A Maker of Modern Ireland.* Los Angeles: University of California Press, 1991.

Gottheimer, Josh, ed. *Ripples of Hope: Great American Civil Rights Speeches.* New York: Basic Civitas, 2003.

Homer, Jack A. *The Gandhi Reader: A Sourcebook of His Life and Writings.* New York: Grove, 1994.

Howell, T. B., comp. *A Complete Collection of State Trials and Proceedings for High Treason and Other Crimes and Misdemeanors from the Earliest Period to the Year 1783.* London: Longman, Hurst, Rees, Orme and Brown, 1816.

Jenkins, Roy. *Churchill: A Biography.* New York: Farrar, Straus & Giroux, 2001.

Johnston, Tim. 'In Australia, From Apology, a Hit Song Grows.' *The New York Times.* 29 April 2008.

Kutler, Stanley I. *The Wars of Watergate: The Last Crisis of Richard Nixon.* New York: Norton, 1992.

Macmillan, Harold. *Pointing the Way, 1959-61.* London: Macmillan, 1971.

'Mr. Obama's Profile in Courage.' *The New York Times.* 19 March 2008.

Moraes, Frank. *Jawaharlal Nehru.* New York: Macmillan, 1956.

Oldys, William. *The Harleian Miscellany: A Collection of Scarce, Curious, and Entertaining Pamphlets and Tracts, as Well in Manuscript as in Print.* London: Robert Dutton, 1809.

Pankhurst, Emmeline. *My Own Story.* London: Eveleigh Nash, 1914.

Perret, Geoffrey. *Eisenhower.* New York: Random House, 1999.

Purvis, June. *Emmeline Pankhurst: A Biography.* New York: Routledge, 2002.

Raphael, Ray. *Founding Myths: Stories that Hide Our Patriotic Past.* New York: New Press, 2004.

Rowe, David E. and Robert Schulmann. *Einstein on Politics: His Private Thoughts and Public Stands on Nationalism, Zionism, War, Peace, and the Bomb.* Princeton, NJ: Princeton University Press, 2007.

Sampson, Anthony. *Mandela: The Authorized Biography.* London: HarperCollins, 1999.

Schlesinger, Robert. *White House Ghosts: Presidents and Their Speechwriters.* Toronto: Simon & Schuster, 2008.

Stanton, Elizabeth Cady *et al,* eds. *History of Woman Suffrage.* Rochester, NY: Susan B. Anthony, 1887.

Von Tunzelmann, Alex. *Indian Summer: The Secret History of the End of an Empire.* London: Macmillan, 1997.

Waldman, Michael. *My Fellow Americans.* Naperville, IL: Sourcebooks, 2003.

Wright, Patrick. *Iron Curtain: From Stage to Cold War.* Oxford: Oxford University Press, 2007.